MONSTER
BEHIND THE
MASKS

T.L. MUMLEY

Cover Art Copyright © 2018 Clarissa Yeo, Founder, Yocla Designs
Editors: Wesley Thomas, Founder, Thomas Editing Services.
Berkeley Writer's Circle
Interior book formatting: Jesse Gordon

Published in the United States of America, LavenderPress Copyright ©2017

The cataloging-in-publication data is on file with the Library of Congress.

ISBN: 9781370446360 (Digital Edition)
ISBN: 9780578458465 (Print Edition)

Acknowledgements

To Wesley Thomas, my editor, thank you for making an appearance in my literary journey at just the right time, and for seeing the beauty in my work.

Thanks again and again to Jesse Gordon, for his exquisite, efficient layout and fast turnaround in formatting my debut, *Masks of Morality*, and this sequel in both digital and print editions. I would be lost without you!

And to Clarissa Yeo of Yocla Designs—I can't count how many people rave about the cover designs you created.

My entire Writer's Circle, every one of you: thank you, thank you, and thank you a thousand times! I could never have pushed through this process without your honest feedback and critiques. The support is a tremendous impetus to keep me writing.

To the countless friends that continuously offer me support and words of wisdom—whether it be personal edits, a book signing party, encouragement or just pure love. Thank you.

A big thank you to my sweet Mom, Marti! Every little thing you do is magic, adding up to big support: sharing my books over social media, ordering extra copies to give away, lifting my weary writer fingers motivating them to tap out more. Nothing you do goes unnoticed!

There's no deeper gratitude than that which is felt towards my loving immediate family. Tommy and Ryan—you not only saw me through this process and put up with my weekly antics carving out time to write—you became my biggest cheerleaders. Thank you from the innermost corners of my heart!

Quotation

"I say what other people only think, and when all the rest of the world is in a conspiracy to accept the mask for the true face, mine is the rash hand that tears off the plump pasteboard and shows the bare bones beneath."

—Wilkie Collins

Prologue

"I have secrets," the man bragged, his words stumbling over each other.

"*Secrets*? Who the fuck *are* you, James Bond?" Sitting on the edge of her stool, Debra could smell whiskey not only on his breath but permeating from every pore of his skin. Although drunk, there was a certain charm to him.

"I'm more bad-ass than Bond. He's nothing but a cocktail-sipping lush. I've gotten away with murder—"

"*Ah…* according to the movies, 007 seems to have a license to kill. I'm not impressed." Debra scoffed at the irony as he sucked down whiskey like water.

She glanced around the bar—a dive in the middle of D.C. with jukeboxes, dark wood, neon lights, and rather unsavory clientele. Why did she come here, much less accept a drink from this slithering stranger? Something had attracted her to his sophisticated savagery. This seemed a man of culture and intelligence.

But a cold-blooded killer, she guessed, costumed for a mysterious motive. Dressed in dark jeans, dark tee, a leather bomber jacket and black boots, he could have been any of these blithe barflies. Until he opened his mouth or tried to pinch her in the butt.

"What's a pretty thing like you doing in a place like this?" He asked with a hiccup.

"I guess I could ask the same of you, although you're not so pretty." Looking at him she guessed he was once very handsome, but now weathered, battered and brooding. He seems confident yet scared of his own shadows.

"I… I've got bigger secrets than Bond," he mumbled. "I'm a one-man weapon of mass destruction. Even why I'm here in this shit-hole is a secret! I'm rich and powerful."

"There you go again, trying to impress me with your toxic masculinity and a weapon of mass *seduction*—only, I'm not taking the bait." Debra picked up her purse and slipped off the barstool.

"What's ya name," he asked, his words slurring.

Hesitating, she answered, "Debra."

"Diego. Diego Ramírez." He offered a flimsy handshake which she refused.

"Have ya heard of Kryptos?" Diego blurted out as if grasping for something to intrigue Debra and get her to stay.

"Kryptos?" *What's this weirdo stirring up now?*

"Most know nutting' bout it cause they hide it from the public." He pointed an aimless finger at her. "Not that the masses could understand the cryptology—people too stupid to figure it out even after solving the puzzles." Diego's face contorted into a cunning smirk. He cast off a manipulative stare then took another swig of his Jack Daniels. "It's at Langley—"

"What the hell are you talking about? *Langley*? So, you *are* a spy!"

"Wha… Whadda ya think I'd tell ya if I was?"

"*You're* the one spilling secrets in a half-drunk stupor! I can *smell* the bad in you!" Debra was fearing for her life, despite somehow mesmerized by him. She wondered if he had slipped something in her drink.

Diego spoke in a clear, loud and sober tone, looking at Debra through wild-eyes, "Kryptos is an art sculpture at Langley, with four secret messages in deep code. Three were solved by the NSA, CIA and a computer scient—"

"I think I've seen pictures of the art sculpture online—looks like a giant computer print-out with all that '*intelligence gathering*' on it. I don't trust either agency, corrupt as any Mafia." Debra's eyes darted around, seeking listeners.

He turned to her with a devious glint in his eyes. *If looks could kill.* "The CIA *has* to keep it all underground—it gets away with murder even better than I do—"

"So, using art as a political weapon?" Debra sipped from the second wine she never asked for, involuntarily captivated.

Diego tipped his head back, polishing off his whiskey, babbling again with his bad guy Bond act. It was hard to tell if he was performing or really drunk. "You're smarta' dan the rest girl, powerful forces illuminate the whole show. The longa the deadlock trying to solve the fourth lil' puzzle, the crazier people get in attempting to crack it, baby."

"Sounds like American politics—the longer the gridlock stays, the more people shoot each other because of policies of those in power. I gotta go now," Debra announced. The dimly lit parking lot seemed safer than being near this creepy yet somehow charismatic man.

"Okay girlie. Careful in the dark."

Debra turned, "Tell me something, is all this real?"

"More than you can ever imagine."

CHAPTER ONE

Caryssa

Year 2017

They all came. Pretend queens, kings, rooks and crooks—claiming to be selflessly fundraising. The place was packed, everyone dressed as either royalty or villains. Yet, there was no way to differentiate them.

Everyone was attired in high-end masks paired with extravagant costumes. The masks changed into menacing shapes and spoke in robotic voices. I couldn't understand a word. My thoughts zoomed in and out in a hazy netherworld of consciousness, spiraling in my psyche.

Coal black masks looking like Darth Vader, I half expected them to whip out lightsabers. Mixed with the intergalactic masks were heavily gilded Venetian disguises.

I wandered invisible myself behind mysterious black lace, through the elegant ballroom near the White House. The combination of fresh cut tobacco, leather and perfumes cast off a sensual scent. I was not afraid, as I hid my own identity. I floated by the boldest of bankers, most prominent politicians, and ruthless leaders of the world.

I shouldn't be here. But who will know? I mingled like an unseen fly on the wall. The good people came to enjoy the masked political theatre. Fools duped by the masquerade.

I walked up to one of the most sinister of masked figures and ripped it off. Down came the plaster and paint, the cardboard box covering the face. What hid beneath the veneer shocked me. I couldn't help but gasp. What scared me most was—he knew my name.

"Hello Caryssa."

I awoke with a jerk, heart thundering in my chest. George lay beside me, sipping coffee. He sat the coffee cup on the nightstand, before wrapping his arms around me. "Saving the world again in your dreams, babe?" I was drenched in perspiration, shaking off the dream, shedding the unpleasant feeling.

We snuggled. "Man, these dreams are happening more the older Tyler gets." I glanced outside our bedroom window at the blue-green bay and sparkling city. A light fog twined around the Golden Gate Bridge, rendering it nearly invisible. *God, I live surrounded with such beauty and peace.*

George rolled his eyes. "Let me guess…killer robots and the human race forced to go live on a spaceship, fleeing the Mother Earth it destroyed?" He gave me a side glance, one eyebrow raised.

"Something along those lines. Only I was in D.C. at a masquerade fundraiser for *'the people'*—Masks were blurring, cracking and talking in mechanical voices. I pulled off the darkest mask, an Emperor Palpatine look-alike—and saw my former boss's face."

"*Your former boss*…oh, must have been the one that said if you don't work fourteen-plus hour days, you are not *tech-start-up material.*" George altered his voice, mimicking my former boss Debra.

"No, it was not the queen bee bitch boss, it was one I really liked at Unabridged Networks. It was Rob, the one that promoted me to Senior Marketing Analyst! Odd, why would I dream of him as a bad guy?"

"Well…you did mention he went to some tech-start-up, designing robotics warfare. Your dream makes sense to me."

A cold wriggling sensation settled in my bones, digging deep into my marrow as I remembered something Rob had mentioned. He's been dabbling in corporate espionage. This is the man that once had me working undercover collecting competitive intelligence for a tech giant rival. The corporate Chess games.

My creepy dream suddenly made sense—who was under those sinister masks? Politicians, faceless corporations and connected shady government operations. They were hiding accountability for the atrocities against our own nation's people with our wars while poisoning our food and water. They were hiding a violent brand image.

Seeing the big picture twenty years later as a mother is downright scary.

* * *

Tyler tossed his backpack into the SUV during pick-up for tennis practice. *I don't know why my mom gets so weirded out about the D.C. trip,* he thought. He retrieved his cell phone from his pocket. *It would be cool to see the capital.*

He texted his buddy Rowan, fingers whizzing around and prodding at the keys. *Dunno about D.C., might ski.*

A second later his phone pinged. *r u bowing out cause ur mom?*

Tyler frowned, then texted back. *wtf, no just wanna ski.* His thumbs hovered over the keys, contemplating if he should reveal something else when another text appeared.

I guess I don't blame u 4 wanting 2 ski instead of a school trip.

Tyler stopped texting, glancing at the tall palm trees outside the car window. "Hey, Mom? I'd rather ski than something school related during spring break."

His mom started the engine, while giving him one of those looks that always made him wish she would trust his choices. "Are you sure Ty? You have friends going, and it's your first chance to see Washington D.C.? This is your decision, not mine."

"Yeah, Mom. I mean…I kinda wanna go, but I need a break. And…. well…I really wanna ski." Tyler avoided his mom's compassionate gaze, and instead admired the palm trees.

"Well, okay then, skiing it will be!" He swore that it was relief punctuating his mother's sentence.

* * *

Pulling away from the curb, I couldn't help but say to my son. "The fresh air and exercise are a healthier option anyhow."

Tyler shrugged. Then he circled his shoulders while rotating his head, relieving tension with a stretch.

"Are you having second thoughts, Ty-"?

"What? What? No! I'm limbering up for tennis mom, *jeez*."

"Ok, Ok! Go have a great practice, I'll see you when you get home." My fiercely independent thirteen-year-old son grabbed his tennis racket, and eagerly dashed off to hit some balls.

* * *

I had two hours before Tyler would walk home from the tennis courts. Driving home, I mused over my mysterious dreams. I suspected a reason for them was my child's pending D.C. trip.

And—the recent trip back to our roots of New England. *Beautiful, quaint New England.*

Driving through the picturesque green mountains of Vermont, the writing on the wall had hit me when stepping into a rest area. This never bothered me before—*before having a child.*

Pictures of Vietnam are unduly displayed all over one side of the room. A woman walked up to wide-eyed children—*including Tyler* and a young girl next to him—asking them if they plan to "join the army."

America's *Hunger Games* played out on our highways justified with federal money. Luring kids with glorification of our violent culture. How tender traveling through this nostalgic time machine with my own precious child, images of my privileged cherry-blossomed childhood flashing before my eyes:

At my family's serene cottages on the lake in NH—running on the beach, riding on our three boats, snow skiing, trips to Disney. The song "It's a small world" flowing through my mind. All while our spurious little Vietnam adventure raged behind the curtain, shielding me from a cruel political reality.

History repeats.

The contradictory spirit of violence and big glory blending with our nation's surreal beauty. America the Beautiful. America the Turbulent—a contrast of dark and light, beauty and the beast.

Then I thought of Anna's dad from Paris and reminded myself it's a global thing—the global atrocity of the military industrial complex. Yet USA is the biggest player in the deception dance of power, to our own detriment.

Memories of New England—its rustic beauty and colorful landscape coalesce into something as forgotten but familiar as my Dad's voice—flatlands giving way to magnificent mountains I was blessed to ski on as a kid.

Veering into our driveway, I was surprised George's car was already there. He played the keyboard of his laptop, eyes fixed with uninhibited focus at the dining room table while perched at the edge of his seat. I glanced out the window at the tropical turquoise color of the San Francisco Bay, a Mediterranean-style daily delight.

"Working from home this afternoon?"

"Yup." He offered, without prying his gaze from the screen or even slowing the pace of his rapidly typing fingers.

"Well, I won't disturb you…. but Tyler is going skiing with us rather than to D.C.." I informed.

"Hmmm…surprising." Again, he managed to respond without hindering his work progress.

"Why? He loves to ski."

'True. Yet it's a great chance to see his nation's capital, Caryss, and with classmates."

"Well…It breaks my heart that as parents today, we have to question whether having our kids go to our own capital is high on our bucket list. It's far too gilded and corrupt."

"It *always* has been. Someday, Tyler will go."

"Of course, and he mustn't think to glorify any of the violence displayed with our war helmets from hell. It's how we end up with money monsters in the White House, and once innocent kids shooting down others."

"Sometimes I wish you never connected the dots of tech corporate America to mass surveillance, endless war and secret networks." George shut his laptop as if on cue to escape cyber spies.

"And remained blissfully ignorant? You *know* they all answer to the same corporate masters—connected to the secret CIA spy networks around the world."

"True...but don't forget it's not just D.C. or New England buried in the destructive '*defense*' industry. California has its share of—"

"You have no need to tell me this...I told you from the start I connected the dots to my beloved Silicon Valley." It conflicted me how both the NRA and Silicon Valley put profits before the people in the areas of gun sales, weaponized ads, social manipulation and military contracts.

"And now we have beautiful San Diego as the national leader of the drone industry." George added.

* * *

The following day I headed over the Richmond-San Rafael Bridge into Sausalito to visit Anna. We dubbed our weekly girl time as "high tea" at her charming loft in the hills. Today, I would again meet Julie, who was quick to correct my tea time etiquette. Julie, a firecracker with flashy outfits that matched her vibrant red hair.

I dropped into the eclectic village of Sausalito, passing dozens of quaint shops. Sail boats were sprinkled along the water's edge. I rolled down my window, soaking in the smells of garlic and fresh seafood wafting through the sea air. Purple and pink wispy clouds dotted the baby-blue sky.

After passing through quaint downtown Sausalito, I turned up the hill towards Anna's loft, enchanted by the Tuscan-style villas and Spanish Mediterranean condos. Remembering the impossible parking on her tiny, winding road, I parked on the street below. Art-deco-esque pillars stood at the entrance of steep steps that would bring me to Anna's deck. *And to the narrow, winding road her daughter was killed on.*

A chill trailed my spine and settled deep within my motherly soul. My heart clenched for Anna, tightening with sorrow. That woman has suffered so much loss…starting with her father killed in the Vietnam War when she was just a young girl. Tragic.

Late afternoon fog snaked across Angel Island like a long, low dragon breathing cool air. I stood on Anna's deck overlooking the bay, taking deep meditative breaths after having walked up 108 steps to loft haven. The views from up here are spectacular—an expanse of San Francisco Bay, pleasure boats, islands and palm trees. The air saturated with the scent of eucalyptus. Bougainvillea wrapped fences and trellises.

Anna came to greet me. "You're the first to arrive! It will be only the three of us today." She had just returned from her home city of Paris and decked herself out bohemian style. "Let's stay out here for tea time and enjoy this amazing sunshine."

I offered to take the tray of finger sandwiches and dainty desserts from Anna's hands, placing it on the bistro table. "Wow, you've got the tousled, sexy bed-head look going on, girl! A Parisian fashionista!" Anna was squeezed into her dark skinny jeans paired with an oversized white shirt and a Hermès scarf. A light breeze tussled her scarf. "So how was your trip to Paris?"

"Hectic yet enjoyable. I sold a handful of my most valuable Indonesian and Indian arts while there, so it's all good! I might be able to sell my inventory after closing shop after all…"

Julie appeared through the sliding glass door wearing a smile, so there was hope in remaining in the happy place I felt on the way. "Hello, ladies, nice day for afternoon tea with a view! Who needs Japanese Tea Garden when we have Anna's lovely loft?" I couldn't help wondering if the boobs spilling out of her white sundress were real.

"Exactly! No fancy tea rooms required here!" I smiled at Julie, appreciating her wide brim tea hat. Red hat, red lips, and red-hot temper lay beneath a flashy surface.

Julie turned to Anna "So, I heard you sold *Exotic Exposure* merchandise while in Paris?"

"Oh yes, I sold five of my most prized possessions to collectors in Paris, mostly online. Now I just need to ship the items to them." Anna's grin stretched from one side of her face to the other, in an uninhibited expression of excitement.

"I loved visiting Paris," I mentioned while reaching for a salmon-cucumber tea sandwich. "The bon vivant lifestyle, romantic streets, and such a blissful simplicity of life. And all the art galleries!"

"So…where's your peaceful Paris today, Caryssa?" Julie burst out in a snide tone as she scraped a yellow wicker chair across the deck.

Deep nostalgic emotions tugged at my maternal heartstrings, provoked by Julie's question. *Where did her bitterness come from?* "I…I was referring to nearly fourteen years ago, a trip with my husband, Julie. Our only child was conceived in Paris, so there's a special bond."

"Speaking of Tyler, his trip to D.C. is coming up, right?" Anna asked, steering Julie away from her geopolitical rantings, seemingly sensing a pending eruption if she didn't act fast.

"Yes, only he's not going. I hafta admit, I am relieved." *Come to think of it, my kid's near-happening trip may be what's making me feel sensitive to Julie's edgy viewpoints.* I added "Why, pray tell, would I want my precious child near the dysfunction afflicting Washington?"

Anna's gaze fell from me to Julie. With composure, she replied "Yes, Jules, Paris was peaceful when Caryssa went there. But I passed by riot police and masked protestors during my recent trip. I was afraid a Molotov cocktail would be tossed my way. It was sad to see my home city like this."

This revved Julie's engine again, with more purposely televised fearmongering "That's what I mean, and the terrorist attacks there and—"

"Julie, may I say something?" I interrupted. "I'm from Boston and like Anna, my heart cries for my home city. But look at the big picture. 'Terrorism' has risen 6500% since the horrific façade of the 'war on terror' started."

The sun reflected upon solar panels of a wooden building down the hill, with bright pink bougainvillea flashing back at us. Such beauty contrasting with my thought: *Mere fallouts of the perpetual beasts of battle…the NATO alliance we share with France which is anything but the peacemaking pact it's touted as.*

I desperately wanted to divert the topic from Julie's dramatized flippant logic. She must watch an abundance of our choreographed reality TV acting known as news.

Today, rather than correct me for not raising a pinky while sipping tea, or my fashion sense, it appeared Julie's only wish was to correct my '*political correctness*'. Hence, I let Anna take the wheel.

Anna put out more Lenox French Perle tea cups and saucers, as the kettle whistled again. "Jules, do we think maybe…these attacks are planted on purpose in the most developed, civilized, fashionable areas to scare people into submission—*New York City, London, Paris, Nice, Las Vegas, Boston—.*"

"Oh no, not you too Anna!" interrupted Julie, throwing her arms up. A disappointed look befell her face. "You are freaking sounding like Caryssa with her nutcase conspiracy theories. Come on, *scare people into submission?*" She rolled her eyes so hard she no doubt caught a glimpse of her brain.

I was about to take another bite of my sandwich, but nonchalantly placed it on the table instead. "I…think we should change the subject. Oh look! Beautiful sailboats in the bay!" I aimed a finger at the picturesque seaside, hoping to derail the escalating tension.

What I wanted to say was *Yes, scare people into our state sponsored televised battle to death against global military created beast of terror, all played out over our sensationalized news to look like some good humanitarian deed.*

Anna let ginger and lavender tea spill into each cup. "Did you bring the sprigs of lavender from your garden, Caryssa?"

"Oh, yes, let me get them." I pulled a little wax bag out of my purse, teasing it open and scooping up sprigs of lavender. I let a sprig plop into each cup. With any luck, the lavender would serve its calming therapeutic qualities to ease Julie's deep monarch programming. I pray for the inner peace of people falling for the propaganda machine fanning the fabricated flames since even before the Spanish-American war.

Anna shot Julie a serious look. "There's a holy union between political manipulation and showbiz, Jules. Not only within America, but my beautiful home city of Paris now dredging up Gestapo-like militarized cops as well."

"I can't believe you two" Julie shook her head, while nibbling her lip. "I mean…We need to protect our national security and freedom!" She spat, outraged.

"*Holy buzzwords, Batman!*" Julie's use of twisted tongues and loopy lingo almost saw me choking on my pastry. "Do you really think the creeping militarization of our sociopathic economy has anything to do with 'national security' or 'freedom'?" *Among the many outlandish clichés that should be relegated to the dustbin of history.*

"Sure"…then Julie noticed Anna shaking her head. "Are you two fucking high?"

"Oh yes, high on this wonderful thing called life." I was enjoying the soothing tea, killer view, and scrumptious finger foods—such contrast to the topic I wished Julie never started. "It's certainly not about maintaining world peace."

Freedom. It was a word that got into its own way. It was a word that held itself a sense of its own limits, an echo of death.

"I suppose North Korea and Russia will peace out the planet with polite poetic justice." Julie yelped, having just taken a sip of piping hot tea. "*Ouch!*" she jerked, the tea spurting out her nose, running like a leaky faucet.

I carried my tea to the other side of the deck, glancing over the Sausalito Bay in all its glory. *Deep breaths!* I called over my shoulder. "Must we continue to label the entire world our '*enemies*'? Those two countries spend *way* less than we do on military!" I visualized the tiny drone cameras hov-

ering over community events, and imagined Julie blaming Russian spies—
or "illegal aliens" bringing in drugs.

I can't imagine how this educated, sophisticated girl from Sausalito can
be so anti-intellectualist. A fear-induced propagandist. Meanwhile, the
gun manufacturers seek their next new lucrative market on school shelves
and in the hands of teachers across America, with a deceptive tagline of
"protecting our kids."

A huge palm tree graced Anna's view of the bay lightly kissed by the
breeze. Sailboats and the city skyline glimmered their magnificence. Despite
the flare-up of the lady in red, I was deeply at inner peace. *Ignorance is not
bliss after all. It enables the worn-out war bandwagon to continue rolling.*

Anna's soft voice, peppered with that magnificent French accent, came
from the kitchen as she fetched more tea "Julie, our political system is connected to multinational corporate profit. Why can't you calmly admit we
are an outrageous war economy?"

"Seriously, no country profits from war more than the USA." I gestured toward Julie. I wanted to change the topic. Afternoon high tea in
chic Sausalito isn't the place for her hawkish diatribes. "So, Julie, where did
you grow up?"

"Right here, in Sausalito. My grandfather settled the family here years
ago, we have local history. He was a shipbuilder during WWII. He was
CEO of Marinship Corporation. He helped the war effort in building all
those Liberty ships and Fleet oilers that saved *your* friggin freedom!"

"Ah ha!" was all I managed. *Even the most progressive, stylish areas of
California have people blindly accepting of our mindlessly militarized society.* I
kept this thought locked tight in my brain-vault, else the red-firecracker
would detonate again, exploding with her fiery programmed viewpoints.
Either she is tirelessly gullible, or I underestimated the media's impact.

A stark reminder of how much the grand opulence of America, not unlike France, Italy, Russia and other developed nations are built upon devious
war profits. Yet now *we* are the most violent developed nation in the world.

Will we ever be a moral economy?

CHAPTER TWO

Julie

As evening settled, I trekked back to my modest apartment. Maybe if rent wasn't daylight robbery I could afford a house—or I could marry some rich gentleman. There must be swarms of wealthy suitors in Sausalito. I should join a Singles-over-Sixty meetup and hunt down my Mr. Moneybags to lift that financial weight from my shoulders.

I strolled through The San Francisco Bay Model, picturing my Dad working here in 1942—back when it was a military shipbuilding warehouse. I'm so proud of him, climbing the ladder of Marinship from the assembly line to CEO. Without such wages, my parents could never have bought their house perched on the steeply sloping Sausalito hillside.

I stood at the U.S. Army Corps of Engineers structure thinking of my parents. As a little girl in the late 50's, both Mom and Dad came home in their Bechtel uniforms, joking how Daddy didn't have to go off to fight because he helped the war effort at home.

I'll always remember the excitement ebbing from him as he told us about building the ships. His face glowed. His words were punctuated with enthusiasm. Even his gestures implied great fascination, as if he molded a cloud, adding the contours and colors with a face lit with wonder. Beyond the patio and rocks, were boats and the golden rolling hills.

"You have a far-away look in your eyes. Have you just seen a ghost?" I turned towards a male voice and was hit with the sexiest eyes I've ever seen, a striking emerald set deep in a smooth chocolate face.

"I guess you can say that…I always feel my father's spirit here." My voice trembled a smidge talking to this handsome stranger, whom I was disheartened to see was at least thirty years younger than me. No chance of him swooping me off my feet. He threw a curious look my way, so I elaborated. "My Dad worked here—of course, most of the shipyard he worked in is now long gone."

My eyes wandered along the grounds and returned to the young handsome black man in a work uniform. Fighting the internal demons conditioning me to clutch my purse tightly, I snatched a glance at his name tag. "So, Marc…I'm Julie. What do you do for the Bay Model?"

A foghorn emitted a low moan in the distance. "I am a volunteer tour guide for kids on school field trips. How about yourself?" He peeked at my boobs, stuffed into a Wonderbra, creating the illusion of perky cleavage belonging to a younger lady.

"My office is just down the street. I work for a non-profit, the Historical Society preserving our heritage, including the Marinship Exhibit here. Do you take the kids through that display?" Nervousness tightened my throat, words escaped my lips shaky and strained. *Was I trying to impress him?*

"No, most teachers want us to focus on the environment, and it takes a while for the children to walk through our scale model. No time left to waste on rusty warships. We want to preserve the bay and delta and teach them the effects of pollution on the watershed. I have a degree in Geological Science, so I love to talk about ecology and natural history with kids."

Rusty warships! How dare he? "But what about preserving our history of defense of our country?" I asked, perhaps a little too forcefully.

Marc rolled his sparkling green eyes while shaking his head. That simple gesture spoke volumes. Before words spouted from his mouth, it was clear he didn't share my feelings. "My generation grew up on dark money spent by a faceless few—it's not about defense now, and some unsustainable history I'd rather forget."

Oh no, not him too! What's the world coming to? Rational and otherwise sane individuals so anti-military. My father must be rolling in his grave.

With my fists clenched, my voice rose several octaves. I stamped seriousness into each word. "Back then, our leaders put our parents to work during the great depression, defeated fascism, and built a middle class on the G.I. Bill," I informed him firmly.

I was not going to let this young progressive buck crush my parent's livelihood.

Marc's eyes and mouth opened wide, his eyebrows reaching for his hairline. "Back then...we had a decadent star-spangled propagandist cartoon character named 'Captain America' blurring the lines between fiction and reality. We never defeated fascism—rather American-flavored fascism is alive today with the same war propaganda as narrative. And the *GI Bill?* It is nothing but an oppressive carrot dangling to entice youth into war. I'm *happy* it left out many blacks," he declared.

"Are you calling Hitler fiction or a cartoon character?" Heat bloomed in my face, I could feel it. My heartbeat quickened, a pulse tapping my eardrums.

"No...my great grandfather who lived in Austria during WWII left plenty of commentaries behind, verifying Hitler was real. A real monster. He was a military man who thought he was doing the right thing. Like our *own* totalitarian leaders today, the people voted Hitler in. I am speaking of blind apathy—we have our own history of killing and marching people into oppression." He explained, tone unwavering, retaining his cool. Unlike myself, ready to explode at any minute.

"But he had to be stopped. Don't you—"

"*We* have to be stopped, for our own goodwill! Imagine investing in things like education so we have free college like other nations? My generation is swimming in a mountain of student debt. And too many of my friends, men, and women, went off to Iraq and Afghanistan. It's not something I glorify."

I fought for the spotlight, but this was one stubborn SOB who wanted center stage. His eyes wandered the surroundings, avoiding my gaze, darting around. Perhaps he was ready to lose his cool but simply hid it well, afraid that locking sight with me would tear at the fabrics of his composure?

"Well, we can't just let genocides happen with extremist regimes ruling society," I said. The people whose opinions differed greatly from my own seemed to increase at an alarming rate. *Caryssa, Anna, and half my crafts class. Perhaps half the world…*

"That's what our blind apathy is *enabling* us to do. Do you think Andrew Jackson, Abe Lincoln, Harry Truman or even JFK were not responsible for horrific genocides of our own youth? Our own historic tyrants sending kids off to die. We need to stop using Hitler as the gold standard of all evil. War is for profit—was then and is now."

Better not mention my family was once part of the 'money class' that profited from the good war. *'The faceless few.'* I was about to shuffle away from this uncomfortable conflict when Marc spoke softly.

"Where do you call home, Julie?"

"Here…I grew up in Sausalito and have never left. For over twenty years I had my own rented space within my parent's beautiful home I grew up in —but my mother and I were forced to sell it last year at a loss after my Dad died. The house hadn't been renovated and needed work." I replied.

His eyes met mine, suddenly full of compassion.

"I'm sorry." His face sagged with empathy.

I wasn't sure if he meant the loss of my Dad or home. "Thanks. He was nearly ninety-four, so he lived a good life."

Silence stole the next minute or so. The tables had turned as it appeared Marc wanted to physically and metaphorically checkout of this conversation. But something in those captivating ivy eyes drew me in with no less thrall than the call of a sea siren. Despite this strange political debate with a stranger that had been rife with awkward disagreement, I trusted him. The cogs of realization were turning.

"How about you Marc, where do you call home?"

"I also live where I grew up—it's hard to leave family behind. I just bought a condo unit in Marin City, worked three jobs to save for it." His gaze settled comfortably on mine.

"So…this job, and you have two others?"

"Oh this…This is a volunteer gig, I volunteer to help kids. I am also a Big Brother. My paying jobs are in my field. After graduating from Stanford, I got a job in the city as an Environmental Consultant. I—"

"*You* graduated from Stanford?" I felt jealous, maybe even pissed.

"Ah…yeah, guess you Sausalito hill people have a hard time thinking of us ghetto-down-the-street black folk as being Stanford material, hey?" He sighed and twisted his head. A look landed on his face, speaking louder than any words he could utter. That look wasn't subtle; I nearly heard his thought: *a typical white supremacist.*

"No, no…sorry to imply that." I searched for words, stumbling through a sentence. My heart once again danced to a faster rhythm, this time from embarrassment. "I got rejected by Stanford and realize how bright you must be," I shoved out, eager to justify myself, which seemed ludicrous. I hadn't meant it offensively. He offered me nothing more than a slight nod and a crumpled-lip smile, continuing to speak volumes without uttering words.

The silence between us droned on, Marc had nothing more to say, so I mumbled, "Don't forget though, Stanford was an early epicenter of tech-innovation for military—"

A solid shake of his head stopped me short as he walked away, with a mere lift of his hand as if swatting unwanted flies away.

As I traveled the last stretch from the Bay Model to my shoebox of an apartment, I realized I was wrong about the millennial generation. It was I who felt a sense of entitlement. Could I also have been manipulated by the throngs of media about our militarized society?

I realized in a flash Caryssa and Anna may be right. I'm holding on a bit too tightly to my father's Liberty ship legacy—which has become more a *lunacy* praised by the lunatic fringe.

* * *

A beeping cell phone welcomed me as I entered my apartment. I immediately prodded the play button. A jittery voice echoed, soaked in anxiety. I know that voice. My brother. I froze.

"Jules, this is Jackson. I am sitting in the back of a police car, they've arrested me for taking pictures in the Times Square subway station. Cops are claiming it's illegal to take pictures here for commercial use. Even mentioned I may be a terror threat! Oh shit, can't talk anymore—"

The voicemail stopped. Dread chomped on my stilled heart. What if they took my sweet-natured brother to jail? I had flashbacks of him as a little boy, trying to "save" all the critters he snapped shots of. My little bro was one of the gentlest, kindest men I know—and was prone to panic attacks. That nugget of knowledge filled me with an insatiable urge to help him. I could survive a night in a dingy little cell. He'd choke on fear, wracked with fright over his uncertain future and possible criminal prosecution.

My neighbor's Basset Hound, a little bundle of attitude, had howled relentlessly since I approached the neighborhood. The never-ending barks drowned out my wind chimes, fraying my nerves even more.

An attempted callback to Jackson went instantly into his voicemail. *Shit!* I palmed my forehead in frustration. I needed answers to a sudden barrage of questions streaming into my consciousness. I left a message in the vain hope he'd hear it.

"Jack, its Jules. What the—why the fuck would they bother to arrest you? Please call me if you can, love you." I held back angst as much as possible but feared it was stapled into every word.

My brother's family hadn't used a landline for years, and his wife Amy and I had never emotionally connected, so I had no cell phone number for her. How else could I—*Facebook!* I sent her a private message.

'Amy, have you heard from my brother? He left me a message about being arrested at the subway station for taking photos! Call me please.' I typed in my cell phone number.

While retrieving pots and pans to whip up dinner, I remembered my cell had rung while at the Bay Model, but I was so mesmerized talking to the mysterious black dude I ignored it. A pang of guilt quaked through me, as I realized it was my little brother seeking emotional support.

When we were kids, we called him "Action Jackson." As a young boy, he never stopped moving between sports, catching frogs or taking snapshots of everything in his path with his Kodak Instamatic. By age seven, he'd returned from adventures with instant snapshots of turtles, snakes, squirrels, and even raccoon poop. Nobody could perfect a lens focus of the feces like Jackson. My mom often hauled him into the hospital to check for ringworm, afraid of what he may have been in contact with during those Kodak moments.

Since relocating to New York City for his job, I barely see him. An Art Director for a railroad magazine, they transferred him to cover the on-again, off-again high-speed rail project. Between his demanding job, juggling family time and nonstop sports with his kids, Action Jackson is still on the move, not hindered by age or a laundry list of responsibility.

After the fancy finger foods and tea at Anna's and worrying about my brother, my appetite vanished. Maybe I can salvage these overcooked mushy noodles by sautéing them with olive oil and garlic tomorrow? Hunger was the last thing on my mind.

Nausea settled in my stomach as I thought about my little brother who would save rabid raccoons as a boy and now wants to save people from being tragically killed due to USA's crumbling infrastructure. *There is no way he belongs in a jail cell.* That would be a complete perversion of justice.

I googled the law as it pertains to taking photographs in the Big Apple subways, and found it was permitted but may be questioned when using professional equipment. I stumbled upon several links concerning totally innocent people being cuffed, with cops and MTA workers invalidly claiming all picture taking in subways was illegal.

This concerned me. I tried to contact a couple of my attorney friends on behalf of my brother. I didn't get far.

My cell rang, I partly hoped it was an attorney returning a call. I swiped it to answer. "Amy!"

"Hi, Julie. Yes, Jack called but the communication was clipped." I could hear my niece Hayley crying in the background. Amy continued, "He's being detained at the station as a suspected terrorist. Can you imagine? My sweet husband being treated like a suspicious criminal! His crime? Taking pictures of Manhattan's dilapidated subway to advocate funds for an upgrade." Her voice cracked with emotion, choking down sobs.

I stayed calm for Amy's sake but inwardly trembled. "Did…did he have his tripod or lights with him for this photo shoot or—"

"No! I mean no he…he did not have all his equipment with him, not to mention he had a press pass to get an angle for a piece about stopping derailing tragedies. God, this royally sucks!" My nephew Hans shouted, *"my daddy's a hero, not a terrorist!"*

"What's up with the cops back east? Are they freaking republicans who hate trains?" Amy seemed to appreciate my political satire and laughed, breaking the tension. "And Jackson should know what the law is about taking pictures in a sub—"

"He *does* know the law about photography in subway stations, including that it's not against the law! The NYPD has been overly edgy ever since 9/11 and subsequent terror threats following, systematically harassing artist and photographers. It's hogwash." The kids sang in the background escaping the reality of injustice to their dad.

"For Christ sakes, that was seventeen years ago, they need to let go already and stop bullying innocent civilians." I gritted my teeth in anger, realizing the absurdity of the situation.

Amy lowered her voice for the kid's sakes, as she practically whispered "Seriously, they treated him like a street creep. He's a productive citizen out doing a damn photo shoot for his company!"

"Street creep? Nope, not my bro." *He is an amazingly talented photojournalist with his work recognized globally.* I silently remembered how he'd simply post photos to his blog and they spread like wildfire. The little boy that saved vicious dogs from being put down could not have grown up to become a terrorist. *Could he? No.* I shrugged off that ridiculous morsel of doubt.

I glanced at my wall clock. It was almost ten-thirty at night on the east coast. "Well, it's getting late there so I'll let you go, but please call me if you hear from Jack."

"I've tried calling him three times, and he doesn't pick up. Which can't be a good sign. None of us will get much sleep tonight." Amy's voice warbled with nerves.

"Well...you did call directly into the station, right?" Amy was somewhat flaky in my opinion, but I couldn't imagine her not checking in with law enforcement for their version. Surely, this would be common sense? Call the authorities.

Silence.

"Amy?"

I currently despised silence. Before receiving that voicemail, I adored silence. It allowed me to listen to the far-off music of nature, soak up the present moment. Now silence was my enemy. When questions and unsettled situations tugged me every which way, the last thing I wanted was soundlessness.

"You know, I didn't even think of that since Jack specifically said they were detaining him at the station. What else could they say? Besides, I'd just end up telling them to fuck off." I sensed anger, understandable.

Something clicked inside me, with three people within three hours of hinting at our growing police state. Yet, I tried to cloak myself in calm. "Jack will get through this, people get arrested every day. Give Hayley and Hans a hug and kiss from Auntie Jules, and let's talk tomorrow." I ended the call with sadness rolling down my cheeks, dampening my face in salty tears.

To balance my nerves, I glanced around my studio apartment with gratitude. The original listing description had never exaggerated. It offered raised hardwood floor. Brightness poured inside, giving an open airy feel. Let's not forget the built-ins. What it lacked for in size, it made up for in character.

Upon moving in last year, I spent hours with funky arrangements stacking my books, adding large pieces like statues, pottery, and plants. When Anna and Caryssa came over, they mentioned they loved my eclectic collections and how it resembled a mini-library, but with classic décor that kept it from feeling like a workhorse study.

Of course, this didn't stop Caryssa from opening my books with notepad in hand, scribbling down metaphors and moral messages she claimed matched her writing. She had lifted my coffee-table book about the San Francisco Bay housing market and announced: "see, says here the tech industry that made the Bay Area rich, is inching out the middle class!"

I couldn't understand how with her former Silicon Valley fat paycheck and her big house in the hills, this could be a concern. That woman drives me nuts.

Although I gotta admit, paying $3,500 a month to live in a sophisticated shoebox in Sausalito is not helping me save for a house. She may have a point. I grew up in a house in Sausalito Hills people would die to live in today and can barely afford to live in my studio apartment.

While letting steam and hot water wash over me in the shower, massaging my tense muscles, I thought about what Anna said about our cities dredging up Nazi Gestapo-like cops. How Caryssa links our tech-crazed crime fighting R2-D2 robots—looking straight out of a Sci-Fi movie to our perpetual war economy.

There's even talk of a "Space Force."

They just might be right. Star Wars has come to America. And we couldn't rely on Obi-Wan.

CHAPTER THREE

Anna

"Anna, it's Sergeant Coral. Another dead dove was found, with the same bloody symbols on it. It appears to be connected to your art gallery ordeal. And...well, call me back on my cell, NOT the station."

The voicemail followed me everywhere, anchoring me to dread, drowning me in anxiety. Running errands couldn't distract me. My heart dominated my head, its *thump, thump, thump* accelerating my fear. I had to call Jason back sooner or later. It was unavoidable.

This can't be happening. Both girls that robbed my art gallery and murdered my security guard were sentenced to prison after the trial. *Weren't they?* Perhaps I should have checked the news occasionally for updates? Rather than burying my head in the sand.

As I was gathering my emotions, a slice of inner peace gets crushed. Overall, life is good again—Pierre and I are behaving like newlyweds, I closed my shop and am back on the teaching front. From the comfort of my home, I teach children the magnificence of art. We recently flitted off to Paris. And best of all, spending time with our grandson Jared. Then this came raining on my parade.

I returned Jason's call and caught him on the first ring.

"Sergeant Coral," he answered with a firm and confident voice.

"Hi Jason, it's Anna Beauvais. So...another dove?"

"Yup another baffling bird has come back to haunt our peaceful community. Look, I know I shouldn't tell you these things, but because of our past dealings..."

Silence veered his sentence off course.

I filled my lungs. "Yes, Bianca's fatal skateboarding accident thirteen years ago, and then the murder at my art gallery six years later. And now you want me to never forget the past—"

"You're right, I'm sorry I called." Sergeant Coral cleared his throat. I realized I didn't want him to hang up, strangely enough.

"Wait! You've got me spooked. I wonder why you think this is connected—the dove could not possibly be found behind an art gallery I no longer own." My mind now raced faster than my heartbeat, a tornado crashing through my consciousness. "Where was it found, by the way?"

Sergeant Coral paused as if to ponder his response. "It was found just outside the Redwood City women's prison—the facility detaining Paige Watson...and where Ava Ramírez was also sentenced to go yet never made it." He explained.

This snatched my attention. *So, it is connected.* Then again, what was I thinking? How many blood-soaked doves are found lying around the peaceful, palm lined streets of California? Not too many I'd hope.

Ava...I learned her name is from the Latin "avis," meaning "bird." *Surprise!*

Still, I didn't want to believe it. These girls were only eighteen and nineteen respectively when they committed this horrific crime. "Maybe it was one of those pigeons stuffed with cocaine and cannabis. You know, those 'drugs doves' we hear about used by prisoners to smuggle substances in. One of the guards got spooked and shot it."

Coral snorted amusement, picking up on my subtle joke to settle the sea of my nerves before moving on. "Anna, you know what I say stays between us, you are the only civilian I've ever conveyed so much detail. There's more found at the scene of the second dove beyond bloody drops."

The tension thickened. My chest tightened. My panic grew. "Jason, please don't tell me one of my friends or family member's blood was on this dove. And…how did it get there anyhow, with the girls in prison? What do you mean Ava never made it into prison?" Unstoppable questions flooded into my mouth, streaming from my tongue.

Images of my girls flashed before my eyes. Lithe little Bianca flying down the street on a skateboard—the skateboard she was killed on. Cassidy, all giggles with her Monet French easel. Her personality as bright and colorful as the art she created. Until her little sister's tragedy, when she took her own life. Until…

I silently cursed Coral for reopening the wounds and bringing back a fresh lease of my grief.

A huge sigh echoed across the electromagnetic waves from the overworked police sergeant. "We don't have a match on the blood yet, for all we know it could be the doves. I expect to hear from forensics soon. But…" Another sigh, equally as heavy.

I waited. Ruckus from a bustling police station oozed into the telephone line. Phones rang monotonously. Conversation barged into conversation, words tangling in an indecipherable chaos. Slurps of officers taking their shots of caffeine through creamy coffees no doubt serving as dipping sauce for sugary donuts. Types and clicks from admin slaving away at computers, playing the keyboard like a symphony pianist on speed.

"Ava Ramírez's well-off dad raised millions with his business associates to post her bail." Jason continued in a near whisper. My guess, he stood outside the station, possibly beside the entrance if the pandemonium was any indication. In the eleven years that I've known him, we've become friends of a sort. He's never been the "Officer Donut" type, slumped in his car dunking sugary shit into a takeout coffee like most law enforcers.

"Ah *merde!* Typical…the wealthier defendants go free while the poor remain locked up." My chest tensed, as I wondered how Johnny's family felt about this. I had to ask the next question, "And what's this about something else found with the second dove?"

"This is really why I called you, why we know it's connected to the murder at your art gallery. There were three other items found: An olive branch was stuffed into the dove's right claw, thirteen sticks in its left claw. And a Picasso painting with *Exotic Exposure* printed on the back leaned against the building."

The Picasso painting! Not until I cleared out my inventory to sell my art gallery business, did I notice my copy of "La Paloma" *The Dove* was gone. It wasn't just the Bronze Sculpture and Delacroix they stole. "Ah double fucking shit—there's the missing piece of my art puzzle."

"At least this painting is not ripped to shreds like your last one. Is it worth a lot?" He inquired.

"It's worth the oil paints, brushes, canvas, time and effort. It's my personal attempt at playing Picasso." I crafted a vision of my painting, and was reminded of how awesome it came out, down to the soft tones of the silky feathers. People with uncritical eyes thought it was a Picasso original. If I was among the asshole con-artists that sold copies as the real deal, I'd be rolling in it.

"Anna, I wasn't going to mention this as I'd be fired if the boss knew what I've told you already, but the name of your art gallery was not the only thing written on the back of your painting." He spoke with a hushed volume, clearly wanting to avoid being overheard. I didn't blame him if his career was on the line.

I wondered why he *was* so willing to put his job on the line, trying to forget the time his hug lingered a bit too long after losing Bianca. "You saw a number. I numbered all my art pieces according to where I'd show-case—"

"No, I'm not referring to any number." He jumped in, somewhat harshly. "There was a sentence *'I stand for life against death; I stand for peace against war.'*"

"Oh, *come on!* They bashed Johnny's head in and now quoting Picasso? Sticking an olive branch into the dead dove's claw—like some biblical saint seeking peace and harmony?" Anger boiled inside me. These psycho chicks had disrupted my happy place again.

"Ava Ramírez owned two white doves. Looks like she killed the lone dove and may have murdered another person." Something whistled, either the wind or a cell phone notification. "Did you say that was a Picasso quote on the back of your painting?" he asked.

"Yes, I recognize it from his speech during the 1949 Paris Peace conference. Picasso had painted that dove out of a thirst for peace during the Spanish Civil War, and it was used during the Conference. I know this, as it was drilled into me through history classes in Paris as a young girl." My stomach churned. Something clawed its way through my mind. But before I could ask, Coral cut in again.

"Anna, the reason I'm pulling you into this—even though it may be turned over to Redwood City jurisdiction—is your stolen painting left at the scene. It's physical evidence that can be linked to the perp if anyone else was murdered. Plus, I trust you will keep this all confidential. I had this case solved. Now, this." Jason echoed frustration.

"I'd rather not be pulled into anything but will help if I can. Which reminds me of a thought I had—Ava Ramírez, is she the one you mentioned whose father is a former huge search engine executive?"

"Oh—yes, DataRodent. He now works for the CIA, or NSA. Not sure which. He has been questioned in all this, but we can't find solid evidence implicating him."

So, he works within the shadow government controlling America. "Well he certainly wouldn't have been the one with the peace and love message on the dove, if he is connected to secret sniper spies." I couldn't help myself, the words tumbled out with no restraint.

Jason seemed to hesitate with some unknown fear. "We do live within a twisted political reality Anna, one never knows. But I am wondering if bail-out daddy and dove-less daughter are working together on this." A commotion erupted in the background. "I gotta go now Anna, no word to anyone, and let me know if you think of anything that could connect your painting to this mystery."

"One thing, Jason!" I burst out, wanting to get my last question in before the dial tone resounded. "When *do* I get my pretend Picasso back?"

"We'll be in touch after it's no longer physical evidence. Take care, Anna." And with that, the police sergeant hung up and left the dial tone droning into my shaken consciousness.

* * *

As I went back to packing for my upcoming trip to Mendocino with Pierre, my mind fell back to when my art gallery was broken into. Not forgetting the brutal bludgeoning of Johnny. Jason had explained that forensics insisted the blood on the dove had a symbolic or cryptic meaning left by the girls, a societal message. What did he say?

"The bloody teardrops could symbolize being blinded to phantom enemies. The three blood drops on the breast could symbolize removal of the heart. Forensics' implication was that this represented violence for profit, a blind vengeance, and lack of a social heart investing in perpetual war while robbing from our children's education."

Something along those lines. If this is the case, it would be the girl that wrote the Picasso quote without a shadow of a doubt. But did she kill anyone else in the process? I remembered also that the girls claimed they never killed Johnny but were terrified he would shoot them. They merely wanted the art to sell at their school fundraiser, giving the students programs for success.

Really? Ava's dad can raise millions to bail her out of prison, but not for his daughter's school? And if they didn't kill him, who did?

My cell rang. Sergeant Coral. This nightmare's never-ending. "This is Anna."

"Anna, the forensic test came back. The blood on the second dove belonged to a prison guard."

My heart thundered.

* * *

My mood immediately lightened as I crossed over the picturesque Richmond-San Rafael Bridge, drinking the gorgeous views. I often enjoy the hills, expanse of the bay, ships, and islands seen from this bridge, even more than the Golden Gate.

Soon I made my way up the hill to Caryssa's beautiful house. More amazing views hypnotizing my emotions, calming my spirits. This thing about Ava's dad working for either the CIA or NSA bugged me. Both part of an invisible government operating in plain sight, making millions of decisions involving peace and war outside of public view. Caryssa connected the dots between Silicon Valley, or the high-tech industry itself and these shady ops. I wanted to talk to her before she headed skiing with her lovely family.

I wonder how much of a shocker the details may be, and the negative influence this man had on his daughter.

CHAPTER FOUR

Caryssa

It was late February, a warm day with snow like mashed potatoes. We skied for a few hours, before hiking to a picturesque backdrop.

The knowledge that Tyler was enjoying fresh air and exercise rather than his mind indoctrinated by sinister souls in Washington D.C. made me breathe a little easier.

The sun-drenched, panoramic views of Lake Tahoe sparkled, jagged mountains surrounded us. A few butterflies flitted among plants, retreating to the pine trees for shelter. The snow patches and ice sent me sliding as I lost my footing. I walloped the ground, landing on my rump, laughing. After grabbing my balance by the horns, I stopped to take pictures as George and Tyler forged ahead on the trail.

The air boasted pure freshness, rife with the smell of the great outdoors. You can't beat it. Fluffy white clouds sailed across the baby-blue sky. I breathed deeply. Man, Life is good!

My conversation with Anna before leaving for Squaw Valley pecked at my mind, insistent on drilling its way into my consciousness. I wasn't going to let it ruin the moment.

But learning about the second dead dove and murder in beautiful, peaceful Sausalito had undeniably rattled me. I battled these thoughts regularly now, attempting to veer this unpleasant news off course, propelling it from my mind. But it was difficult. Especially knowing how it rubbed salt in old wounds for Anna, nightmares of her daughters rushing back to haunt her.

And then there was the part about Ava Ramírez's dad working within our invisible government. Whether it's the CIA or NSA, both conceal unscrupulous activities. I swatted the thoughts away. Politics will not plague my thoughts. Politics will not flow from my mouth. Politics will not interfere with my Zen. Politics suck!

But it was not to happen, as the bleak political reality we live in stalked me to the peaks of paradise, casting its ominous shadow on this tranquil setting. My failure to escape from reality for the day presented itself in the form of a delightful twenty-something couple we met while hiking.

"What a day, huh?" I smiled at the young lovebirds, sitting on a bench overlooking the glistening lake, as I glanced ahead and saw Tyler perched high up on a rock.

"Shalom! Yes, it's amazing! Ey, we hate to ask but could you please take a photo of us?" Asked the girl. "It's our one-year anniversary and I suck at selfies." She sat at the edge of the bench primping. She scrunched her hair to rub volume into it.

"Sure, happy to!" She handed me a real camera—a nice Nikon, not some stupid smartphone like myself and most people use for pictures. "Ah…how do I—" I stared at an abundance of buttons, feeling technophobic.

"Oh em. Sorry. It's all set up. Press the shutter button here." She wagged a finger at the confusing buttons on the side of the camera. I hoped not to make an ass out of myself.

As I positioned the camera and brought the viewfinder to my eye, the girl's companion asked: "ey, Maya, did we remember to pack sendwichs?"

"Do I detect a German accent?" I asked, while positioning myself at what I hoped would be the best spot to take their picture, not wanting to appear to be a total novice with the camera.

"It's Hebrew accent, we are from Israel. My name is Maya, and tis is Ariel." Long glossy chocolate-brown hair flowed from Maya. Big brown eyes glimmered on a canvas of pure, pale skin. She reminded me of the Ivory soap girl ads. Ariel was all tan, toned and wiry, with jet black hair framing grey eyes with the longest lashes I've ever laid eyes on. Each were remarkably fit.

"Caryssa." I offered them each a handshake, which they accepted. "Ok, one, two three…smile, you are on candid camera!" I suggested two poses.

We struck up a conversation, as the three of us caught up with George and Tyler. They still stood at the lookout on a cliff high above Lake Tahoe. "These are my new hiking buddies, Maya and Ariel."

A shalom and hello were issued all around. From there, we easily fell into step together, traveling the trail as a group for the next couple hours.

As the hike progressed, obstacles became more difficult. Tree trunks and huge rocks stood in the way, requiring us to climb over them. Treacherous mountain slopes and loose gravel gave cause for hesitation. In sections of the trail, icy terrain was carefully negotiated. Tyler, forever ahead, stopped to climb another huge jagged boulder.

As we ascended, fields of lupine, mule ears, bright red and orange paintbrush, penstemon and California snow flowers seemingly bloomed with gratitude, providing a fairytale-like path.

While hiking the steep trail, Maya casually brought up the alliance the USA has with her home country. *Oh no, politics!* My stomach tensed. This can't go anywhere well.

I attempted to resist the pull of the conversation. It would tug me away from the Zen moment. "I prefer not to discuss geopolitics; my heart rate is high enough with the altitude and this steep hike. And check out the holy-mackerel views!" I threw her a smile before looking over at Heavenly Ski Resort across the smooth turquoise-blue water. Its lower base resembling an upside-down Y.

Wearing my yogi om on my sleeve, I openly commenced chanting the mantra: *ooohhhmmmm…ooohhhmmmm…*I had set my intention, pressing the bases of my palms together lightly. *I won't think politics, I won't talk* *politics. This family hike is my politics-free zone. It is my haven from the harassment of political dialogue and heated debates.*

But Maya insisted, to my chagrin. "Well, em, I tink da relationship is important. All dat military aid does not protect my homeland as Americans tink, as been a waste of your tax monies—" She revealed, shocking my senses.

This stole my attention—the type of politics I don't mind, more calming and refreshing than the deceptive supremacy freedom act. I took a breath and allowed the conversation to flow freely, prepared to listen. "I could not agree more, and think it rather jeopardizes both our nations." I was all ears now.

"I tink America's 'stand with Israel' ting is the worst policy ever." Maya's lips curled upwards slightly while declaring this, straightening her shoulders. She looked directly into my eyes, yet still toyed nervously with her lustrous mane.

How shocking yet enlightening to hear this young woman speak from the other dark side of our foreign policy. "Again, I agree, and would love to hear more about your stance on this." I urged her to continue. "My take is it's only about money, what do you think?"

Ariel took the wheel. "Em, Maya and I were raised within the Israeli society with deep tensions between religious and secular beings. We've both been to war, our government expects all youth to serve their time. Yes, we tink it's all about da money, religion, and elitist power. It's time we stop the occupation of Palestine."

I cringed. It sounds increasingly like USA's invasions—this same exploitive philosophy—with repressive ROTC programs permitted on school campuses across our nation simply because the public schools get federal aid.

"At least Israel terminated its horrific occupation of Gaza." I offered, maintaining the calm.

"No! I mean, truthfully? I tink da Palestinian-Israeli conflict is sensationalized speech-make. I tink my home state of Israel is and always was the occupier and oppressor. The land was never bequeathed to us Jews by the Almighty—as if God is in the real estate business! Palestinians were never 'terrorist.' Israel and USA share the same spin and gloss!" Insisted Maya firmly, seriousness nailed into every word. "It's all Western/U.S./Is-raeli propaganda lies."

"We do need to stop our illegal money and weapons flow to Israel." Added George, who hiked beside us. "It's disturbing world peace—"

Maya surprised me, blurting out "both nations dehumanize their pop-ulation, dese top secret nuke deals are done secretly betraying our own—"

Shadow government? Oh, fuck the Zen moment! "Seriously! If I were to take a choice between me being raped or my only child joining 'the war effort,' I'd take the former in a flash." I announced. "It wouldn't be as op-pressive."

The serene rush of a waterfall and nearby creek blended with the pro-found topic, making it a healthy release rather than negative energy. Turned out, my inner peace not only remained, it thrived. This was good to hear. A relief that others in this crazy world are capable of rationalization.

"Ow! Hearing that kills me," exclaimed Maya, her stunning mahogany eyes near tears. "I work at an RCC—a Rape Crisis Center. My job is to help people with da emotional part of rape. But I can understand what you mean." She glanced at Tyler as he approached a bend in the trail, a bunch of wildflowers gathered in his hand. "I am frightened to bring chil-dren into the world, after what I went through. I had PTSD big time from war."

"Did you feel like your soul…your moral conscience was attacked with war?" I questioned while glancing at both she and Ariel. Gorgeous people. The same deep empathy clenched my heart when I see youth across war-like America in their army fatigues at airports, clutching at their pillows on the way to their "stations," completely oblivious.

Maya's eyes glazed over while she glanced at the Mediterranean-like wa-ter below. "Em…I was put into minimal combat. But I saw and heard enough to cause trauma. Dat is what got me into my career path. I vant to help people." Her words wavered with unresolved turmoil. I could only imagine what horror she'd witnessed. It no doubt ravaged her dreams and fought for dominion over her day-to-day conscious thoughts.

The others went ahead, nowhere to be seen, while Maya and I held back among a succulent garden. Although I had vowed not to talk about politics, this conversation remained therapeutic. I often wondered how any Israeli's could accept the USA-Israel treacherous buddy system. Just like Americans. A blind apathy.

I shared my deepest concern, confiding in this worldly stranger. "It pains me that Silicon Valley—where my most lucrative career years were spent, is married to Israel's military market. Silicon Valley sold its sexy high-tech soul to Israel's defense sector."

"Em, yes. We 'ave our own Silicon Wadi. Both focused on 'security' and 'defense'. I tink both tech areas do lots of good tings for humanity, but I try to seek Yahweh and his truths by stepping out of a box of mind control—" she explained.

"I read that Israel was not supposed to have a standing army according to 'God's words' in any bible. There were no foreign alliances, no taxes to fund a permanent military—"

"Em, yes—both our people wrongly relate the biblical text to modern Israel." Maya piped in. "Dere's no relation, as that covenant forbids militarization. Dere was no true order from Yahweh to conscript anyone into military service. Militarization is a sin, a form of idolatry," She answered.

"We are high-tech war pals going on high-speed invasions!" I responded light-heartedly. "I went to Tel-Aviv on business back in late '99, to pitch my company's technology over a competitor's in a bid to acquire a computer networking start-up with a military-missioned customer base. I understand where you are coming from."

"Ow is it dat so many don't see it's all about da money, politics, and religion?" Maya questioned as she plucked a lupine and tucked it behind her ear. "Dey don't see the connection to terrorism," she shrugged, befuddled.

Maya and I hugged like long-time friends and even exchanged cards. "You ave redeemed any negative sensitivities I ad about western military intervention. You are a beautiful woman on da inside and da outside!" She grinned, restoring my faith in humanity.

There are like-minded individuals out there. People are switching on, little by little. More folk are yanking their heads from the sand and taking a good look around, leaving behind ignorant bliss.

* * *

My new Israeli friends Maya and Ariel veered off, taking a separate trail down, while I joined George and Tyler. We went to a rustic-chic restaurant in Tahoe City, sitting outside on a deck by the Lake's shore. Colorful umbrellas adorned the setting as we ate *al fresco*. Pleasant chit-chat and a gentle breeze was music to our ears.

"Can I go to the beach? I'm not interested in eating those bugs." Tyler didn't wait for an answer. He snatched his cell phone and flew down the stairs, headed towards the water.

Teens! While sipping wine and enjoying grilled prawns—or "bugs" with basil, I turned to George. "Meeting people from all over the world and hearing their perspectives intrigues me."

George swallowed, dabbing his mouth with a napkin. "That was a surprise to me, what the Israeli couple said." He scooped up his glass, the scotch sloshing with the ice ranging from pale gold to robust amber. Staring into the glass, as if pondering the shifting shades of color, he continued: "America remains in the grip of complacency of its disastrous war economy. That is what haunts me the most. We are our own worst enemy."

A delicious combination of sage, thyme, and onion blended with the scent of fresh pines complimenting the scenery. There was a light stirring breeze, joined with the sounds of children laughing gleefully, uninhibited from the stresses of adulthood they're yet to experience. I glanced at the shoreline and surreal snow-powdered mountains.

As opposed to plunging into frigid Lake Tahoe, Tyler hung out with other kids skimming rocks off the lake. A couple of boys argued who skimmed the longest distance. You'd think they're in an Olympic competition, their voices amplified over the water. Concentration stitched their features together as they each took turns competing for the furthest rock skimmer.

"You're stupid dude! Use flat rocks, not those boulders. Oh man, you toss like a girl! Spin it! And three skips, not one. You lost, you didn't win!" And on and on their banter went.

Whatever, if they're not skimming rocks off each other's heads it's all good. I raised a glass of Screaming Eagle—the quintessential cabernet of Napa, and swirled it around, examining the ruby liquid washing the base of the glass, arousing its flavor. I slotted my nose deep into the glass and inhaled its wonder.

"Will you finally take a sip? You're not in Wine County!" George rested between irritation but amusement. "We paid more for a damn glass than we typically spend on a bottle. Or a case!" He huffed.

"Not to worry, one glass of this vintage—some Screaming Eagle can cost up to seven hundred bucks a bottle! I was surprised to see it by the glass at such a reasonable price. Consider this a splurge for my serenity!" I raised the glass to my lips and sipped.

The bunch of wildflowers Tyler picked stood in a glass of water beside me, to be treasured in every corner of my heart long after they withered and died. One moment he shows the typical growing pains of adolescence, while still being that sweet boy I knew and loved.

Kool & the Gang played in the background. The deck was brimming with people, some waiting in line to be seated. I figured its happy hour, time for a happy dance. I didn't care what anyone thought or how many eyes were on me, heavy with judgment. I stood and let the rhythm take hold.

Get down, get down, get down. Ahhhhhhhh! Jungle Boogie! Get it on!

Someone in the corner smirked to the waitress, "I want what she's having." Mimicking a flash mob, a group of about twenty people joined in to feel the funk. The entire deck transformed into a dance floor, with a couple little girls performing cartwheels.

Jungle boogie, let me jump in. bruhuhuhu.......

Halfway through the song, I found myself dancing on a table like a wild thing, my body a slave to the music. *How did I get up here?* Must have been some exceptional Screaming Eagle! From this level, I saw further out into the lake. Tyler had braved the chilly bite of the water and was lounged on a flotation device. Surrounded by the deep blue of the lake, snow-sprinkled mountains, and sailboats—he looked up at his crazy parents dancing like fools. We were likely traumatizing him with embarrassment.

We drove the scenic route around Lake Tahoe before heading back to the Bay Area. The runoff from the snowmelt was high, making the glacial views more spectacular. The transition from snow skiing to beach destination reflected within the shorelines. Gotta love Lake Tahoe, people skiing, kayaking and sailing on the same day in late February, a wetsuit haven.

Finally, home. I said goodnight to Tyler as my eyes fell upon a book he had chosen nearly six years ago in third grade. There was a tiny part of my Catholic brain that had thought *how sweet he chose a Bible as a book!*

"Oh, look, the book you chose when you made your Holy Communion. I didn't even know we still had it." I delicately picked it up and started turning the pages of disturbingly violent biblical stories depicted with Legos. It sent shivers stomping down my spine.

It was titled *The Brick Bible*, a new spin on the Old Testament. All heart-wrenchingly designed with kid's love of Legos. Luring young souls into sinful warrior mode, glorifying it all as an "act of God." Shameful. America's relationship with religion is unhealthy, to say the least. Some can't see logic through the haze of petulant beliefs.

"Why wouldn't we have it? I still read it." Tyler seemed almost hurt through his defensive fragile tone. "I picked both those books as a gift to myself after suffering through nine months of religious education, remember?"

Smart ass. "Really? But you've outgrown Legos." I couldn't decide if that was a question or statement, neither could my tone.

"No, I still like Legos. Just don't have time for…well, I kinda outgrew them but it's fun reading that book. Both of them—"

Ah, now I remembered. He had selected two books, the other a gentler version of the New Testament—the story of Jesus. Both twisted tales of violence, beheadings, and hate, with Lego massacres galore, splashed across the pages.

"It's okay Tyler, you don't have to justify anything. It's kind of bittersweet. Good night." I took both books from his bedroom, as I recalled mixed feelings about them from the start.

I slumped on the living room couch and cracked open the Old Testament version. There, with dreamy-childlike Lego pictures and written like the Holy Bible, were the extremist words:

"Then Samuel said to Saul 'Yahweh says, go attack the Amalekites. Put them under the curse of destruction. Kill the men, women, children and babies, cattle sheep, camels, and donkeys. Spare no one."

Enough. Maybe if I turn to another page—I flipped randomly and read. "And the Israelites took possession of their land."

The visuals and text went from bad to worse as my eyes reluctantly skimmed over pages. "Moses called all the Israelites together and said 'When Yahweh your God brings you into the land which you possess, many nations must be cleared away. You must put them all under the curse of destruction."

A children's book. How dare they? This is appalling! I had to admit the author's Lego artwork illustrations of blood, death and wreaking havoc on humanity was magnificently rendered. Still, the context was hugely inappropriate for anyone, most of all children with young impressionable minds.

I slapped the book shut. Somewhat miffed. Meeting the young couple from the Holy Land on the same day as coming across these violent children's Bible books seemed too much of a coincidence. I wondered if Tyler had pulled them out of his bookshelf after overhearing our conversation on the hiking trail?

Something clicked in my head. What was that Maya had said? "Religion, politics and money are the cause of terrorism."

Or war. Fallouts? Who is this elusive enemy? This mystery entwined my consciousness.

Chapter Five

Julie

We sat in a hipster coffee shop called Bricks' n Beans, feeling like antiques among the twenty and thirty-something crowd of newer merchandise filling the place with chatter. The clinking of cups and saucers echoed while cutlery clattered. Workers flurried around, scooping up coffee mugs and plates carrying cake crumbs before setting them in their grey plastic tubs. Caryssa suggested we convene at this trendy little café, as to market her book to the counter-cultural mindsets. She had stacked three copies on the side shelf as we entered, hoping to ignite some intrigue from the younger clientele.

I had to admit, it was relaxed while chic. A happening spot with a bohemian, vintage look etched into the upholstery and furniture—and the best espressos I've ever had. The furnishings were an artistic collaboration of various textures, woods, and styles, all blending to give off a unique and introvert vibe. Youngsters were buried in books and iPads, attention held captive by either written words or the blast of social media, wearing thick-rimmed nerd glasses and intellectual-looking t-shirts. The coffee shop had been sprinkled with people from every stereotype of youngster: the vapid airheads, the thinkers, the fighters, the oddballs, the trendy, the gothic, and the expressive. But the thinkers were the dominating stereotype by far.

We'd found a table in the corner, away from the bustle and shuffle of employees and singsong of conversations. The cushioned seat embraced my rump with surprising comfort as I eased into it. No doubt the youngsters cared less about comfort and more about their devices. I remember when I could lay or sit anywhere. Now, I appreciated comfort. In fact, I sought it out, refusing to dine or frequent places unless my tush got ample cush.

"So Caryssa, you had to drag me into this young yuppie hotspot, so I can stand out as the old lady crashing the party, hey?" I was likely viewed as the ridiculous rappin' Grandma trying to be 'down' with the kids, using slang and dressing inappropriately.

Surrounded by youngsters squeezed into skinny jeans, young ladies boasting a lack of cellulite, and smooth unwrinkled skin yet to be ravaged or lightly tugged by age, I didn't fit in. Their skin still held onto that natural dewy youth, plumping their full faces, void of lines or creases. They didn't require a strict skincare regime yet, or to worry about the aging effects of the sun.

"I rather like being the menopausal mom doing the cool thing," Caryssa replied, her L'Oréal anti-aging serumed eyes rounded in excitement to see all three copies of her book in hands among this well-educated hipster land. "Look! I'm making traction already!" Caryssa hyped, face gleaming.

Anna laughed, "Shhhh, be quiet! They've got excellent hearing." She pressed a finger to her lips and hunched, wearing a smirk. "But you know Caryss, we are likely old enough to be their mothers."

"Yeah, like the dude over there with the tattoos and messy shag cut is going to give a crap," I replied, nodding subtly at the man decorated in body art. As the younger generation would say, he's significantly 'inked'.

"He's too busy rolling his cigarette with his hand-woven bag of fair-trade tobacco," Caryssa mocked.

Caryssa turned. Dude also sported a Confucius Says t-shirt: "*Think for your damn self.*". She spanned her eyes across the room. More independent thinking t-shirts: "*Feel the Bern, The Book was Better. Question Reality.*" She slathered apricot jam and cream cheese on her bagel. "I think we are in the right place. These young peeps think outside of mainstream bullshit. They're industrious and aware. They won't be manipulated by the words of news reporters and fake news. We need more youngsters like this in the world."

Caryssa had the patrons all figured out. Which is why her reaction surprised me when she turned to Anna and yelled louder than the thumping guitar music in the other corner, "Hey Anna, did you hear who was elected new PTO President for Tyler's school? What? Was Pol Pot unavailable?!" She laughed. Recognition dawned on her face as she muttered:

"Shit."

Shit. Shit. Shit.

From Caryssa's wince and covering of her face, you'd think the words "PTO" and "Pol Pot" had barreled through the café like a revolting homemade stink bomb. I whispered to Caryssa "What? Community service has got to be viewed as way cool with these sentimental fools—"

"No, it's not the parent-teacher thing I'm embarrassed about—this crowd is too smart, too much the critical thinkers not to question if Pol Pot was more a tyrant than our own leaders. A few gave me skeptical looks—"

"Who cares? It's not like these cool cats even recognize our existence—nobody has even batted an eye at us. We're ancient in this crowd. And don't worry, I just saw two of them leave with your book tucked under their arms." Did Caryssa forget what we met for? Mutual support. *Will I get a word in about my brother detained as a so-called "terror" threat? Perhaps I should soak up as much enjoyment as I can, while I can before I drop a bomb into the conversation.*

I turned to Anna, as she sipped a 'Conflict-Free' Latte. She had been unusually silent, words barely slipping from her lips, rather than shooting us with them. "Why so quiet Anna, we have hardly heard a peep from you?"

Anna took a deep breath, before blurting out "another dead dove was found, same bloody symbols—this one behind the prison. And another murder, a prison guard." *Dieu Tout-Puissant* she muttered under her now-unsteady breath.

This not only caught our attention, the patrons no longer thought we were too boring for this copycat café of faux-Scandinavian design. All eyes lay on us. "Well it couldn't have been the girls who murdered your security guard, they're in pris—"

"No! I mean yes, Ava Ramírez, the one with the pet doves, was bailed out of jail by her father." Anna's lips sank into a grimace. She curled a hand over her mouth.

Caryssa kneaded the back of her neck, while narrowing her eyes. "Ramírez...Ramírez. That name rings a bell. My old boss at Unabridged Networks was a Rob Ramírez."

I snorted. "So? We had a José Ramírez play for the Cleveland Indians. What are you getting at, Caryssa—?" I asked, with a stronger dose of irritation in my voice than I'd have preferred.

Anna jerked backward, before leaning towards both women, "Is that the boss in your dream, the one you pulled the menacing mask off?"

"Correct!" Caryssa pressed her fingers together forming a steeple shape, bringing her hands to her chin.

"Caryss? Anna?" I asked delicately. "Are you two connecting your creepy conspiracy theory dots again?"

Now Caryssa was wringing her hands as if attempting to drain herself of confusion. "I...I don't know..."

Anna butted in "Not so sure about 'conspiracy theory' Jules, I've done some research on this family wreaking havoc on healing from my own family tragedy. Turns out, Ava has an Uncle Rob—this Rob Ramírez works in Silicon Valley at some AI start-up cozied with the Pentagon. Designing lethal autonomous weapons—"

"Killer robots," Caryssa interrupted. "My dream has come true! My former boss, I remember him saying he was involved in espionage. And Ava's dad, you said he's a CIA agent."

"Yes, after working for a search engine giant called DataRodent. Both think tanks for political parties. They're brothers...they write policy—."

"Oh my God! The connection between these two men is slithering down my spine!" Caryssa knocked her 'Avolatte'—a latte served in the skin of an avocado, coffee streamed off the counter, forming a creamy beige puddle on the floor.

The barista who'd served their beverages came to the rescue, "I'll take care of that."

I intercepted these two with their drama queen scene, muttering "Hey ladies? We are on stage here. Do you mind if I add to the performance?" I spoke up for the benefit of our attentive audience. "My brother Jackson has been in jail for two weeks, a suspected terrorist!"

Caryssa and Anna froze, kicking any comedy from our conversation. I'd whacked scares and seriousness into them, evident by their agape mouths, jaws scraping the floor. Their eyes roamed wildly, shock sparking in the whites of their eyes. The hipsters hung on my every word, perched on the edge of seats as if watching a matinee. The guy attired in *The Book was Better* t-shirt jumped in "Hey, don't stop on account of us."

We were hip after all. Not even these young cool cats ever saw three fifty-something women—or in the case of Julie, sixty, discuss bloody doves, murder, espionage, and terrorism, while sipping coffee from an avocado shell. They were a captive audience.

Mission accomplished—If getting this market to read Caryssa's books was a goal, we've peaked their interest. Their eyes—and attention—was glued to us.

With a mix of embarrassment and excitement, we paid our bill and left. Caryssa turned to the t-shirt man on our way out "I promise, the book will be better than the movie." She handed him her last copy.

* * *

Back to the safety and familiarity of my apartment. My new parakeet, tweeting to be fed, provided a pleasant distraction. He wasn't short a word or two. His melodic tweets were music to my ears, helping derail my stressful thoughts revolving around my brother's questionable fate. At this very moment, he no doubt slumped in a grungy, dirty city jail cell, sinking deeper into depression or racing faster towards a crippling panic attack.

My plan of sagging into the sofa and channel surfing through mindless TV shows while teaching Feisty fresh tricks was knocked off course by the doorbell.

Before reaching the door, my brother's childhood buddy screamed, "Jules! Jules! It's Steve, you home? I need to talk to you about Jackson!"

With feathered friend perched on my left shoulder, I opened the door with one hand while holding onto Feisty with the other, so he wouldn't fly out, and coerced a smile.

Steve's handsome, unlined face leaped from a look of strain to enchanted surprise. "Wow, beautiful bird!" His eyes pulled taut, mouth gaping.

"I tell you, everyone who tried to talk me out of getting a parakeet claiming it's a stressful event, stand corrected. Feisty has proved nothing but pure unruffled feathers! He's a delight!"

As if on cue, Feisty chimed in "Pretty Bird!" His constant chirping, almost a chatter, never ceased to entertain me. He could converse with the best of them. "Good boy!" I replied, feeding Feisty a pellet. His beak tickled the tip of my finger as he sucked the pellet from it, munching it down.

"I thought he was a she, being such a pretty bird and all." Steve playfully swooped his finger closer to Feisty. The bird opened its beak, singing whistles and screams. Abruptly, it bit him. Steve retracted his hand swiftly. "Whoa, I see where he gets his name, feisty bugger!" he laughed, shaking discomfort from his hand. "Amazing colors on him."

Steve's fingertip held a tiny splotch of blood. His tongue smeared it away before he rubbed his fingers together. It wasn't a good feeling, inflicting further discomfort on Steve. I bought this bird on a spontaneous whim, as a diversion from my own anxiety about Jackson. I hoped the feathers and chirping would cheer me up and occupy my thoughts, barging out panic of my brother. But panic was an untamable beast. It would take more than an animal to distract me.

"Oops, sorry, he is a bit wary around strangers—and yes, he's a beauty." I grinned at Feisty, appreciating his vibrant green body, bright yellow head, and patches of purple on his face. His *tsssk, tsssk, tsssk* resembled singing. "No biting Feisty! No pellet this time."

The bird flapped his wings, trying to draw my attention for more pellets. I ignored his pleas and instead offered him a warning, "I'll be putting you back into your cage if you bite again." I threatened with a firm tone.

My gaze found Steve's tired eyes, flashing back to him with my brother Jackson as kids. Partners in crime who brought potentially rabid raccoons' home to "take care of." Or perhaps partners in passion, with their deep love of animals. Both obsessed with mending wounded birds and pissed at me for keeping wild turtles as pets.

"Soooo...Steve...you sounded anxious before I opened the door. What's up?" Although deep down, I knew his plight.

At this, Steve paced back and forth. Feisty became animated again, watching the tension rise in the unsettled man. Each step cranked up the tension. He clicked his beak, chirping loudly. A sensitive bird. Steve uttered through heavy breaths. "It's overwhelming, my best friend tossed into jail for taking photos in a Times Square subway station! Psycho cops calling him a terrorist threat! Our nation has gone nuts. Fuck!" His fist clenched as if he could squeeze away the angst.

Feisty flew off my shoulder, landing atop his cage. A squawk left his beak. "Fuck, fuck, fuck!" The bird blurted, as if capable of engaging in human conversation, sensing Steve's dismay and aptly responding to it.

Steve's nose crinkled while his forehead scrunched "What a sewer mouth," he joked weakly, "How did you teach Feisty to say the f-word?"

"Oh, I didn't need to teach him. This here is a budgie from Australia, one of the most talkative parakeets in the world. He mimics human speech. And actions. Watch this: "Feisty, stand on one leg!" I demonstrated how to stand on one leg. The bird followed suit, perfectly balanced on top of its cage. I gifted him another pellet.

"Impressive. But Jules, back to what I was saying." Steve's eyebrows squeezed together, forming a crease in his skin, stitching dismay into his features. "Your brother is just another innocent American falling under the government's warped definition of so-called 'terrorism.'"

Feisty's head bent down. His body tightened. He rocked from side to side, then screeched "Brother a terror!"

Steve turned on my feathered friend, yelling "No, brother not a terrorist YOU belong in a fucking cage. Not Jackson!" He shook a stiff finger at the squawking bird, frowning fiercely.

I finally placed Feisty back in his habitat. As if to defy my irritation with his behavior, he skipped joyfully in his modest cage, singing a lullaby. His food was nice and full; I could leave him be while I battled Steve's heightening worry.

When I turned back to Steve, he ran his hands through his hair, trembling. His lustrous dark hair without a trace of gray. It reminded me that he and Jackson are considerably younger than I. A pang of sorrow shot through me. "Steve—"

"Look, I'm sorry Jules." He looked to Feisty. "Even sorry about yelling at you, Bird of Terror." At this, Feisty merely clicked his beak and answered, "Pretty Bird."

Steve huffed through a half smirk.

I shook my head. "Steve, there's no need to apologize. I understand…I feel the same way. Do you want something to drink? Water? Wine?" I offered, hoping to calm his storm.

"Water would be great, thanks. I wonder—how the heck does that bird know your brother is being held as a terrorist?" He asked, words tied in part confusion, part amazement.

As I walked to the kitchen, I answered "I told you, Feisty mimics everything humans say. He's heard me talking on the phone about this horror."

While rummaging for glasses and pouring water over ice, Steve calmly spoke with Feisty. "You know, bird, you're much smarter than what passes for our so-called intelligence community."

I came around the corner armed with two glasses and watched. Feisty hopped up and down, as Steve built trust between them. He chirped energetically, then shocked us both with what sounded like "CIA."

Steve's jaw dropped, as my grip tightened on the glasses. If I'd have been any stronger I'd have crushed them, sprinkling the floor in pebbles of glass "What the—?

I jumped in "I don't know! Only thing I can think of—I had two friends over the other day and they kept repeating how corrupt the CIA is. And other feds. They repeated it again and again." Feisty cheerfully chirped, as he stretched his body tall and proud.

"That deserves a reward! Mind if I give him a pellet?" He asked.

"Oh, please give him either a carrot or celery stick, next to his cage there." I pointed to the right. "He needs his veggies."

"Well, back to the CIA—and other criminal agencies. That's partly what I came to talk about." Steve gestured towards the couch. "Can we sit? I promise not to ruffle the parakeet's feathers."

"Of course!" I l placed a glass of water on each end table. We sat. "Talk to me, Steve."

He kept his voice low, drilled with wariness. "Jules, your brother is being held on a $1M bail as a 'terror' threat as you know—I think. Of course, it's not yet hit the media waves, if it does at all. Many systematic mistakes are buried, not headlined—"

Now it was my turn. Outrage stole my words. "What the fuck!" I half expected Feisty to repeat the fuck word again, but he was engaged chomping a celery stick and singing. "Nobody is left in my family to tell me these things, Steve. And frankly, I was trying to stay in blissful denial about my kid brother."

"His wife Amy hasn't told you?" Steve's face danced with surprise.

"Amy and I have never been close, and I think she is trying to protect me by keeping me blessedly uninformed." Oh, how I wanted to slink away and sing with my joyful bird, leaving the chaos and distress behind.

"We can't remain in denial forever, Jules. Listen…this is happening across America. Kids even, innocent high school students are being tossed into detention centers on ridiculous 'terrorist' threat charges for things like posting creative rap songs on Facebook. It's because of the draconian "Patriot Act." And yes, agencies like the CIA, NSA, and FBI are all guilty of collecting data on innocent citizens."

Panic churned in my stomach. Perspiration drenched my brows. "How the hell are we to come up with a million bucks to bail my kid brother out?" Nausea hit me hard, and the contents of my stomach rose to my gullet. I barreled to the bathroom and filled the toilet. I stood shakily, stress poisoning my senses and damaging my equilibrium. After washing my hands, and rinsing my mouth, I stared in the mirror. I was paper-white, wearing a glossy sheen of sweat. Now I know how Jackson felt, prone to anxiety attacks all his life. *And they've him locked up.*

I returned to my living room steadily, stomach empty and throat burning from acidic vomit. Steve was at Feisty's cage. "What's up with the mirror in there, Jules? Is it so pretty bird can groom himself?" He attempted to lighten the mood, for which I was thankful. I felt as though I'd just awoke from a coma, fragile and unhealthy. Now I understand the expression 'sick with worry'.

"Oh, it's to make him feel like he has a friend. Makes him chirp more as well." I investigated Feisty's cage and watched him scratching against objects. Sign of a good meal. The bird's gaze landed on me, his pupils expanding and contracting. He stretched one leg back as if that was our signature move. "He's getting nervous Steve, let's go back to the couch."

"I can't stay long, but Jules—there is a team of us—all your brother's friends. Like the Fight for the Future cause, we are fighting back. We will get him out, don't worry. Just know that there is a huge 'security' apparatus strangling American citizens. Choking us, like an octopus. Your brother is innocent. You know this, right?"

"Of course." A tear trailed my cheek. Steve brought me into an embrace and promised he would be in touch. "I love you Jules. You're like a sister to me." He left with the same strained facial expression he arrived with, if not with a heavier strain than the one he brought.

I returned to my wonderful feathered buddy, my best friend. "You don't like being in your cage, do you bud?" I freed Feisty and held him in my hand. He happily chirped, glad to be away from his confinement. If only I could free my brother with such ease.

Perched on my finger, close to my heart—Feisty and I sang songs. "You're a free bird, Feisty. Able to come out of your cage. Now, let's do that for my brother." What came next was unmistakable.

Feisty pecked me on the nose, and uttered, "I love you."

CHAPTER SIX

Anna

Even though Pierre and I have been reunited for five years, sex is like a new relationship. Fresh. Exciting. Exhilarating. Not a fiery passion, but an intense calm. As if we never want to let each other go ever again. It was the perfect antidote.

Our thirty-two-year marriage had come unglued with grief, buried in Pierre's flashes of lengthy anger. I guess we're trying to make up for the nearly six years apart, experiencing separation anxiety. The shared grief of losing our daughters blended into the deepest emotional closeness possible, molding us together with an even stronger bond

Pierre's grip echoed his angst. In the throes of lovemaking he whispered *Anna, mon amour ma chérie, je t'aime,* tickling my ear with his soft breath and sensual words.

We lay beside each other, sated with love and laughter, soaking up the post-sex ambience. Pierre wrapped his arms around me, warm and glossed in sweat. His eyes fell on me, full of amazement. "Just look at you—glowing with youthful beauty, after all these years. How is it I've aged while you're still the young gorgeous gal I married in '93?" He asked, full of pride.

People flatter me. They state I have the same creamy ivory unlined skin, chestnut-blond highlights, big almond eyes and willowy body I was blessed with in my twenties. Yet, all I see is a woman in her late fifties, her yogatastic past given way to a champion limper. A case of body dysmorphia?

"A good hairdresser and regular facials, perhaps?" I answered with an air of humor on my way to the bathroom, somewhat embarrassed at the compliment. Glancing at myself in the mirror, I had to admit—the after-glow of lovemaking had turned my face the pinkish blush of a school girl with a major all-consuming crush.

"This goes beyond any beauty salon, Anna." He called from the bed. "You experienced the same tsunami of grief I did with the death of our girls. Yet it nearly killed me while you grew stronger. You plunged ahead, opened your art gallery—"

"It nearly killed me as well. I just knew to seek professional help while you withered away with bitterness…"

I peered outside the bathroom door, unsure if my words had been too blunt and bashed him with depression. I stopped short at the look on Pierre's face. I drank in the handsome man I married. Still so handsome, yet he sagged with sorrow.

Pierre's hair, once a thick sandy blonde—was ravaged with gray, as if he wore a furry ashen hat. His face was lined with pain. It wasn't always this way. Before the death of our twelve-year-old daughter Bianca while riding her skateboard, then the suicide of our other daughter Cassidy, things had been fine.

But such tragedies had taken a toll on both of us. Only apparently, my turmoil wasn't evident through a haggard face, but an inner pain. Before the spiraling chaos tearing our marriage into pieces—Pierre was a vibrant spirit with a youthful spring in his step. That spirit had since been frac-tured, and the youthful energy dented.

However damaged, he was still the man I loved.

Our eyes locked. At least one thing never changed. His striking jade green eyes glistened like a sexy wolf's, sending electric shocks down my spine and in-between my legs. They held endless depths of struggle deep inside, but on the surface, their shimmer hadn't faded. It was akin to star-ing out at the ocean, stars dancing on its waves.

I rushed over and cradled him in my arms, reminding him we still had our sweet grandson Jared. Things could be worse. We held each other close remaining quiet for a while, then we both got dressed.

Not wishing to bring up the subject but knowing I had to, I reminded him of a visitor we were expecting. "Pierre don't forget that...FBI man is coming to visit in a couple hours." I pulled away and watched confusion weave into his features.

"I don't understand why the FBI is getting involved in a local crime. I didn't think FBI gets involved in this stuff." A deep line burrowed between his brows.

"Coral said FBI is getting involved because it involves an art theft. The FBI has an Art Theft Crime Division and handles galleries under security attack." The thought of an FBI agent coming to our home, with the agency itself having a shady history like the CIA, had my stomach in knots continuing to tighten.

* * *

The doorbell rang too soon. My throat dried, and a fresh lease of nerves writhed in my stomach. Pierre looked at me, stern as can be. "Remember Anna, the FBI has no power to make you answer questions, or anything." He breathed shakily, not as easily able to manipulate his vocals as he could his stiff unreadable face. "You have a right to silence and privacy—"

"Why the big concern?" I shrugged. "It's not like we're suspects. Coral said it's because the murder at my art gallery is connected to the murder of that prison guard. And both involve my stolen art." I approached the front door, suppressing sparks of anxiety.

"Anna stop, let me get it." Pierre jumped up and strode with intent to the door. He opened it, and there, at my doorstep, stood a young man looking fresh out of college in a job interview. At least 6 feet tall with jet-black hair, dark heavily-rimmed sunglasses, a charcoal power suit, crisp white shirt and no tie. He was armed and toting a large briefcase.

The man held out his hand with the tiniest tilt of his lips, as if a fully formed smile would crack his face. "Hello Mr. and Mrs. Beauvais, I'm FBI Special Agent, Timothy Blake. I am assisting Sergeant Coral—"

My lips trembled. "Yes, yes, he said to be expecting you, Agent…ah, Special Agent Blake. Come in please." I shuffled to the side gathering myself, while Pierre shook his hand. Pierre mirrored the agent's emotionless face, on edge but not wanting to give anything away.

"We can talk in my living room, come this way."

Simple snacks lay on my glass coffee table, in preparation for his arrival. A tiny teapot, water, crackers, and cheese. "Please help yourself." I gestured toward the refreshments, assorted neatly.

The agent helped himself to a cup of tea but did not partake in any food. "Thank you kindly. I'd like to talk about the murder at the prison." He took a load off. "And the connection to the murder at your art gallery." He didn't waste any time, cutting straight to the point. His tone was all business, much like his attire.

I chewed with the decision whether I should say we preferred not to answer questions without a lawyer present. Would that rattle the cage? It certainly wouldn't put us off to a good start. He seemed to sense our hesitation. "Neither of you is being questioned," he informed, as if capable of reading our minds and uncovering our concerns. "This is just a formality. There's been a twist in the case—" He snuck off his glasses and tucked them in his jacket pocket. His eyes were more readable than his still features, only just.

"A twist?" Pierre burst out. His hand stopped short of his mouth before he took a sip of tea.

"Yes. Well, let's start with this." Timothy unzipped his briefcase, and out came my painting.

"My Picasso painting! How did you get it?" The FBI Agent held my "La Paloma" *The Dove*, to the side, then turned it around, revealing the handwriting on the back. I had a suspicion of how he got my painting. My asking was more out of unease, to fill the tense space between us. I wanted the air brimming with words, drowning any awkward tension.

"Sergeant Coral handed it over as evidence. It's your painting, Mrs. Beauvais?" He asked. His words leaned into the question, but his face was stolen and emotionless. It was almost impossible to read him. Usually one can read a person's eyes, but he was expertly controlled, not giving anything away. He didn't blink unnecessarily; his gaze didn't dart madly. Every movement was controlled and thought-out.

"Yes," I answered, wetting my parched throat.

"Okay. The writing on the back has been positively identified through forensic handwriting analysis. It matches that of Ava Ramírez." He hesitated with his following words, before pointing at the Picasso quote written by Ava.

I read it again: *"I stand for life against death; I stand for peace against war."*

The FBI agent cleared his throat, his lips pouting just a touch, "So Ms. Ramírez was an anti-war activist."

"It appears she had an ounce of conscience, while she bashed in my security guard's head." I blurted out rather flippant, the words flowing of their own accord.

At this, the agent jerked to attention, straightening his back like a soldier in the presence of his superior. I half expected him to salute. *Oh no, I've irritated a military mouthpiece.* Pierre sat his hand on my knee. He gave me a squeeze, as if twisting a faucet off, only not stemming the flow of water, but hindering the stream of my potentially offensive words.

But damn if I need to stay quiet, knowing what happened to my Dad in Vietnam. Already my heart thudded with greater purpose. I wanted to ask when I get my Picasso painting back, but the agent stole the spotlight.

"A couple of questions—what do either of you know of these young women wanting to seek political or social change?" Timothy now looked overly stiff with tightly drawn features, as if to intimidate us. I wondered if he was more concerned about collecting "political intelligence" on people rather than solve murder cases. But Pierre's silent warning worked.

"Well, they were upset school budget cuts were so drastic and how expensive college tuition is. Supposedly, that's why they robbed my art gallery. For tuition fees." I didn't know what to say beyond that. I didn't want to test him. I certainly didn't want to irritate him. Be polite and cordial. Remember, you haven't done anything wrong. As he said, this is just a formality.

Timothy scribbled into his pad, filling the air with a scratchy ruckus. "What do you know regarding the symbolic messages left in blood on either dove?" He asked, eyes bouncing from his pad to me, seemingly trying to get all the information on paper. Especially if he felt they contradicted with my answers. Knowing how efficiently they are trained in reading responses and facial expressions made me nervous. I ought to weigh my words from now on and simmer any emotion capable of contorting my face.

I wanted to say that the girls were allegedly trying to uncover a secret society behind America's wars. A shadow government operation. Yet, I'd be sitting on the lap of a potential perpetrator—feeding him his own bullshit. So, I just repeated. "According to the forensics team, bloody teardrops were left under the dove's eyes, which symbolize being blinded by an elusive self-created enemy. Three blood drops were left on the breasts to symbolize a removal of our society's heart." I explained with a dull monotone, measuring not just my words, but my overall responses.

His pen wiggled some more as ink swirled along the pad. From what I could make out from a sly glance, he had doctor handwriting. Even if I had the balls to read his notes, it would likely be fruitless, especially upside-down. Then again, how do I know his notes aren't written to merely keep up appearances? Maybe he'll toss the notes as soon as he leaves? No, that's too far, surely? His eyes squeezed almost shut, then opened and shot straight at us.

"There's no doubt these girls robbed your gallery and killed the doves. But we have unseen evidence not looked at by local law enforcement. A low-resolution video that shows a male visitor to your art gallery the night of the murder in Sausalito. We zoomed in, and it's no doubt Diego Ramírez." He paused, as if for dramatic effect. "A rogue CIA agent—"

"Ava Ramírez' father!" I blurted, losing control of my previously controlled demeanor. Words sped from my mouth without thought, soaked in emotion. "Oh my God, he visited my gallery that night? What does this mean? Do you think he murdered my security guard, not the girls?" I questioned, shock wedged into my sentences. My hope of remaining calm and collected had dissipated.

The agent stuffed his hands into his pockets. "I shouldn't be telling you any of this—" he leaned in ominously. "But we have surveillance footage of Mr. Ramírez also at the prison at the time of the second murder." He stood, slotting my painting back into his briefcase, throwing an idle glance at his watch. Guess I wasn't getting my painting back yet. "Look, I can't say more, but the two young women may have been framed and blamed—" he snapped the briefcase shut, looping his fingers through the handle.

"By her own father? That doesn't add up—the DNA, fingerprints, their confessions…" I was wondering why both Sergeant Coral and this guy tell me too much. Am I that trustful or inconsequential?

Timothy withheld his answer, debating his response. Instead, he chose to derail the conversation with a farewell. "I've got to get going. Thank you for your time and hospitality," He said, avoiding eye contact, as if losing a handle on his eyes. As if secrets and answers would tumble out should his sight catch ours.

He paced towards the door, then hesitated, his hand hovering before the handle. He turned, still not letting his sight meet with ours. His gaze skimmed the floor and rooted to his shiny shoes. "Mr. Ramírez is capable of covering up anything, and silencing anyone. He's an expert at espionage. And he's gone off the wall since working intelligence operations in Afghanistan." His words were clear but peppered with fear.

And with that revelation, he walked out the door. He sat in his car and sped away in a mist of gasoline, leaving us with agape mouths and heavy frowns.

* * *

Pierre had to drive into the City to stop by his work. He is crazy busy, after being promoted to Director of Sculpture at The Academy of Art University while still teaching sculpture classes. He barely had time to breathe.

My workload was equally as hectic, with twenty-four kids coming for a watercolor workshop tomorrow. My ten-year-old students can be discerning, visualizing their paintings not only framed but gallery-wrapped.

Being highly skilled at crafting frames, I had made a grand plan to do all the matting and framing for my student's oil on canvas projects myself. I wanted to surprise them with their finished product, as a reward for their amazing efforts.

This would be excellent for driving my material costs down, but what was I thinking? My motivation was squashed after that FBI Agent invaded my private space and stuffed it with disturbing revelations and buckets of dismay. I found it hard to swat away the encounter from my mind, repeatedly buzzing in and around my consciousness and subconsciousness.

"You look absorbed in your work." Pierre stood at my studio doorway, carrying his art portfolio case. The words "Burning Man" among other iconic projects he has been involved in, showcased on the front cover.

"You haven't left yet? I thought you were gone?" Upon the sight of him ready to leave, I couldn't help but miss having an office to go to. Not to mention, missing owning my art gallery. The simplest things can pluck at my nostalgia, however recent or not.

"I got almost to the 101, then realized I needed this." He finished the sentence by lifting his art case, implying that slippery devil was the reason for his return.

Shaking my head with a mighty sigh, I rose into a stretch, relieving tight and cranky muscles. A couple of my bones even popped. "I'm really not into my work and need to go for a run to shake off the FBI episode," I moaned.

"Good idea, I'll be back in a few hours." He planted a kiss on my forehead, then left. His lips provided a brief distraction as that simple kiss caused butterflies to flutter in my stomach. Yet, in no time, it was gone. I was consumed with work and fighting off thoughts involving the FBI visitor. I felt heavier with every second. Try as I might repel it, the FBI visit sunk deeper into my consciousness.

With a dusty chunk of chalk, I wrote on the whiteboard. "Today's first assignment: Make your own frame!" So what if frame making was not on the original syllabus? This is a highly self-motivated group. My guess, they will gladly accept the additional challenge. I know them well enough. Plus, it'll teach them to be industrious.

I gathered all the materials and organized them in a central spot for the kids to choose the tools to craft their individual masterpieces. While sorting the pre-cut frames and mat sets, I decided to up the ante on the assignment. I added to the whiteboard message:

"A contest for the top three designs based on:

1. Frame-to-painting proportion.
2. Best combination of mat to frame.
3. Most unique design. Layering: Glazing."

Perhaps this will ward off those parents protesting their perfect kid needs "more challenge" in the classroom. Little Billy in the corner has a tiger mom constantly assuring me he is the next Van Gogh. His abstract watercolor drying on the easel at his station was impressive. I couldn't deny the boy had talent. A beautiful work of art. But little Billy is a nuisance, frequently disrupting the class. I find myself wondering if he will be cutting off his own ear. Or will someone do it for him? Or will he choose another body part? With any luck, his tongue! Let's see how disruptive he can be without a wagging tongue.

Already squeezed into my yoga pants and padded running shoes, I was almost ready for a run. All I needed was water. So, I grabbed a bottle and off I went, seeking peace in the great outdoors. Leaning against a eucalyptus tree to stretch my calves, I glanced at the San Francisco Bay and Angel Island. I felt better already. There was little *that* sight couldn't cure, or at the least, soothe. You could swim in the backdrop and scenery, shedding your worries and problems.

Twenty minutes later I was at the bottom of the hill, turning towards the Bay Model. I eased up when I passed Julie's apartment building. Her parakeet, Feisty, chirped through an open window. I decided to stop in. She would be working from home after all.

After lightly rapping my knuckles on the door, shuffles came from her home. The door inched open, eventually revealing her gaunt face. I stared into sunken eyelids bordered with dark circles. "Are your allergies bothering you, Jules?" Although deep down, I knew allergies wasn't her plight. Her eyes held sorrow, panic, and a weakened spirit. The pallor to her face was significantly paler as if color had been drained from her visage.

"Anna, I have not slept all week, worried sick about my brother Jackson." Her voice was croaky, no doubt raw from multiple torrents of tears and the relentless grip of anxiety. "He was in jail for over a month for taking photos at the Times Square subway station." Julie retrieved a tissue, blowing fiercely into it. No doubt about it, she'd been crying.

"He...*was* in jail. So, he's out now?" I tried steering the conversation onto a more positive track.

"Yes, he is home. After we realized the one-million bail was too much to afford even as a team, we secured a bail bond. It's like a loan. So, he's home, but it's been hell for him. Still is..." Subtle sobs squeezed her words.

I wished I had just continued my run, with my own stress surfacing again, this time with a vengeance. "So...you guys borrowed a million dollars to bail out your innocent brother—"

Julie cut in "No, the bond agent comes up with the full posted bail amount. But Jackson had to come up with the premium bond fee, I think around one-hundred thousand. He does well financially, but really this is a lot for anyone with two kids. So, his friend Steve and I helped. I drained my bank account." Her hand armed with the soiled tissue trembled as turmoil strangled her words.

"At least nobody can say we live a boring life, Jules," I smiled a little, attempting to calm her.

"Well, this is the type of excitement I could do without." She patted her eyes with the crinkled, sodden tissue. "Oh, and he had to fork over collateral to assure he doesn't skip on the upcoming court dates to prove he is not a 'terrorist.' This meant his property. The bail bond company can sell his house from under his feet if he 'fails' to come to one court date."

"Basically, everyone in our nation is a terror 'threat' according to our feds. Even Grandma." I wanted to laugh, but this was no laughing situation. This was deadly serious. "The real perpetrators walk the halls of the White House, wearing two-thousand-dollar suits."

To this, Feisty chirped. "Bird of Terror. Pretty Bird."

I glanced at Julie's feathered friend. She is way too attached to this animal. Gotta get her a man. "That bird knows too much. Says too much." I murmured as if concerned the bird could hear and—most importantly—understand.

"Yup. Feisty will get himself into trouble one day." Julie wandered to the cage and spoke softly to him. "You are way too smart for your own good, Feisty," She punctuated the sentence with a firm index finger pointed at the feathery animal.

I wanted to get back to my run; feel the sun and feast on those much-needed endorphins. The last thing I needed was to dive into more stress. Anymore cracks and I'd crumble. "Well, I am happy to hear Jackson is out of jail at least, so sorry for all the family stress. We had our own rather unsettling visit from an FBI Agent today." I announced, deciding that maybe a good vent would help me and distract her.

"What? A freaking FBI Agent came to your home? Now that's creepy!" Feisty took flight in the confinement of his cage, wings flapping wildly, nearly knocking his home off the table. The unsettled bird didn't help with my festering angst.

"He seemed to indicate the two girls sentenced to prison for killing my security guard Johnny, may actually not be the perps—"

"I knew it! I knew something was not right!" Julie's eyebrows lifted, her mouth open, revealing her molars. "Something was strange about two girls from the outskirts of Tiburon knocking off two big men."

"The FBI Agent mentioned he was saying too much, but that didn't stop him from implying that Ava s Ramírez' Dad, the CIA Agent, may be the murderer of both the security and prison guards." My happy runner's high had worn off, having been overtaken by dread. I looked forward to trekking up the hill to blow off steam.

"Why is it that law enforcement tells you so much, Anna? You'd think they'd know better—"

"Oh, come on Jules, we have cops and CIA getting away with murder of innocents on our streets and abroad, and you think they really care about any simple code of communications ethics." I surprised myself with the vehemence of my words, especially after wondering the same thing myself.

"Well, we have plenty of good cops left, don't demonize them all." Julie hesitated, then placed her hand on my shoulder. "But the cops arresting my brother sure are crooked." She hesitated again, before saying. "Come to think of it, how did we get from two young women killing your art gallery guy to a CIA Agent? One of the girl's fathers, no less!"

The FBI Agents chilling words haunted me, ringing in my mind, drumming on my heart. "He's CIA Jules…I know we've been conditioned to believe the agency protects our 'national security' by spying on bad guys—"

"You mean James Bond was Hollywood hoopla. Oh no, my girlhood crush destroyed." Julie smiled through hollow eyes, the attempt at a joke falling flat and empty.

"007 was a womanizing killer. James Bond aside, American spies—the CIA is running USA's wars, buddied up with the private banking cartel. Espionage is called the 'cloak and dagger' business for good reason." I reminded her.

"I always thought they subvert our enemies." Julie picked up a celery stick for Feisty, who squawked. "CIA, bad guys."

"Wow, that bird…" Had a human blared such statements, they'd no doubt have been killed and had it made to look like a suicide. I said nothing about that disturbing vision. She had enough on her plate. "That was once their function, yet its main job today is killing. Mostly fictional foreign 'enemies' for our presidents."

"Well, if that's the case," Julie said, "today's CIA has no cloak. It's all dagger."

CHAPTER SEVEN

Caryssa

We alternated our weekends with camping and hiking in Tahoe or enjoying a multitude of outdoor activities in the Bay Area, soaking up nature wherever we could. There was little that fresh air and exercise couldn't fix, or at least significantly help. When one lives in the company of such natural beauty and splendor, it would be foolish to not take advantage. Then again, the same could be said about being alive and living your life to the fullest capacity.

On this balmy early autumn morning, I indulged in an invigorating mountain bike ride with Tyler, then my green thumbs—and fingers—got to work in the garden. Today's project involved an abundance of succulents—a mix and match of color, form, and textures.

I sipped an afternoon latte while absorbed in a novel in my backyard. Now and then my sight would stray to my garden creation, filling me with pride. So much color, with flowers sprouting off many cacti, palms skirting them casting off a purple and pink desert-like charm.

I drink in the Golden Gate Bridge with fairylike streams of fog rolling over and through its fiery beams, then continue reading. Anna was on her way from Sausalito. I had been looking forward to hearing the latest of her mysterious life events. The second dead dove discovered with symbolic messages in blood, and she hinted at an interesting twist in the murder case. I couldn't help but be intrigued.

My iPhone pings. A message from Anna. *Stopped 4 gas. I'm just over the bridge in Richmond. Will b there soon!*

Through clicks and flicks courtesy of my thumb, I replied. *Great! Just come through to the backyard, I'm living the moment in paradise!*

Closing my book and leaving the fictional world, I dashed to my kitchen, programming the espresso machine for a vanilla ginger latte for Anna. Multitasking, I steamed milk while washing the newly plucked berries from my garden. I couldn't wait for her arrival, this beautiful, sophisticated friend from Paris, with her tragic yet exciting background. With her huge heart, able to think first of the life of a young man before her own tragic loss of her daughters.

By the time I'd returned to my wicker sofa, Anna arrived. "Bonjour! Oh, you have lattes! I brought a bottle of Château-Grillet, straight from France, and some goat cheese stuffed apricots."

"Do you prefer wine? I can always save the latte for George who should be home—"

"Oh, nonsense! I'll enjoy this lovely latte. I can smell it from here, blending in with the delightful scents from your yard—you've made my favorite, with ginger! This bottle of wine is for you to toast your love of life. Share it with your hubby tonight at the dinner table."

I motioned for Anna to sit, scooting her latte closer to the bowl of berries and apricots, boasting a visible freshness complimented by the sun.

Anna picked up my book, a smile setting into her face as her eyes glazed over the cover. "Sounds interesting, and a fifteen-year-old boy wrote it?"

"Yes, it's an amazing story. I have to say; your life sounds like a novel. All art and beauty, architecture, symbols and mystery, murder and—"

She derailed my positive comparison with a drearier dank comparison, cutting into my sentence with darkness. So unlike Anna, with her forever optimistic attitude.

"Death and tragedy, and questioning the religious, political and legal powers that be if doing what *they* expected of me—burying my daughters in more family tragedy, could be the moral thing to do." A giddy, nervous cackle spoke volumes of her struggles.

I wanted to kick myself. "Oh, I am so sorry Anna for bringing this up." It dawned in my gut—I wanted to learn to balance my captivation with having a friend with such suspense in her life while remembering her sensitivity and engaging in conversation appropriately. With the horrific reality of it all. "How are you doing?" I asked, tickled by a slight breeze.

"I must be okay, as right now I see penises. One, two, three penises in your garden!" Anna laughed so hard her face glowed red as her eyes puddled.

Looking where she pointed, my eyes landed on the Phallic Cactus plants resembling prickly green penises. "Out of all my beautiful plants, you notice those…are you sure you're getting enough these days, Anna?" I teased.

"Oh, I'm getting plenty enough lately. Pierre and are like newlyweds, we can't keep our hands off each other!" Anna smirked, a cheeky laugh slipping out. "You must not be getting enough, so you need to plant penises!" She winked.

"Well, when I planted them, they didn't look so much like dicks." I chuckled. "My landscape is a place of beauty and relaxation." I sipped my latte while staring at the bay, the sun warming my face and wind tussling my hair, also stirring a smile on my face. "I think you brought up the 'prickly' cactus as a distraction from the subject."

"No, I want to talk about my situation. So…you know about the prison guard murdered at the Redwood City correctional facility—where the two young women wanted for the murder of my art gallery security guard are held. You know there's another dove, same symbolic message in blood?" Anna hesitated, satisfying an itch on her nose.

"And I know about your *La Paloma* painting with the Picasso quote written on the back by one of the girls." I decided wine did sound good after all. What better pairing is there than wine with art and murder mysteries?

"Okay. But what you don't know is, the two girls may have nothing to do with the murders." Anna gawked into my eyes, gauging my reaction.

My mouth fell open, shock landing on my tongue while I raised a finger. "Now this is getting good. We need to savor that wine you brought—be right back." I ran up to get a corkscrew and two glasses.

I popped the cork and filled the two wine glasses with the fruity refreshment. Glugs echoed from the glasses as I served generous portions to Anna and me. I clunked a glass in front of her, and one sat cradled in my hands. Anna had hardly noticed this, caught in her mind and determined not to tangle the tale and keep everything straight.

"Tell me more!" I continued, enticed by intrigue.

"Well, an FBI Agent came to our home—"

"What? Now the freaking FBI is involved?" I blurted, words streaming from my mouth. "What happened with Sergeant Coral?" I couldn't believe it. I was being blasted with revelation after revelation.

"Let me finish, I was getting there! The FBI has an Art Theft Division. They went through my surveillance videos, discovering a man was filmed both the night of my art gallery break-in, as well as at the prison. He was positively identified as Diego Ava Ramírez's dad." She explained, eyes as round as dinner plates.

Recognition clicked on in my head. *The CIA Agent.* Something seemed strange, not sitting well with me. "Why didn't Sergeant Coral look at that video?"

Anna inhaled heavily, fortifying her lungs with air. Needing to take the edge off, she took a sip of wine. She admired the panoramic view from my backyard as if to drink not just wine but the serenity. Then persevered "He had asked me for security footage, and I told him I had not used my security cameras in a while since the crime rate is so low in Sausalito. The cost of running all that high-tech equipment was too much. I didn't even know my security cameras were streaming videos that night—" she shrugged, sitting the wine down. I watched it slosh for a moment before it settled.

"I remember now. You mentioned Johnny had called you earlier in the evening, saying he saw suspicious activity." I alternated a sip between my latte and wine, which as horrid as it sounds, made a delicious combo tempting my palate. Like a Ginger-Sangria made with white wine. I relished the combination of flavors while Anna continued.

"Yes, isn't that sad? Johnny set up the surveillance camera that caught his own killer on tape." Anna plucked a goat cheese filled apricot, popped it into her mouth, and closed her eyes.

"So, they're sure it was this Diego dude, the CIA Agent? Hmm, not surprised. He is the brother of my former boss, who now makes killer bots. They're all in bed together, creating the America we see today—defined by militarism, surveillance, and shadow government." I topped off our glasses with more wine, sensing we'd need it.

"Oh, I'm on the same page with you on that one, USA is like the former Soviet Union. But what does surprise me is it means he set up his own daughter and her best friend." A hummingbird swooped to my feeder, hovering for a few seconds. Anna smiled as it flew backward, up, down, sideways then flitted away.

"Why does that surprise you? You acknowledged agent provocateurs are among the head of our foreign policy. And here's America, with youth perpetually going off to war to spill their blood for the invisible money power working to enslave mankind." My neighbor started playing music, and Airstreams *Electra* sent Buddha-like relaxing tones flowing through my yard.

"Invisible money power?" Anna scooped up her wine glass and fiddled with the stem. She stared at the fluid, as she absently swirled it, watching the alcohol lick the inside of the glass.

Why is she questioning this, when she was the first to tell me her dad died due to this? "Yes, the Triangle of Power: corporations, executive government and US'CIA-led coups against foreign governments. That spy agency was created not to discover secrets for 'national security,' but to fabricate ideologies and disinformation to finance both sides of wars—"

"I overheard, as a little girl, that the Vietnam War was created by the CIA." Anna's face contorted into a sneer. "Imagine….my dad could still be alive today."

I sat my hand on Anna's shoulder, my lips sank in sadness. Nothing need be said. My heart forever cried for her inner child.

After a moment, acknowledging her turmoil and hoping to distract her from it, I continued "Okay, so back to Diego dude—you said he was a former executive of DataRodent. The tech giant is a political think-tank for foreign policy formation funded by the CIA and NSA. Throughout history the CIA has been framing and blaming whole nations, governments, and people to instigate wars."

"I'm trying to see the connection between the conspiracy theory and the murders—" a line burrowed between her brows.

"Oh, come on, Anna!" I flung my arms out. "The phrase 'conspiracy theory' has devolved into a freaking cliché! Why should we question if a crazed agent who worked intelligence ops in Afghanistan would do such monstrous things to his own kid?"

Anna kept her head down, sight running along the table as if answers would be hidden in the furniture. "Because I still don't understand why he framed his own daughter. What was his motive?" She asked, face drawing tighter in confusion. Her tone was one of frustration as if deliberately being kept out of the loop.

I wondered if her self-inflicted remorse for her own daughters' tragedies held a blanket over her eyes, keeping her from seeing this man's true identity: A scheming murderer. Like many other military officers, perhaps his once vibrant soul has been ravaged by PTSD provoked by his ill-fated career.

"Motive? Anna, he's implicated in the murders of Johnny and another innocent man. He works for a covert operation that has committed atrocities for decades. The CIA has been placing social activist on a watch list. They don't *want* people to be humanitarians. It interferes with their clandestine operations. Motive? His daughter is an antiwar protestor who wants peace and money for education. My guess? He wanted to silence her." I shrugged, having explained it as clearly as possible.

"But…makes no sense, he bails her out of prison then implicates her?" Anna was not buying my idea. Although she does have a valid point, I wondered if he didn't frame her—then got buried in parental guilt...I found a finger running along my lip as I pondered this possibility.

As if on cue and capable of conscious thought, the neighbor's music switched to the song, *World*, by Dan Bern. I couldn't help but wonder if they wanted to imbue our conversation with mental clarity to forestall the world's careening drunkenly into madness.

We sat for a moment enjoying the gentle, flower-scented breeze as my consciousness drifted back to when I first discovered the dark side of the CIA and other federal agencies.

I worked in the alluring world of computers and the internet. Contracts for the overseas sales of IT systems crossed my desk daily fueling our permanent war economy... *My mind flits there, but it won't land.*

Anna swayed to the music, smiling into the sunshine. I love how we can engage in an intense conversation while maintaining the calm. She said, "Well, I do think worldwide corruption keeps going, with people not even blinking an eye."

I took a dollar out of my purse. It crinkled in my fingers. "This creepy eye sure doesn't seem to blink, just keeps staring at us." I pointed at the Egyptian pyramid with the all-seeing eye glowing on top. "It's a Masonic symbol. It's—"

"Supposed to be the Eye of God watching over us." Anna completed my sentence.

"Bullshit!" I scoffed. "More evil has been carried out in the name of God than anything. FDR ordered this symbolism placed on the dollar back in 1935. With 'In God We Trust.' The mystery behind all these symbols is a puzzle. I've heard it's an Illuminati symbol."

"Which makes more sense. See the writing under the pyramid?"

I glanced down at the dollar bill again. "It says, *Novus Ordo Seclorum.*"

"Which means New Secular Order." Anna seemed to sense my discomfort at this further revelation. She continued, "secular as in non-religious."

"Which matches the Illuminati objective yet clashes with the trust in God line," I said. "Maybe the ambiguity is on purpose. There's always been a blurred reality and rivalry between science and religion—"

"What does science have to do with any of this?" Anna interrupted.

"It's directly connected to money, including dark money when it comes to military science. It's no coincidence this symbolism ended up on the most powerful currency in the world—it's all about secret power and control."

"Violence has always been connected to religion. I've heard that our wars are indeed about GOD. —Gold. Oil. Drugs."

I was riding on a little buzz courtesy of the wine. "This is the best white wine I've ever tasted."

Anna laughed, "It should be, I brought it back from France's premier Rhone Valley wine region—not that I paid a dime for it. I know the growers. A bottle can sell for as much as $295 a pop!" Her eyebrows reached for her hairline.

"What? Whether you were given this wine as a gift or not, this is an extravagant rendezvous. You should have told me, I wouldn't have opened it." I gestured to the half empty bottle.

Anna's hands moved outwards in a rapid twist of the wrist, brushing my worry away. "Nonsense, we are talking money, why not drink it?" She pointed to the dollar bill still in my hand. "So, where were you going with that? The Illuminati?"

I hesitated, taking a greedy gulp of air. "I don't want to go there. Yet, there's some covert shit going on besides what's fed to us in the media— the world is controlled by three corporations: The City of London, Washington D.C. and the Vatican."

"More like the high military, the corporate executives and political directorates—"

"Same thing," I insisted. "Only broken down by department."

Anna snatched a sprinkling can from my garden rack, and started feeding a few plants, focused now on my potted palms. Her eyes didn't falter from the plants as she spoke, "The high-tech industry so linked to global arms sales is frightening. Imagine if we let the money flow into something like clean energy instead of spy satellites and war machines."

The sexy high-tech world I worked in. I tried to chase away the almighty semiconductor chip and its early link to military contracts. "Having dictators' spit 'fire and fury' over the world coalescing into today's forever wars, coupled with raging hurricanes and wildfires, mass shootings, and the heartbreaking opioid epidemic is too much!"

"And on a lesser scale, having my tiny art gallery in upscale Sausalito robbed and a security guard bludgeoned to death?" Anna's head tilted to one side as she asked this as if it was the weight of the question that knocked her head off-kilter.

It's like a symbol of an apocalypse now. "Are you still questioning if the CIA Agent framed his daughter—"

"No, I am convinced he set up the girls to be implicated with the murders. I think he master-minded the entire art theft—likely mind-controlled the girls to help carry it out. There's a standing joke in the art industry that the CIA has quite an art collection at their clandestine art gallery in Washington. Who the hell would sell artwork to the CIA?" Anna questioned, scraping hair from her face that had slipped onto her forehead thanks to the meddlesome breeze.

"You certainly wouldn't sell the agency artwork, after their little sneak performance with Vietnam," I insisted.

Anna nodded, adding, "The CIA secretly used modern art as a political weapon back in the 50's and 60's. A covert op to support Cold War propaganda."

I crossed my arms in defiance of the hideous arms race that brought us to where we are today, with nonstop violence. "Yes, I read that culture and art was driven into the Cold War, to make it look all 'sexy' at taxpayers' expense." I couldn't help blurting out.

My sight was driven to the landscape and the shadow of a figure on the nearby hill cast by the sun.

It moved. I tensed.

"Girl be subtle; look down there towards the trees. I think someone's watching us." I muttered, reigning back anxiousness. Were we deliberately being watched? Mountains of questions forced their way into my racing thoughts, matching my now-racing pulse. Then I realized I was being ridiculous, acting like one of those people insisting they are a 'targeted individual."

Anna's gaze drifted across the hill and settled on the fleeting shape. "He left. Maybe he's just a hiker enjoying the trails. After all, you live in this beautiful setting near open space." She spoke with such calm, not a spec of nerves. *If only I could say the same.*

I didn't want to alarm her, but it seems that someone is always hanging in the periphery whenever I get together with her or Julie. But of course, I also think my Google Home Mini is listening in on everyday conversations. I chased the thought away.

Anna continued, "I still think that Ava Ramírez' killed her pets and left the symbolic messages and Picasso peace quote behind."

My hand went to my neck as I thought of the girls transferring the victim's blood, drop by drop onto the dove's breasts and beneath the eyes like teardrops. A symbol of fire and death. *Did they?*

"This murder and art theft cases are shrouded in mystery, I still wonder why the girls' fingerprints were found on the weapon…I mean your bronze sculpture."

Anna raised her eyebrows while shaking her head decisively. "You were the first to mention the CIA is famous for framing people. DNA evidence can be fabricated and planted at crime scenes." She reminded me.

"But fingerprints? It's not just DNA how can—"

"Why do we keep going back and forth like a ping pong ball? Caryss, this is the CIA, experts at espionage and secrecy. I imagine they know a few fingerprint forgery methods." Her head rested on her fist, which unraveled as she spoke behind her fingers as if someone was tuned into her debate.

I topped off our glasses, laughing internally how two wine lubricated mothers had turned into private investigators in a backyard paradise. As if alcohol had turned us into ruthless sleuths unearthing lies and deceit. "So, Ava and perhaps her friend killed the doves to—"

Anna jerked forward, index finger in the air, connecting another dot, "Maybe it was a rebellion against her dad for the chaotic society he helped shape? Doves resemble peace. CIA agents don't want peace. They make money from war. Besides the emotional pollution her father's job brought her, I forgot to tell you something else."

"New mystery! Oh boy, do we need some more wine?" I teased.

"Heck no, I'd never get over the bridge back to Sausalito. Anyhow, I researched Ava's family background and found out her Mom vanished in 2008. Her body was never found."

A new weight landed on the conversation, bringing my jaw to the table and widening my eyes.

"Oh my God, this sounds too much like stories of other CIA agent's wives gone missing or murdered." My mind raced back to an artist, Mary Pinchot Meyer, murdered in Washington D.C. in the 60's. She challenged the CIA and US Foreign Policy. The story was she had just finished a painting at her nearby art studio...I chased the thought away. "Tell me, Anna, you're not talking to any feds, are you? Don't talk to the FBI again—"

"I haven't spoken to any law enforcement for a week, not even Sergeant Coral who I'm beginning to think was fired for saying too much to me—" She slipped out.

"The FBI has also entrusted you with their secrets. You are too beautiful Anna, inside and out. People talk to you." I looked away, willing a hummingbird hovering over my feeder to blanket my mind in stillness.

Anna crossed her arms, a gesture I rarely see in her. I hoped I wasn't creating a barrier between us. She lifted her head, "Well, the dove, symbolic of balance and peace of the deepest kind, is also the symbol of motherhood. I wonder if the message left behind in the blood drops was meant to not only represent lack of social justice and world peace, but her inner calm crushed when her Mom went missing." She guessed, kneading her temples. Clearly, this intense discussion came with a physical weight lodging in her skull, expanding with every new speculation and consideration.

I thought about this. "If you kill the dove, you kill peace." I declared, hitting the nail on the head.

"Yes...a symbol of love and peace, silenced."

As for the next few minutes, our chatter was also silenced with this sudden realization and its unnerving presence.

* * *

"Julie wants to have a gathering," Anna told me, while leaving my house. "Her brother is in town with his wife and kids. Pierre will be on a business trip, but I'm going. Next Saturday if you can make it."

I stopped rinsing my wine glasses and turned to her. "So, Jackson is out of jail? That's great!"

"Yes, especially since he is innocent. This is hard on him, and Julie. It's hard for the kids. They never know if law enforcement will accuse daddy again." Anna lacquered her lips in gloss while fishing for her keys. The girl from Paris is quite the multitasker. "It will be at her adorable little apartment in Sausalito—you know where it is."

"Sounds great…are kids invited?"

"I think so, but her place is so small, can't imagine her entertaining kids. No place to run." Her eyes joined her hands in the hunt for her keys.

"Come to think of it, George and Tyler will be on a father-son camping trip next weekend anyhow. So, if I come alone she can't shove her political viewpoints down my kid's throat."

Anna's lips puckering into a frown, her huge almond eyes narrowing. "I haven't heard Julie talk politics in a while. I wouldn't worry about it."

"Well, she uses phony buzzwords like 'freedom fighter' or 'national security' imposing opinions on extremist foreign policy. Condoning political violence goes against the enlightened morals I try to instill onto my child. I won't tolerate—"

"Caryss, we've been through this." She jumped in, speaking through glimmering lips made even shinier by the sun. "Don't worry. She's letting go of her hawkish views, after her brother's ordeal. I talked to Jackson, he told me today his sister has been knocked off her fantasy freedom cloud."

That's a relief!

I hugged Anna goodbye, then my eyes found hers. "I'll try to make it over. I have a community fundraiser to go to." I had been supporting several causes including donating to the hordes of families affected by California's smoldering fires.

"Well, there's something you could discuss with Julie. She too is involved in a local fundraiser. It's called *Foundation for Innocence*, supporting the victims throughout America accused of terrorism. It's become a huge problem." She informed me. I felt for her, I really did. But I didn't agree with her political views. Understatement. Unless she really had seen the light? I hoped so. While I don't like to let political views stand in the way of friendship, I couldn't help judging someone with such a lack of awareness—or pity their gullibility. However, I am human. Her situation did tug at my heartstrings.

My mind drifted back to reading about the multitude of innocent young teens arrested for "terror threats" for simply posting political satire on Facebook or playing online video games, including a 13-year-old girl. Our federal government has become what our forefathers sought to destroy. It's outrageous. If it weren't for people pulling the wool from their own eyes, I'd be deeply discouraged about the fate of our planet.

No bloody war ever destroyed tyranny. I thought of a James Madison quote, "If tyranny and oppression came to this land, it will be in the guise of fighting a foreign enemy."

It yanked at my heart and tortured my soul.

CHAPTER EIGHT

Julie

How am I going to do this? How *can* I do this?

My brother's in town. The idiot checked into The Gables Inn to waste money when his family could stay here. He said they're jet-lagged and stressed from the horrifying ordeal of the terror charge leveled against him. Understandable, but still. Why waste money after enduring that financially and emotionally draining situation?

I'm convinced it was carried out by white supremacists or foul feds against infrastructure investments. An unseen force wanting to make the dollar bills rain on troops and not trains. What better way than to feign another terror threat at a New York City subway station? *Oh no, I'm thinking like Caryssa and Anna. Damn it!* I gave myself a firm face-palm.

A call to Jackson asking if he'd like the kids to sleep over landed in his voicemail, unanswered. A romantic night alone at the Inn with his wife would be good therapy. After this testing experience, they needed to strengthen the foundation of their marriage. Not unlike a house that had been shaken by a minor earthquake, you needed to check the plumbing, wiring and so forth. Small problems could turn out disastrous if not taken care of. In their case, festering emotional turmoil.

Between them and the girls coming over for dinner and drinks, I'm attempting to make creative space of my 500-square-foot studio apartment. However small my shoebox apartment may be, I had one thing going for me: the rooftop garden! That made up for the lack of space. I let my access loft ladder unfold, climbed up and looked around. Perfect, we'll hang out here.

Considering how little I tended the garden, the plants in the border containers were nice. Brimming with ferns, Spanish lavender, sage and what I think are butterfly weeds, there's a modest rustic charm.

My gaze rested on the small stone-clad outdoor fire pit and at once I knew I'd be lighting it tonight. There is no wind. I'll run to the store for S'mores and treat my niece and nephew. Oh, this will be fun!

Now back to the quandary of how to sleep the children, if not the four of them. I was relentlessly determined. I won't be turning on a 'No Vacancy' light. I suppose the kids could be strapped to the rooftop?

That's it! Strap the kids to the rooftop! Bingo!

I flew down the ladder and dashed to my shed. Retrieving the pop-up tent I never used, I struggled to get it back up the ladder, never mind setting it up. "Voila!" I announced aloud to no one, waving my arms in gesture of my achievement. "A bedroom for the kids!" Wouldn't an eight and-ten-year-old love to camp out in a rooftop garden beneath twinkling stars? I'd have killed to at that age! Heck, it sounds magical at my age.

Down the ladder again. I scavenged for my air mattress, cozy blankets, plump pillows, and a sleeping bag. I wrestled with the items, re-climbing the ladder, and spent the next half hour inflating the mattress and arranging everything. What's missing? Lights! Once the fire fizzles out the darkness will flood them.

This most certainly warrants a trip to Target: flashlights, chocolate, graham crackers, and marshmallows. I happened across solar string lights and picked up a box of those.

Returning to my rooftop haven, I twined the solar lights around the railings, sat candles and kerosene lamps on bistro tables and stepped back, in awe of my work. *Wow! I love this!* Needs more chairs though—which is not something I'll tackle now. Action Jackson to the rescue!

Taking a breath and stretching my back, I soaked in the view. The San Francisco Bay and city lights will be so enchanting while we sit by the crackling fire.

I texted Caryssa and Anna: *No heels tonight ladies. You'll see why!*

* * *

While prepping dinner, Fiesty chirped from slumber. Just in time for my first guests to arrive. The bird won't compromise my attention tonight. I'll focus on my brother and his family.

I had my door open, allowing a fresh breeze to gently whoosh in. Giddy, Hans and Hayley charged into my pad. "Wow Auntie Jules, is this one of those tiny houses? We learned about the Tiny House Movement in school, this is so cool!" Hans turned toward the chirping. "Double cool, a tiny house with a colorful bird!" He commented, eyes as big as dinner plates.

At this, Feisty greeted Hans with "Pretty bird!" Both kid's eyes popped even wider.

"Wow, a talking bird!" Hans scooted towards the cage, lured by the colorful winged animal.

"Come over here and hug your Auntie Julie and let's leave Feisty alone. I planned family time tonight, not bird time." My high-spirited feathered friend wasn't stealing my energy tonight; I planned to spend it on myself and my family instead.

Hayley wandered around my apartment. "I love California, I want to move here! Pretty palm trees and hills!" She gleamed with that youthful innocence and magic. I envied her. I wished I had the filter on my eyes that she and all children had. Before adulthood bogs us down and happiness becomes something we consciously strive for.

I reached out for a hug, and the children fell into my embrace. As we enfolded in a circle, I peeked over Haley's shoulder. My brother and Amy stood at the door throwing a grin our way.

I froze, then attempted to hide my concern. Jackson was gaunt, almost completely void of color, and seemed to have aged ten years in the three months I hadn't seen him. I raged at what the twisted system did to him.

"Jackson…" the word came out in a gasp, almost one of disbelief.

"Jules, good to see you." We greeted with a hug while I helloed Amy. Remembering she's not the touchy-feely type, I extended my hand for a shake with my sister-in-law instead.

I looked at Jackson while scratching my chin, narrowing my eyes. In his late forties, he's still handsome, slim yet well built. His face, typically clean-shaven, was a forest of black stubble. His dark hair was unruly, almost greasy. And he had bags under his eyes big enough to pack up and go to Europe.

As if reading my mind, he mumbled, "If you think I look bad, you should see Manhattan. It's an apocalyptic showdown." Defeat still leeched onto his tone, faint but evident.

Amy swiftly changed the subject of impending disaster. Who could blame her? "Nice little spot. Classy décor." She commented languidly, her shoulders rising, voice shallow. There wasn't much for her eyes to roam. I wanted to say, *sorry I don't have your spacious house.*

I wiped my hands on my apron. "It works for me, I love my tiny space. So…can I get you guys anything to drink? I've got wine, water, beer, and a mix of non-alcoholic beverages in the cooler outside."

"The kids have their juice boxes, but we would love some of this red wine. I know you like people to help themselves," replied Jackson as he poured two glasses and handed one to Amy, the burgundy liquid swishing as he did so.

"Can I help you with anything Julie?" Amy offered while plucking an olive, cheese, and cracker from the appetizer arrangement. She wore jeans paired with an oversized black blazer and sizeable orange scarf. A casual chic-look.

"No thanks, it's a simple dish," I replied. I secretly thanked Trader Joes for the ready-to-cook entrée. "Actually, Jackson? Could you please fire up the grill? It's beside the cooler."

Haley came skipping towards me, lugging her favorite stuffed monkey. "I found the bathroom, but where are your bedrooms, Auntie?"

"Uh," Amy went to speak but hesitated.

I laughed. This isn't what they're accustomed to. "Afraid this is it, missy." I spread my arms in an arc. "Over there is my kitchen." I pointed to the itty-bitty kitchenette. "And this room we are standing in serves as my bedroom, living and dining area," I explained, gesturing emphatically.

"It's charming," Amy proclaimed decisively. "An eclectic sophistication without the clutter of our home," She complimented.

My brother re-entered, "The grill's fired up!"

I figured this was as good a time as any to show them my garden rooftop. "I'll toss the kabobs on but want to show you all something first. Follow me!" I instructed with a mysterious tone to my words.

We marched behind the kitchenette to my rooftop ladder. "I don't know if you want to carry your wine glasses up—"

"What do you mean, Jules! This ladder is more like stairs. It's sloped to make the climb easier." Jackson moved towards the ladder, but his son beat him to it.

Hans sprung up like Spiderman, "Come on, Haley, your monkey will love this!" Once on top, he yelled back, "Wow, this tiny house is a tree house, check it out, dude!"

Jackson grabbed our drinks and walked up the ladder carting three wine glasses. I didn't stop him, after struggling with an abundance of items earlier. Haley followed, and the two children squealed about the tent as if bats were swooping around.

As I stepped onto the rooftop, the kids were already inside the tent, giggling. "Looks like they might like to sleep here tonight!" I covered my suggestion in a joke, hoping it would loosen his firm stance on staying at a hotel.

Jackson shook his head firmly, expression stiff, "Oh, I don't think so. We are set up at Gables Inn. But it's sure quaint up here, Jules." He sipped wine, glancing at the fire pit. "Want me to fire that up as well? It would be cozy to sit up here."

"Yes! That's what I was hoping!" Going nuts to get organized for their visit will not be divulged. I'll let my brother think it's always this welcoming here.

I pointed next to the fire pit, "There's the tinder—those sticks, twigs, and leaves. There's wood in the corner. My candle lighter is on the bistro table. While you do that, I'll throw the shish kabobs on the grill."

Amy had crawled into the tent with the children, using her wriggling fingers to elicit giggles.

"Okay sis consider it done. When you get back up here it will be a camper's heaven."

Which made me stop, and repeat, "Speaking of camping, I meant it about the kids staying the night. They can sleep in my apartment if you think it's unsafe up here. You two are welcome to stay as well of course. I can make it work—"

"Do you have a poker?" Jackson jumped in, cutting me short as he lit the fire. The flames roared to life, flickering in the gentle breeze.

"You're ignoring my wish." I give up! "Yes, behind the pit. Look, I'm going down to cook."

"Wait! Jules, I'll come down with you and help." He scampered to me. "Have you ever grilled the rice for the kabobs?"

"No, but you've always been a more creative cook than me." We descended the ladder, Jackson at my heels remaining silent on the descent.

At the bottom, his hands landed on my shoulders and lightly squeezed. "Jules, did you set up the tent for us?" He asked with a lingering suspicion. I didn't want him to feel like an imposition or inconvenience, but I didn't want to flat-out lie either.

I recalled all I went through with the grand delusion my brother and his family might want to stay with me. I wanted my baby brother back. I wanted his innocence back. "Sort of, but I'll sleep under the stars if none of you want to," I shrugged, feigning casual.

Jackson inhaled heavily before letting it out. "My dear, big sister. I know we're twelve years apart, and you once changed my diapers." He paused to punctuate with a smirk. "But I'm not a baby anymore—"

"I know, say no more." I stepped in. "I realize you guys just flew in today and are three hours ahead. You must be exhausted." I slid the kabobs onto the grill.

"Thanks for understanding, do you have some aluminum foil? I want to do the rice on the grill if you don't mind," He tossed me a grin, which helped. I know he's his own man with his own family now, but I still see him as my baby brother. I'll probably always see him that way to some extent.

"Are you kidding? That would be great." I replied enthusiastically. "In the left drawer by the fridge."

As Jackson rummaged around for the foil, he mumbled. "I thought you were having a couple girls over tonight."

"They should be here soon, I planned it so you and I could chat before they came." While turning the kabobs over, I glanced at Jackson. He was folding and creasing the aluminum foil. He cut the top, let the stream of rice pour inside, and added a pat of butter with water. He shook it vigorously, his frail body ready to crack with each jiggle. He tossed the packet of rice onto the grill.

"About twenty-five for this, I'll flip it halfway through." Jackson stood at the grill with me. Nervousness played on his features. "So, it's Caryssa and Anna stopping by, right?" He asked, no doubt attempting to distract his nerves.

"Is that why you don't want to stay?"

"No!" Jackson's hand stopped midway reaching for his wine glass. Instead, he reached out to smooth the crease from my forehead, then brought my wrists to his heart. "Jules, please…this is not about you or your friends. My family is just in desperate need to chill. Amy wants to use the spa in the morning, we all need sleep. We've been at each other's throats since what happened to me." He confessed, sorrow and guilt gripping my heart.

We stood soundlessly for a moment, staring at the grill as if to will the rice to cook quicker.

He glanced at his watch. "It's nine pm our time in Manhattan, in an hour the kids will turn into pumpkins." He joked, lightening the mood.

I realized how selfish I was behaving, thinking only of my needs. Basically, my need to hold onto the only blood I've got left. I showed my palm to him, dismissing any further explanations. "Jackson, you don't need to explain further."

"And you wouldn't want the kids sleeping on your rooftop anyway, they'd be hanging off the railings, running around burning your place down." He chuckled, though I sensed the laugh was more for my benefit.

"Well, I'd have the sense to put the candles and fire out—"

* * *

"Hello!" Caryssa sang from the street. I realized I was relieved not to be stuck with family hospitality duty. I love my brother, but now I can just kick back, and enjoy the company of girlfriends. Perhaps I'll sleep under the stars myself. After all, I did go through a lot of effort turning it into a teeny paradise, someone ought to prosper.

Caryssa and Anna stepped from the darkness, into the creamy light of my doorway. They were radiant, carrying wine and nibbles. I placed the wine, shrimp cocktail, and baked brie on the table before we leaped into a three-person hug, our various fragrances intermingling.

Stepping back, I stared at the two women. "What, did you call each other and plan to dress like twins?" I asked, commenting on their attire. They were decked out in fitted casual black sweater-dresses paired with knee-high black boots.

"Ha, nope! Total coincidence. Great minds think alike." Anna responded matter-of-factly, throwing a wink Caryssa's way.

Caryssa countered, "Or fools never differ?" She chortled.

"You must be Jackson," Anna extended her hand for a shake, and Caryssa followed suit. Jackson, historically the most blithely untroubled man in the world, did not smile at first. But as he registered the warm charm of the beauties before him, his smile surfaced. First, with his mouth, moving lazily up his face but never quite finding the light switch to his eyes.

It pained me to see my brother this way—the boy who always had a smile for everyone and saved every animal from impending doom. The boy who has never laid fingers on a gun in his life, wouldn't even go to the shooting range during Boy Scouts because he was too full of life and love to ever use a weapon. And now, wanted as a "terrorist" threat by self-indulgent law enforcement.

As introductions were made, a loud thump, thump, thump came from above us. The two others stared towards the roof, with perplexed faces. Jackson laughed, "My kids, sounding like a herd of elephants. Guess they're letting off steam."

Caryssa looked at me with alarm widening her eyes somewhat. "The kids are playing on your roof?"

"Get yourselves a glass of wine, and after I finish cooking I'll show you my rooftop garden!" I instructed, enticing them to the magic of my rooftop haven.

Anna's brows raised. "Rooftop garden? When did you have that installed?"

Jackson was keeping an eye on the grill and cut in: "Jules go ahead and show them, I've got this."

"You da man, Jackson! Gotta love a guy who rules the grill." Caryssa complimented, giving my brother a high-five, the slap resounding for a second or two.

"I've always said the barbeque is a man's domain. I only wish I bought a couple of steaks to add." Jackson smirked.

"What? My kebobs and rice aren't enough?" I teased.

"Plenty enough. Just realizing we came empty-handed."

"I asked you to!" Caryssa and Anna had already gone ahead and were strolling through my apartment. As I followed behind, I noticed Feisty asleep on his perch. That bird gets ten hours of sleep a day, tough life.

"Where's the roof access? Asked Anna.

"Behind the kitchen area." As we neared the ladder, we heard Amy and the kids belting out the song *It's A Small World*.

We waited at the base of the ladder, listening. We didn't move, as if ascending to the top would disturb the peace.

"Kind of bittersweet, after what my brother's family just went through." I shrouded my voice in discretion, "I didn't tell you, somebody called me recently to ask me about Jackson. An FBI Agent."

"What? That's preposterous! They're like leeches!" Anna spats.

"Seriously...I have all respect for law and order, except when they bring a lawless chaos," Caryssa added as she admired Julie's family wall photos.

"Don't worry, I told them I had nothing to say. They're the ones terrorizing people, including us! What about you Anna, have you spoken to anyone again about your art gallery horror?"

Anna did a backward hand flip, "Are you kidding me, Jules? No way. I don't want to draw attention to my gallery, tarnishing its reputation. Why let the media drag my business through the mud because of murder?"

With a hand to her heart, Caryssa answered, "Oh my, I agree. They would bat your business around like kittens in a box with a ball of string."

"Ha, more like a tiger attacking a child at the zoo." Anna shook her head. She had enough media frenzy with her daughter's tragic case. "But enough of me, how's your brother? He looks..." she searched for the right words. The polite words.

"Like crap," I finished Anna's sentence with half a smile. "He is drained, emotionally and physically."

Jackson called from the kitchenette, interrupting the chatter, "dinner's ready!" Speak of the devil!

I hoped the family singing drowned out my harsh analysis of his appearance. "Going up to get the others, Jack, thanks!"

At the rooftop garden, Amy and the kids sat by the fire pit cozy and happy. But their conversation stopped me in my tracks. It made me realize how parents have to worry about the America their kids will grow up in. We eavesdropped...

"The kids at school are bullying me too, Mommy. They say my Daddy's a terrorist and should be suicide-bombed." This from eight-year-old Haley, squeezing her stuffed monkey, pressing it close to her heart as if the stuffed animal would shield her from the cruel comments.

"Has anyone hurt you like they have Hans?" Amy's voice was tender, as she kissed her daughter's forehead, choking down emotion. It's times like these when parents have to be their child's strength. They can't break down crying. They must be a symbol of hope and resilience to endow those qualities to surge in their offspring.

"No, but it makes me sad what they say. And they don't let me play with them at recess." She stroked her monkey, sadness resounding in her tone.

"Dad's not a terrorist! He was just doing his job taking photos of the train. I think some cops have become the bad guys!" My nephew Hans wept. In that instant, I thought of the bruises on his face. I assumed they were sports-related injuries—Hans is forever getting lumpy and purple playing soccer or falling out of trees. *Was he beat up in school?*

My chest was caught in an emotional vice, tightening as the conversation progressed. Dinner would get cold, yet I couldn't move. Guilt and a fear for my nephew's safety glued me to the ground. Caryssa put an arm around me, stilling me with a maternal instinct I lacked.

"Why are they calling? Daddy's out of jail. Why won't those men go away?" Haley shook her stuffed "Funky Monkey," as if trying to shake sense into the men that haunt her dreams. Her face crumpled, and her mouth wailed, tears spilling down pink cheeks. Those tears may as well have been mine.

I watched the words, the ones Amy was no doubt trying to avoid, find their way to her lips. They rolled over and under her tongue dropping out of her. The words weighed a ton. "It's not over yet, sweeties. Daddy has to go to trial. Even though he did nothing, that's…that's just the way it is. It's a small world. It's a beautiful world." Amy gathered both children close, ruffling their hair. "But it's not a perfect world."

I whispered, "God, this makes me glad I didn't bring children into this fucked up world." The moment I uttered those words I winced. *Anna!*

Anna brought children into the world—and they left it too soon. I hoped Anna didn't hear, otherwise, I'd have put my foot so far in my mouth it'd be splashing in my stomach acid.

The cogs were turning in my brain as I wondered if my sister-in-law sensed our presence. I realized it's not just my brother's innocence being robbed. My niece and nephew's childhood is being ravaged by this ridiculousness.

Anna turned to Caryssa, "Let's head down for dinner, and give them family privacy."

With a renewed promise to connect with Amy, I strode with intent to the fire pit. "Hey guys, time for dinner!" When Amy stood, I flung my arm around her. "Let's have girl time, just you and me before heading back to New York City."

Amy uncrossed her arms and stared at me, bewildered, too shocked to speak. But gradually the words came. "I always felt you were kind of standoffish, like you never cared to know me."

Now it was my turn to be shocked. This woman standing in front of me is the love of my brother's life, and it occurred to me that I had closed her off. "Amy, I've always been protective of my brother. I admit I was wrong. I guess I saw you as a threat." I confessed.

Amy's mouth opened, and her eyes narrowed, "A threat?" The kids had raced down the ladder and were out of earshot. Not a bad thing since their biggest hero—Daddy—has already been deemed a threat to society, crushing their lens of the world.

"I thought you might deprive Jackson of his happiness. Now I realize, you are his happiness. His biggest joy, you and the kids. You're his family, his life." I paused, instilling genuineness in my following words. "I'm sorry."

The fire in Amy's eyes glistened with a cocktail of relief, anger, love, and sorrow. "Tomorrow's a rest day, we won't be playing tourist. Let's do lunch at Gables Inn at noon," she suggested.

My to-do list can wait, this can't. Getting closer to Amy would be the best way to support my brother. "Sounds great, I'll be there," I replied enthusiastically.

"Splendid! And Jules? Let's talk about us. Not the man in the middle. Your brother brought us together, but let's connect over what makes each of us tick." She suggested.

I felt a fight, and in response, my spiny old shell emerged. That spiny shell protecting my brother's image; my dad's image—my blood. As quickly as my defensive armor rose to the surface, I softened my hardened heart.

What was I protecting? Seriously? In a desperate attempt to preserve the privileged bubble of my childhood memories, I'd forgotten what's important to my brother. Never having married, it's like I married Sausalito, holding onto the money and social status my family once had. I'd looked at my sister-in-law as the interloper that's crushing my dad's honor or my brother's spirit.

Settling into Amy's gentle eyes, it dawned on me that she is no interloper. I'd made a horrible mistake. She is the mother of my brother's kids. *My blood.* I now know what she means to him.

Seeing my brother's life spin out of control with the disintegration of America's politics opened my eyes. She'd been a part of my family for years and I've stubbornly refused to give her a chance. No more. Fresh starts. "I'd love to hear more of your life in New York City."

The group had dispersed between the garden rooftop and my kitchenette area for dinner, and now everyone slumped around the fire pit. Jackson yawned "We need to get you two little rascals off to bed soon, it's nearly midnight east coast time. Look! Haley has turned into an orange gourd!"

The girl, indeed, resembled a pumpkin in her oversized orange sweatshirt. Half asleep she sprang up with a wired energy, "And look! Before I become a carriage, I'll lose my glass slipper!" With that, she kicked off a shoe for show. The shoe somersaulted into the air before gravity yanked it straight into the fire pit.

Hans laughed, taunting his sister, "Cinderella, you did lose your slipper. But now it's burned up and you won't get your Prince Charming." His face crumpled as he burst into a fit of laughter.

"That's not funny!" Hayley stomped petulantly, starting towards the pit. Luckily, her father blocked her path.

"I'll get it," he nudged her away from the pit. "Looks like it didn't land directly in the fire." Jackson plucked out the shoe, piping hot and powdered in ash, but salvageable. "Okay, that's enough baking over the fire pit for one night. Give Auntie Jules a kiss goodbye, we'll see her again this week."

"No, we can't be back by the stroke of midnight. My Cinderella sister has to turn to rags and the mice will pull her home." Hans announced humorously.

"You're a meanie and would make a horrible prince!" Hayley wailed, giving him the tongue.

"No, I'd be a great prince," he puffed out his chest. "Because I'm a hero about to save the night! We haven't had s'mores yet! S'mores to the rescue!"

The kids were beyond overtired, acting sillier than ever and ready for a bickering boot camp. Jackson rolled his eyes, famished. I offered, "Let them roast a quickie bro, it takes minutes." I grabbed two marshmallows, stuck them on the whittled sticks and passed them to the children.

Once their marshmallows had a toasted tint, knowing from experience their insides would be gooey and warm, I laid out graham crackers and layered them with chocolate. "Here kiddos, squash the marshmallows into these crackers, you have s'mores to go."

"Mine's not done, it needs to be burnt!" Hans objected with a high-pitched voice.

"Hans just do it! Your marshmallow's almost falling off the stick," Amy seized the stick from her son and snatched it off, her patience clearly dwindling.

"But it needs to be brown!" Hans picked up the bag of marshmallows as if to start another.

"We need peanut butter to make them yummier," Hayley added to the whining session.

"Listen to your mother Hans, put the bag down now. We are not having your Aunt lug a jar of peanut butter up here at this time of night Hayley." Jackson turned to me with a smile forming beneath exhaustion-filled eyes, "Hey sis thanks for the hospitality, we'll be in touch. Gotta get these kids to sleep."

Caryssa and Anna were enjoying the fire, working on their wine in-be-tween conversing. They either weren't bothered by the kid's annoying an-tics or ignored it.

Amy approached me, arms spread wide. We embraced, for the first time in the decade she's been married to my brother. Too long to go with-out having much of a relationship, but at least we'd formed a bond now. "See you tomorrow for lunch, I'm looking forward to it!" I whispered into her ear before releasing from the hug.

And with that, they were off. The jet-lagged sugar-hyped kids vanished. What a great Aunt I am! Although, I am not so sure my brother and his wife would think so, giving kids sugar so late at night. Oh well, at least my 'cool aunt' status is still intact.

* * *

Over the next few hours, the clock ticked past midnight while we sat by the fire henpecking, turning to pumpkins ourselves. The rooftop glim-mered in candles and starlight. A soft breeze perfumed the air with fire and the floral scent of roses.

"Good to see your brother and his family tonight, Jules. He's stressed, but his wit's still there." Caryssa handed me a piece of chocolate which paired well with the Merlot. Much needed comfort food. I nodded, "Yes." I didn't know what else to say in the moment.

"Our broken justice system continues dragging innocents through kan-garoo courts." Anna laid another log on the fire, taming it with the poker. The fire was a calming balm adding tranquility to a chaotic world.

I didn't want my brother's horrendous ordeal to drag the conversation down. I needed to forget his troubles for a while, so I navigated towards Anna's heartbreaking past. "You certainly didn't drag Brandon Garth through the courts after his car fatally struck your daughter. I still don't know if I agree he was innocent."

Anna balled a fist, bringing it to her lips. "He sends a Christmas card every year—how sweet. He's now twenty-seven, still a med student study-

98 · T.L. MUMLEY

ing to be a Pediatric Neurological Surgeon. He hopes to practice at UCSF. I like to think Pierre and I did the right thing." She explained, honorably.

Caryssa added, "I think what you did was commendable Anna, finding it in your heart to drop the case against him—defying our culture of irrelevant revenge. I mean, come on! He's studying to be a doctor to help save children! A warrior of our planet. Just shows if we give people the benefit of the doubt, they'd do better for society than rot in a prison cell because we were unable to settle our festering hate and show forgiveness."

I wasn't buying it. "But if we just let everyone mow people down in the streets excusing it as a 'tragic accident,' we'd have vehicular homicides outnumbering gun deaths." I proclaimed.

"As if that could ever happen," Caryssa poured herself more wine while shaking her head. The burgundy liquid filled her glass as our vocals took a quick break.

Anna steered the topic back to Julie's brother, to my dismay. "Anyhow, we can't deny there's suspicious stuff going down in this nation with an authoritarian flair, shady characters watching and arresting upright citizens," Anna mumbled while watching the fire, as it gently flickered and mesmerized with every movement.

I thought about the men haunting my brother and his family. The man that called me lurking in the shadows. The CIA dropping into Anna's place exploiting information regarding the murders at her gallery and the prison. Hasn't the woman been dragged through enough drama and trauma? Give her a break already!

"Fuck 'em all," I declared. I picked up another log and tossed it into the fire pit, sending a stream of hot sparks to fit the sentiment.

"Yeah!" Caryssa added. "Fuck their honor, fuck their glory, fuck their dance of power!"

We wrapped up the night and the girls said farewell. I met with slumber under the stars, snuggled inside the tent. I'd struggled with the set up for myself apparently. As I drifted off, a mysterious man in an obsidian trench coat and gangster hat plagued my dreams, haunting my unconsciousness. It was the man sitting on my street today—stalking.

CHAPTER NINE

Anna

"I'm so excited Grand-mère! We're going to France to ski Les Arcs!"

Jared raced into my loft, the skis donated by Caryssa raised overhead like a prized trophy. He wore a child's smile that reignited our home with a sparkle that hadn't been present for quite some time.

I loved seeing my grandson happy. "I learned to ski as a kid in the French Alps, so passing the experience onto you, kiddo."

"But I don't have to learn, I'm already ripping it up," Jared boasted.

Pierre hesitated while loading the dishwasher, watching his grandson through curious eyes. "If you're so good, why don't you have your own skis?"

"Pierre don't start!" Josh can't afford skis for his son, but I didn't want to say so in front of Jared. And why undermine the boy's self-esteem? There was no need for it.

Pierre tossed his hands up. "Calm down ma chérie. Just saying. Hardcore skiers always have their own equipment."

I wanted to remind my husband our own equipment isn't the latest and greatest technology on the ski-market either but realized with a sudden jolt why. *We haven't skied since we lost our girls.* My stomach knotted, tightening with that realization.

"Well, maybe I'm not hardcore, but I master the mountain all right." Two teeny frown lines appeared between the boy's eyes. I wondered why Pierre needed to crush his spirit.

"Where have you skied?" Pierre questioned Jared in a juvenile way, resembling a teenager on the playground as if further testing his skill level. I noticed him look down at his feet self-consciously. Maybe his inner-child was speaking with words of love.

"Boreal." Jared cast his own eyes down. I had a sudden urge to kick my husband in the balls. What was I mad at? I chased away memories of Pierre's stages of grief—the deep anger that lasted an age, including him blaming Jared's dad for his daughter's suicide. As if it was *his* fault she became pregnant, and *his* fault she swallowed those pills.

I asked Pierre, "Why are you being such a hard-ass on your petit-fils? Let our boy shine!" This treatment seemed to have become an annoying habit.

"It's okay, I'm fine with this Grand-mère." Jared leveled his eyes with Pierre, standing straight with shoulders back. A warrior stance. He hoisted the top-of-the-line Atomic skis he'd just been handed for free and declared, "I'll challenge you in a race Grand-père! Come on, we have a mountain to tame! Can't beat me, old man—"

"There's my petit-fils! You go tiger!" I high-fived my grandson, inspecting him. Thirteen-years-old, standing at 5'10" with golden hair hung over one side of his face. Something melts inside of me seeing his lop-sided smile. There he stands—pieces of me—pieces of Cassidy. His hauntingly familiar jade-green eyes luminous with excitement.

Pierre flashed matching eyes, meeting the challenge. He raised a finger to make his point, "But, there's one problem young man. Boreal is no training grounds for the French Alps. I will kick your butt!" He warned with one scrunched eye. Words drenched in arrogance spilled from the corner of his mouth.

At this, the boy lifted his own finger in a dual challenge, eyebrows raised, "But I am thirteen, strong, fearless and agile. You are—"

"Fifty-nine and strong, with over forty years practice skiing the steeps and deeps." He counteracted. "The pregnant snowball you learned on is no match, you'll get your ass kicked kid!" He snickered.

I was enjoying the male bonding. But still, I wondered if Pierre wasn't being too harsh. "Don't worry Jared, your grandfather hasn't skied in at least twelve years since you were born. He's as rusty as an old nail."

Pierre's face crumpled, but he didn't speak. Something was going on with him—something more than the lingering loss of our daughters. Perhaps he too, was reliving memories. *Skiing. It was our favorite family activity—and it died with our girls.*

Sensing his grandfather's discomfort, Jared remained silent for a moment. Then, he asked, "Do you still have my Mom's ski equipment?"

I exchanged swift glances with Pierre and noticed the compassion in his eyes as he spoke to Jared. "We do. Nothing of your Mom's belongings, or Bianca's, has been touched." He assured with a soft voice.

Jared did a little dance in place, what I've always called his "happy feet." But I recognized it for what it was: anxiety.

He stopped tapping his feet, and declared, "I want to see my Mom's stuff. Her skis, her boots, her…everything." Jared's voice quivered as his words tumbled out.

Jared was two months old when Cassidy committed suicide. The only maternal bond he has are in the form of photos. Now he's a teen, asking a great deal about the girl-woman who brought him into the world. Then left long before he even said his first word.

My palms were moist with sweat. Tears stung my eyes as I stood zombie-like, wondering what to say. I hadn't been able to step inside the girl's bedroom since the time I sat on their floor perusing heartbreaking photos. Our housecleaner Lily comes and goes weekly, so at least their belongings aren't collecting dust with memories I desperately cling onto.

Lily's words after cleaning yesterday haunted my mind. I quickly brushed them away as they bruised my soul. She had muttered: "habitación fantasma." *Ghost room.*

I decided… Now's as good a time as ever. "Your Mom's ski equipment is in the walk-in closet she shared with Bianca. I might even use her skis for our trip. Let's go take a look together!"

Pierre stared at me in shock. I was finally crossing a boundary, as I led Jared to the girl's room. I was oddly at ease. I would be brave. Here and now and on the slopes, I'll boldly crash through this final layer of grief. Perhaps crash through some ski-racing gates with Jared.

The moment we crossed over the threshold into the girls' room, my heart leapt to my throat. I froze, staring off at Jared as he aimlessly wandered around the room.

Maybe it was my imagination, but I smelled my daughters' being, felt their presence—like lingering perfume. Sweet and earthy. Clean and animal. How could this be, after thirteen years?

The room seemed smaller than I remembered, as if the walls were closing in on me, suffocating me—or telling me it's time for the room to disappear altogether.

My fingers gently touched the girls' furniture, at once comforting and familiar—as I walked towards the closet to grab the skis. Jared was across the room, on Cassidy's side. Looking sorrowful and intrigued, he scanned her walls, rubbing his arms as if chilled. He didn't utter a word. I feared our little adventure into his mom's room might be traumatizing him.

"Jared?" I called. He didn't turn, and I was going to suggest we leave the room when words came.

"My Mom liked art?" he asked while looking at the paintings and drawings on the walls.

"Yes, she showed a lot of talent really early, like age two."

My grandson still hadn't turned my way. He continued to rub his arms. He was uncomfortable, an awkward expression crinkling his face, as he added, "She had lots of friends?"

Both Cassidy and Bianca had picture-crowded walls; giant colorful cork boards loaded with photos of friends.

"Your mother was popular Jared. She had an amazing personality." My voice cracked. Hearing it, he stared directly at me. His eyes pooled with tears. I grabbed Cassidy's skis, and something jammed into the corner of the closet caught my attention. My heart froze when I realized with horror what it was. *The clothes Bianca was wearing that fatal moment.*

Since I had pushed back against implicating Brandon Garth, law enforcement seemed to realize Bianca was in the wrong for riding a motorized skateboard in the street, so close to available sidewalks. It was no longer considered a criminal case. Sergeant Coral had reluctantly handed me back the bag once considered "evidence" upon my request.

Just as I've not been able to ease the pain of change by repurposing the bedroom, I'd clung to this item as if to resurrect my dead child.

My hand trembled as I reached towards the white paper bag holding Bianca's blood-stained clothes. Emotions swilled around me. My heart felt like a pinball machine.

Images wedged deep in my mind since the day I was told the case was closed, floated to the top of the space around me. I saw my arms stretched out towards Sergeant Coral: *Please, Jason…please give me the clothes my daughter was wearing.*

"Why would you want them, Anna? Won't it be too painful?"

"No…it's more painful letting her blood be so disposable," I had answered. Jason had looked at me with what seemed like pity, and said, *"Okay, but this isn't standard protocol."*

I was nudged from my reverie as Jared scooted from the bedroom without another word. In his wake, the last stage of grief presented itself with a vengeance, as if to say, "It's time."

My eyes roamed my daughters' room. In my mind, it transformed into Jared's room. Pieces of him—his personality. Cassidy's artwork changed into a baseball poster, Bianca's skateboard photos were swapped out for Jared's ski adventures. The makeup vanity presented itself as a model airplane. The color palette of the world I painted used brushstrokes of blue, shades of black and gray—fading out the pink.

Something unfolded and glimmered within me. I was letting go—*Acceptance.* The bedroom I kept intact to shelter both my daughters' souls will be purged. I can do this. I am strong. *Where to start?*

The bag of blood-stained clothes in my arms weighed down my grief and tore open my heart. I unsealed the bag labeled "clothes" and found a roll of paper containing what Bianca was wearing when she'd taken that fatal skateboard ride. It was labeled, "blood sample."

My breath caught as I somehow had the nerve to tear it open, revealing Bianca's favorite jeans and t-shirt. *Why was I doing this? Who in their right mind wants to see the bloody clothes their child died in?*

But for whatever reason, there they were, in my shaky hands.

My fingertips grazed over the crusty fabric, hardened through the years. The blood was black, darker than the dead of her life. I brought her shirt to my nose and sniffed, unsure what to expect. Nothing. I kissed my daughter's blood that had haunted my dreams.

My eyes traveled to the edge of a nightstand and found a silver-framed photo of Cassidy and Bianca, grinning profusely. Across their chest was a sign that read; "Good luck in the race."

After I reached over and picked up the glossy photo, memories flashed through my consciousness: a succession of disconnected scenes at track, cheerleading, art contests, Bianca's first official skateboarding race, and school plays.

In a flood of tears, I buried my face in my hands, and let the uncontrollable sobs rule me. In a few moments, an inner calm swept over me, like my body was cleansed of a burden. Closing my eyes, I swallowed my sobs.

I dropped the clothes into the bag, sealed it up and placed it in its creepy corner—for now. It will be the first item to go.

I was relieved when laughter echoed from the kitchen. Just what we need, love and laughter. Grabbing Cassidy's skis, I took one last look. Bringing Jared into the room had served a purpose. It brought this change in me—helped me see I am not betraying my daughters' souls by letting go of their possessions—rather, I am enabling their precious souls to flow forward and rest in peace.

With skis in one hand, I sat on Cassidy's bed and smoothed the comforter with a slight tremble. I flashed to when they were ages three and six, laying on this bed while I read stories. I'd read eight books a night to them. They were book fiends.

Finally, I stood, turned off the light and blew a kiss into the room, "Goodbye my sweet girls, Mama loves you." And to the room, my mind sent out the signal: *You will be restored to the land of the living.*

* * *

"There she is, we thought you'd fallen into the twilight zone. What've you been doing?" Pierre smiled as I walked into the kitchen, skis over my shoulder as if I'm ready for the gondola already. *If they only knew.*

"Oh, just rummaging through Cassidy's closet for these." I propped Cassidy's skis against the wall. We had just given them to her as a Christmas gift in 2007—a month before she died. The year that sealed the fate of our marriage, buried in double grief.

Jared looked at the skis—his mother's skis—and said, "Wow, they're still in the wrapper."

I nodded, still spooked by my revelation in the *ghost room.*

Pierre lifted the skis, "I remember getting these for Cassidy. They were expensive not knowing if she'd use them so soon after the baby—" his words came to an abrupt halt.

He realized what he was saying. The fateful reason Cassidy never used the skis, hung in the air like the smell of an old wet rag. But unlike a smell, this couldn't be ventilated out or overpowered by a stronger scent. This would linger in our souls until we each met our maker.

An awkward silence fell upon us. But it was Jared—that baby—who could pull the moment together with the emotional strength to say, "So Grand-mère, are you planning to use my Mom's skis in France? Look at them, they're still the kind like the newer short shaped slalom skis!"

"Heck yes, I'm bringing them to the shop to have my bindings fitted on the way to meet Caryssa. Maybe they'll bring good luck on the slopes."

Both my husband and grandson raised their eyebrows. I wondered if the same thought occurred to them. The skis as a bad omen, a death wish as if the skis summoned a suicidal spirit. I swatted the negativity away.

There it was again—that emotionally charged heartbeat in our home. It hung in the air around us. The disturbed pulse hadn't come from Pierre's heart, or mine; but it was somehow shared. The empty space between us fed the odd rhythm. The empty pink bedroom down the hall.

"Well, I'll scoot Jared home, so you can get across the bridge to see your friend." Pierre tapped Jared on the shoulder, "It'll be good to see your Dad."

This brightened Jared's eyes. I was grateful to hear Pierre mention he'd like to see Josh. Within his stage of anger, which lasted more than half a decade, I wasn't the only one blamed for our daughter's deaths.

I hoped this was a sign that within the cycle of grief, we're crossing the finish line heart to heart. Hugging the generations of love standing in my kitchen, I whispered to Pierre, "Don't worry about me getting over any bridge, Caryssa has offered to meet in Sausalito."

* * *

Caryssa and I stalked the hostess through the airy French bistro. Candles were aglow, dishes clanked aggressively, while chatter and laughter rose to a louder crescendo. "Avez-vous une préférence?"

We came to talk. I was about to answer when Caryssa pointed towards the outdoor dining patio. "Much quieter out there and check out the view!" she suggested.

We were both dressed in that typical eclectic San Francisco-style casual chic prepared for sudden fog or cool weather. Dark skinny jeans, big scarfs paired with a sweater, big purse or backpacks for layers and a light jacket.

The low sun warmed us as our eyes soaked in the sights. Two huge palm trees cast their pointy, swaying shadows on the patio while a bevy of boats on the bay added to the South of France-like vibe. We had barely settled on which umbrella to sit under, as the waiter asked, "Voulez-vous boire quelque chose?"

I answered with a smile, "Le menu des vins s'il vous plaît." To that, menus magically appeared from beneath his arms, as if tugging off his wings and handing them to us.

"Merci beaucoup." I knew the menu by heart; I was asking for Caryssa's sake. But the waiter disappeared into the dining room.

When he left, Caryssa shook the menu, "Holy crap, it's in French, just like the wait staff. Charming, but how can I order? My bad French will show." She spoke in a hushed tone, eyes dancing around, embarrassed she wasn't more familiar with the language.

"*Merde sainte!* Just let me do the talking. I'm experienced at the French service game." I assured her with a wink. "And by the way, this is on me, as a token of my appreciation for the skis."

"Wow, thanks! Quite a bargain, since Tyler outgrew those skis and they'd just collect dust in the garage." Caryssa scanned the industrial-chic bistro with less embarrassment and more intrigue. "Speaking of garages—"

"Yup, the restaurant's a converted garage, hence its name *Le Garage*. It's got a rustic feel about it—I love this place, the only one in the area with authentic French cuisine. The service is usually excellent, but not sure about this French dude." I raised my arm, waving slightly, calling out to the waiter, "S'il vous plait."

He appeared in an instant. I spoke with perfect pronunciation, "Une carafe de Pinot Noir s'il vous plait."

The waiter nodded. Caryssa asked if we should also order our food now. Upon hearing Caryssa's English, the waiter responded with a thick French accent that rolled off his tongue, "Would you like un apéritif, perhaps?"

I rattled off a list of dishes, including Dungeness crab, raviolis dusted with fresh basil, escargot, and a crispy salad with goat cheese. My taste buds could hardly wait.

Our wine came. We toasted to nothing in particular and everything about life itself. "Ready for the French Alps?" Caryssa asked, sipping her wine.

"No, how 'bout you—packed for your ski trip to Utah?" I asked while snapping a picture of a sailboat gliding into a slip, back-propped by the bright pink and tangerine sky after sunset.

"I'm always packed for skiing. The trick is to never unpack—just wash dirty clothes and toss them back into the suitcase. "

The word clothes tugged at my core, shooting me warily back to that moment in my girl's bedroom. I slapped the memory away. "I guess I do have one item ready for the trip, new skis." I said.

"New skis! How exciting, does this mean you'll finally go skiing with us?" Caryssa had been trying to get me to ski for years, but I…couldn't. The mere thought was too painful. Without my girls, who could no longer enjoy their favorite snow sport, it seemed selfish.

I wasn't intending to bring the topic up—Caryssa and I are forever talking dark thoughts within beautiful backgrounds. Yet, I needed this therapy for my soul. I had to take this final hurdle.

Our tiny dishes came at once. As we sipped while tasting the French delights, I unraveled the haunting moments in my girl's room, dumping the horror on Caryssa's lap so as to share the burden. Judging by the look on her face, she was happy to share the load and help ease my pain. Mothers—we stick together.

"The skis aren't new. They're over a decade old but still the cool parabolic shorties on the market. They're Volkls like yours."

"Oh, nothing wrong with buying used skis, especially since you haven't skied in at least a decade anyh—"

"No."

"No, what? You have skied over the past decade, without me? You're caught, red-handed!" Caryssa laughed, sipping wine. But her humor was stifled with my revelation.

"They're not used, the skis. They've never been removed from the factory packaging. I haven't skied since—" my sentence was cut off by the waiter's arrival.

He came by, asking if everything is to our liking. I shooed him away as if he should recognize a private conversation when he saw one. "Caryssa, the skis were Cassidy's."

Caryssa's mouth fell open; she leaned in towards me, "Wow, that's brave of you!"

"Thanks for recognizing that!" I swirled my wine glass without thinking, allowing the sloshing to settle my woes somewhat, like standing aside a babbling brook and attempting to let it carry away my worries. "I hope her distress doesn't emanate up from her skis, steering me into oblivion."

To this, Caryssa went mute. She waited, as if willing me on. And really, what could she say to such a dark premonition? I'd left her in an undesirable position. The thought ran in circles and I watched it go, run into the distance and close in again, rounding the corners of my mind.

As if to make me feel better, she said to me, "I understand, skiing can be such a mind-game. It's easy to lose our mountain mojo. But try to think of Cassidy's skis as good luck charms rather than a black cloud."

To this, I merely nodded, sipping my wine. Cassidy *was* an expert skier by age ten. Maybe her skiing edge *will* put the spring back into my rusty performance. I tried to let the thought lighten my load, but I'd stuffed the bad omen thing too far into my subconscious.

We ate in silence for a moment enjoying the fresh bay breeze. There was a chill to the air as the sky darkened with my thoughts. The vibe and view commanded more—something uplifting—positive. But getting through the final stage of grief seemed to only come with facing this.

Caryssa waited, as if she sensed something lurked in my psyche that needed releasing. My lips tightened, and the words spilled out, "I found something in Bianca's closet."

"Uh ha, go on." She replied, measuring expressions before letting them sit on her face. This was a delicate situation, the smallest infraction could cause emotional bedlam; she knew that, hence the steady pace of both her gestures and expressions.

"A baggie, with the blood-stained clothes Bianca wore during the accident." I dropped a bomb, which exploded onto her face.

"Oh my God." Caryssa's fork stopped midway between the plate and her mouth. A tremble running through her arm caused crumbs of food to fall from the fork, as if they wanted no part of this conversation, a jump back into the dish being a preferable fate.

"But know what? I'm okay with this. I mean, not okay with losing my daughters, but learning to live with the heartache that breathes within me." I took an almighty inhale, a much-needed one. "I see this as the final step—of letting go."

Caryssa remained silent, having placed her fork back in the dish, confounded in a maze of motherly pain. She sat hunched and fragile. A twinge of guilt hit me for bringing this up. But she was my friend. Who else would I confide in? Of course, I understood her awkwardness. Not only was this topic a difficult one, it reminded her that the very same thing could happen to Tyler. Life was unpredictable. There are no guarantees. Everyone dies, regardless of age, accidents and tragedies can happen. I realized her sensitivity; always afraid something might happen to Tyler. This obviously wasn't my intention. "I promise I'll change the subject, but how do I dispose of it?"

"I...I..." she stuttered, words catching on her tongue like cloth catching in a zipper, until a stream of coherent words slipped out. "There are services that help with that—"

"No, I need something more spiritual." I cut in. Her advice was rational, but I needed something more sentimental, more meaningful. "I mean, I can't give it to Goodwill or toss it into the trash. My daughter's blood is not so dispensable." I explained, biting back a tone of patronizing, not wanting to upset a friend who is merely trying to help. This conversation can't be easy for her, she was stepping through a minefield, concerned that one wrong word or phrase would offend or hurt me.

Caryssa placed a hand over her mouth. I was about to switch to a less morbid topic, but she surprised me. "I don't know how you feel about this, but I've heard of people burning their loved one's clothes and spreading the ashes somewhere they enjoyed."

That's perfect! Not only was it getting rid of the soiled clothing, it could be a sort-of ceremony, and even allow me to take that final step of letting go. I held back tears. I restrained a fist bump, as it didn't seem appropriate. But I was relieved, we'd met with a pleasing resolution. In no time at all, I responded.

I blurted out the first place that popped into my mind: "The skate park."

CHAPTER TEN

Caryssa

"The best things in life aren't things."

We strolled along Sausalito boardwalk working off our feast of French foods. The lingering taste of garlic and butter from the escargot remained on my palette. Anna's words—which language authority might deem "cliché," echoed through the air, bouncing off the churning water.

"That's the theme I used for my baby announcements for Tyler. It read *The Best Things in Life are Worth Waiting For.*" I zipped my jacket up, retrieving gloves from the pockets. A thundering crash of waves hit the imposing rock outcroppings. We turned around, heading back towards the art studios.

Anna drifted along the walkway, rubbing her arms to ward off the sudden chill. "Until now, I couldn't let go of those—*things*—in my girls' bedroom," she admitted. "I held on, unable to accept that they're gone." Sorrow added weight to her voice.

"Understandable," was all I could say. I couldn't even let go of Tyler's belongings now, not wanting him to grow up before I had a chance to enjoy his youth and the treasure of memories it brought. In no time he'll be married, have a job, maybe kids, and a real adult life and responsibilities will be ever-present in his existence. He, and every other child, deserves a childhood.

We added pep to our pace and it wasn't long before we were back to the restaurant, crossing over to the stretch of art galleries. I wanted to ask Anna for an update on the art gallery break-in, the murders, and entire cryptic dove thing, but she continued:

"I'll do it...I'll purge those things in the room and..."

A silence fell between us, amplifying the bustle of shopper's strife in the streets. "Want to sit, Anna?" There was a cozy bench under a gas tiki-torch, the street adorned with tiny white lights.

Without another word, we sat watching people rush by. They were lugging various gifts, filling the air with laughter, or shouting restlessness.

I waited. Anna sighed, then announced, "I'm hesitant to talk to Pierre about your idea how to dispose of the bag of Bianca's clothes."

"Does he even realize the bag's there?" I questioned. How I knew the answer was beyond me.

"No," she replied, her eyes avoiding mine.

My heart skipped a beat. My mind wandered. *Does he want to know? Should he know?*

As if an x-ray vision allowed her to read my thoughts, Anna spoke, "I can't tell him about it. It'd kill him. He is way too sensitive about losing our girls, even more so than me. He'd likely sleep with the bag cradled in his arms as if holding his baby girl again."

Weariness hung in Anna's voice. I announced, "I'm so happy Jared will make use of Tyler's old Dynastar skis." I hoped I didn't sound insensitive switching topic so abruptly. There's only so much advice a person can give.

"He's stoked for the trip!" Anna lifted wistful, bewitching eyes toward me. "Thank God I have Jared. Remember those playdates he had with Tyler? Seems just yesterday."

"Yes, I can still see Jared at age four, with wild, free-flowing blonde hair. He could have been mistaken for a girl. He fit right in with the kids, like the final puzzle piece."

Memories ignited within Anna's eyes. Those bittersweet flashbacks caused her to well up. But within a couple of rapid blinks, they were gone. "Speaking of playdates, do you ever see the others from our former group? Stan? Brenda? And who was that couple with the twins, the ones that had a pile of family money fall into their laps?"

"Charlotte and Bryan. I see a few of them around town, yet we don't get together anymore because we came together for the sake of our children with playdates and sports. Our kids branched out to new friends." I explained.

"Your kids have grown." Mixed emotions played on Anna's face. Nostalgia sat on the bench beside me, hands covering melancholy eyes. I thought she'd cry, but instead, she smiled through the pain of her own children denied the chance of blossoming into fine ladies.

A fresh salty sea breeze brushed our hair, while the beautiful view of sailboats and the marina delighted our senses. It was not quite as chill as it was walking on the boardwalk.

We sat for a moment, each tangled in our own wistfulness. Anna's mention of Charlotte and Bryan Garrity reminded me of when Tyler played baseball with their boys. What an amazing couple. He stepped away from his inherited power after seeing his dad's riches were born from unscrupulous political activities—including war.

The classic white lights illuminated palm trees and succulents lining the street, adding to the charm of the area. The sights and smells delighted my senses.

I turned to Anna, my voice echoing into the crisp Sausalito air, "I admire those two…Bryan and Charlotte. Despite inheriting over twenty-five million dollars from his old man, they both still work in their respective fields doing good for the world. Rather than live high-off-the hog, they donated a ton to humanitarian causes. We need more people like that!"

"She worked in Ecology, I remember—so she still does that?" Anna inquired, a stray hair teased by a gentle kiss from the breeze, which she scraped from her face.

"Yup, still saving the planet rather than being part of the elite destroying it. She sees firsthand the need to link global ecology with a moral global economy. She no longer has to work but does to make a difference. What a gal. And he still runs his landscape architect business, designing eco-friendly properties. They are a power couple for the environment."

"Nice to know *someone* is protecting the planet, perhaps my grandson will have a life before Earth disappears," she said with a tinge of sarcasm. "He is now thirteen and unscrupulous leaders are still blowing things up, destroying his world. It's bomb and build, bomb and build. I want him to stay innocent...young—" she paused for a moment before continuing.

Warier of the massive US Military than "terrorism," and how America has forfeited liberties out of a shadow government-induced irrational fear, my psyche switched from where this could go. The words leaped out, "Seems the kids grow up too fast." I at once wanted to take back the comment. Her girls never had the chance, nor will they ever. Yet, Anna still smiled—focused again on the parents.

"And how 'bout Stan? He's an interesting man—still playing Mr. Mom?"

I shook my head firmly, "Heck no, that ended years ago. Stan finished grad school, works as an Environmental Sustainability Lawyer focused on corporate abuse."

"Wow, commendable, turning his own battle with cancer around to help people!" Her words were heavy with pride. "I remember his illness was traced to chemicals he was exposed to on the job." Anna pondered this further, evident through a far-off gaze.

I shifted quickly on the bench, my heart both warm and heavy with the thought— "Yeah, he's amazing, a human rights lawyer. His most recent case involves a local teen who developed cancer from exposure to toxic fumes blown into her neighborhood from a nearby oil refinery." My hands flew to my heart, as I stilled my mouth from the typical whimsical, esoteric tangents that can fly out of it.

"Local? Where does she live?" Anna asked.

"Richmond, I know the girl, goes to school with Tyler." I pushed the vulnerability of those who live near oil refineries out of my mind. I didn't have enough space left to worry about those too.

Anna mentioned, "We can see one of those refineries from your back-yard—good thing you are far away from it."

"Yeah, the industry culprit can be eerily seen from my house atop the picturesque hill. What a contrast of gorgeous bay view, palm trees, bloom-ing cactus and smokestacks fuming from a rusty petroleum factory— Beauty and the Beast."

Anna clicked her tongue, "good for the local coffers, I suppose." She finished off her words with a shrug.

"Hmm…good for something. Also, a stark reminder how oil mixes with politics, pollution and endless wars seamlessly blending in with the surreal beauty surrounding us." I commented, my eyes stroking the cur-rent horizon, wondering what evils lurked within its beauty.

"Everything's about money, including how the courts wanted to make Brandon Garth a wasted by-product of our unjust legal system." Anna mentioned, referring to the boy who fatally struck her daughter in a tragic skateboarding accident.

I nodded, grateful for people like Anna. Imagine, less needless revenge and more human compassion in the world. Understanding. Tolerance. The planet would be a different place if more people lived by this philoso-phy. Stealing a glance into my Cover Girl compact, I admired the fresh blonde highlights my hairdresser gave me.

Anna moved the conversation along, breaking from any more talk of her daughter's demise. She asked, "Do you still go to PTSA meetings?"

"Heck no…I'm just volunteering at the school once a week. I tried go-ing to one recently and walked out when the discussion turned to choco-late and vanilla cupcakes. Seriously, I was once making million-dollar decisions and then I'm listening to parents and teachers argue over such trivial bullshit!" I laughed at the irony of it.

Deep down, I savored the cupcake decisions, anything to make a child smile in their magical little space, oblivious to the terrors of the world. Inside, I realized those silly decisions to keep the kids happy just might have been more meaningful than a few of those controversial million-dollar decisions but kept that tidbit to myself.

Anna laughed, then rolled her shoulders, straightening. Her eyes caught the soft classical white lights flickering along the street which seemed to blink off and on suddenly. "Too bad the art galleries are closed, it'd be a nice way to end the evening."

"Want to window shop along Caledonia Street?" I asked. Anna tightened her big brown scarf around her simple, yet elegant V-neck sweater, and I noticed the gold and crystal statement necklace she wore. I adored the way Anna always looked so classically beautiful.

"I kind of like sitting here—besides, I'm familiar with the amazing art studios and shops in Sausalito."

"Well come to think of it, I've window shopped enough stores I can't afford. Speaking of art galleries, what's the latest on the *Exotic Exposure* murder mystery?"

"Not such a mystery anymore, it was Ava's dad, Diego who killed Johnny—and the prison guard. He's been arrested." Anna removed a hairpin, letting her chestnut mane cascade, golden highlights shimmered in the night.

"Why didn't I see anything on the news?" As soon as the question fell from my lips, I had a probable answer.

Anna raised her left eyebrow with an incredulous smile. "Are you kidding?" Her eyebrow raised that much further. "The same reason many CIA scandals are covered up."

"Well, there's still plenty of mystery left behind with the two dead doves." Those baffling birds never stop intriguing me. A never-ending enigma straight from a bestselling crime/thriller novel.

"I've heard nothing from the cops, and I'd rather never talk to them again anyhow. But Ava s Ramírez seemed like someone I'd want to talk to…and so, I did!" She casually dropped a bomb as if discussing a school bake fair.

"You—" my mouth dropped. I could feel my face crinkle. Did she really just say what I think she did? Am I missing something? Had I misheard her? Her revealing of such huge news in such a laid-back manner astounded me.

"Spoke to the girl who stole my art, killed her doves, and wrote a Pablo Picasso anti-war quote on the back of my painting. She's fascinating." Again, she spoke as if this was nothing more than some gossip or juicy tidbit.

"So…you casually called her and forgave her for vandalizing your art gallery and leaving behind a dead bird—"

"No!" She cut me off. "Not letting her off the hook—she was involved in stealing at least a million dollars' worth of art which may never be restored. I merely tolerated listening to her side of the story." She raised a hand to emphasize that she hadn't and won't be forgiving the girl anytime soon.

"Which is?"

"She admitted being entangled in the art theft, she and her best friend Paige worked with her dad. He was the ringleader and wanted the art too, but for a different motive. She claims he wanted my Delacroix to use as a political weapon at CIA headquarters." Her voice lowered as if fearsome that someone was eave's dropping on our conversation. They could be—probably were.

"A political weapon?" I gasped.

Anna became animated, "Yes, and it might make sense. The CIA has been said to use modern art by abstract expressionist artists, as pawns of the Cold War—a form of benevolent propaganda." She explained while gesturing emphatically.

"But Delacroix was a French Romanticist—" I was confused.

"Which uses a similar blend of color, religious and political symbolism. The Delacroix he took from my gallery is a reproduction of *Liberty Leading the People*."

I rolled my hands, "Go on."

Anna continued with more hand gestures and melodramatic expressions, "She also reiterated the story about her and Paige wanting to sell the art for college tuition."

"Did she explain her version of why her father framed them for murdering Johnny, then posted a million to bail her out of prison yet has no money to put her through school?" A serious case of bipolar disorder came to mind. This mystery tangled more and more, forming endless knots that I desperately wanted unknotting.

"She mentioned her dad is a misogynist. He thinks women don't belong in college, or in business—have no say in any matter of importance. According to Ava, Diego dude said he'd never considered paying a dime for her college tuition." Anna shook her head, disgust visible through a stiff jaw and flaring nostrils. I echoed the sentiment, repulsed by such sexism.

"Nice father—likely buddies with the current nutcases in the White House." I felt for the girl, to have such a pig for a father. "And odd, since he likely wanted her to join his military."

"I asked her about the symbolic message with blood drops on the doves. She said the forensics team had it right, and she elaborated: she placed the olive branch into the second doves' right claw as a mockery of our leaders claiming world peace can be found at the end of a gun barrel."

Or worse, with big nuclear 'buttons.' I winced, then it dawned on me: "Interesting…so the doves were symbolic of the U.S. Seal?"

"Uh-huh, and the second doves' neck was broken. Ava had positioned the bird's head away from the olive branch, towards the left claw where she had placed thirteen sticks."

I envisioned the U.S. Great Seal, my heart beating to a faster rhythm. "To show the thirteen arrows of the 'power of war.' Wow, this is deep shit." A hand instinctively cradled my jaw as if the information added an actual weight to my brain.

Anna nodded, "Yup…Ava said she tried to convey how the olive branch has never been extended, even though the American eagle faces it—and how this negatively affects her generation. How it kills world peace."

If you kill a dove, you kill peace.

"A true revolutionist." I admired the girl, despite her part in robbing my friend to survive her future. Needs, I guess. "But why wasn't any of this mentioned during questioning, or taped? Why now?"

"There was a lot of intimidation. Diego threatened not only the lives of law enforcement if they exposed his actions. He told Ava, his own daughter, he'd kill her if she talked about the murders he committed and framed on her—or how the symbolic messages she left behind with the doves reflect what he secretly does for work." She explained, with seriousness and compassion drilled into every word.

"How does she know so much about her dad's work, when the CIA keeps its historic involvement in the power-hungry drug and war cabal so secretive?" I asked. I found it hard to believe that such a man would let his daughter discover this or put himself in a position where this information could be easily found.

"She's overheard one too many of his conversations surrounding secret missions when he least expected it. In short, she knows too much." Anna shifted on the wooden bench. Nervous? She turned to see a ferry coming in.

"I can't help but see a connection…the political issues starving America's public schools, over-the-top academic and financial stress, the girls' motive for the art theft, the symbolic messages reflecting our cultural obsession with nebulous 'foreign enemies' and resultant violence within. How it's all about money and power. The dots connect."

George's words echoed in my mind: *sometimes I wish you never connected the dots of corporate America to perpetual war; our cultural ecosystem being polluted and mass surveillance.*

And then, on top of everything, there's Anna's ordeal floating in the periphery. Her daughters' blood-in-a bag staring back at her like a reminder of how we are expected to want a foul retaliation onto the innocent boy who heartbreakingly hit her on a foggy street one day, thirteen years ago. A tragic accident attempted to be turned into profit for the prosecutor and revenge money into Anna's pocket.

"Yup...the elites sell war, fire, and fury—and the American people buy it." Anna lowered her black Prada handbag from her shoulder to the ground, rummaging to grab a lip gloss.

"It's surprising you were able to get Ava speaking to you on the phone—"

"Oh, no...no. She wouldn't speak over the phone. She had said in a guarded tone, '*Let's meet in person.*' We met at my loft, and she opened to me. She said her dad and his team eavesdropped over the phone, spied on any emails, or other communications. Then she dropped a bomb on me..."

Anna trailed off and seemed reluctant or afraid to say more. I became uncomfortable on the bench and asked if she wanted to have a latte at the enchanting corner coffee shop.

I looked around, reminded we are in one of the most popular and pretty places in California, right over the famed Golden Gate Bridge. Again, the surreal outer beauty of America while the hidden beast within preys its power upon us.

A man in a leprechaun hat started playing music on the sidewalk. The melodic twangs of his guitar filled the air, bringing our discussion to a halt. Mournful tunes flowed from his silky voice. As we strolled, each of us dropped bills into his tip jar. He tossed a smile our way and continued to sing.

While walking, Anna whipped out her cell phone and said, "I bet Ava will meet us now at the coffee shop. She lives right at the edge of Tiburon."

I stopped short and brought my hands up, crossing them over my chest. "You're *serious*? You've become attached enough to this cagy girl that robbed your art gallery and killed her doves to just call her on a whim—"

Anna interrupting me, "Shhh! Her phones ringing." Then she walked a few feet away and I sensed she wanted privacy.

I whispered, "Isn't she in prison for the art theft?"

"She's awaiting another trial, leave me alone while I— "Hello, Ava?"

I used the moment to check my own messages and realized there was a text from George.

Utah is booked. Tahoe is booked. Get pumped for some great skiing!

My heart raced with excitement, especially getting Tyler on his first trip to ski Utah's steeps and deeps. He'll love it, and we have a ski in-ski out condo, hot tub and pool at both Squaw Valley and Snowbird ski resorts.

Anna called over to me from the other side of the sidewalk, "Ava is on her way! I think I succeeded in gaining her trust, as I hadn't kept harping on about the art theft. I showed her I care."

"You care, about even those who hurt you the most. Such a compassionate humanitarian." I flashed back to the biggest demonstration of this, when she dropped the case against Brandon Garth. "So…what should I expect with this girl?"

"You can expect to see a very pretty nearly twenty-year-old Mexican girl with long brown hair, big brown eyes and an award-winning smile—too skinny to be called healthy, with an edgy outlook."

"I guess the anxiety can be expected, with her shithole of a dad." I felt bad for the girl, despite her appalling acts of helping to rob Anna's art gallery, then killing her pet doves for show and tell.

Glancing around spellbinding Sausalito, my mind drifted back to being on the French Riviera. It looks so much the same to me. People sipping fine wines by the waterfront, the sun-kissed coastal palm trees and quiet charm wrapped in bougainvillea. Brilliant white boats sparkled the waters' edge.

We meandered on cobbled sidewalks towards the café, passing unique waterfront hotspots. Art galleries, antique shops, chic-bars and restaurants were plotted along the streets, warm and inviting. The bitter tang of coffee issued from the stores, blending in with the scent of desserts intermingling with the sea-born fog. And other scents, of burning wood from beach bonfires and eucalyptus. It was nearly empty, just a few stragglers wandering along browsing and chatting. The lightest breeze tapped wind chimes and shook palm trees.

Arriving at the cute café resembling a craftsman-style bungalow, a bald man in a blazer and bow tie looking every bit the fierce gentleman he was held the door open for us.

We took a seat in a cozy corner on a swank orange sofa. Anna ordered a decaf coffee when the Barista came by and I got a classic frothy latte. He asked if we'd like to order something to eat, and we decided to share a macaron with raspberry. The pastries were huge here, more like a small pie.

I glanced around the rustic café and delighted in the contrast of bay view and fireplace, warm atmosphere with relaxing music. It felt like being in someone's house. "You must be getting so excited for the French Alps, Anna!" I was thrilled that in a few days, we'd both be swooshing down the ski slopes and loving the great outdoors.

"You don't know the half of it, it's been too long since I've felt the adrenaline rush of my skis gliding over snow-capped peaks." Anna's eyes glazed over, and I could see the pleasure mixed with pain.

We sipped our coffee, and I declared I needed to use the restroom. On the way into the lady's room I discovered this quaint café offers more than gourmet coffee. I passed by a myriad of plants and flowers, room sprays, and an entire section for wine tasting under vintage-looking lights.

Upon leaving the restroom stall, I was greeted by lovely bouquets of roses and several decorative baskets full of toiletries. I started smelling and trying out the lavender scented lotions, rosemary and sage soaps, and salon-grade hairspray. Last, I rolled a Tahitian Gardenia perfumed oil over my wrists. *Charming.* I realized I'd been gone for at least twenty minutes and headed back.

I rounded the corner and saw Anna talking to Ava. We were the only patrons left in the café this late, which was a good thing to help the girl feel comfortable enough to talk. She needed to lift and lighten the mental load she carried.

And what I heard stopped me in my tracks….

Ava was crying, letting it all out. "My dad brought me to a dark place in the city; lab that looked like a secret prison. I saw like…seven young men and women—teens I think, strapped to tables with IV drops, all drugged in some way."

"What the—" my mouth flew open as if that knowledge physically pried my lips apart. There goes my bathroom stress fix. Both women turned their heads towards me, and Anna said, "Caryssa, this is Ava."

I approached the delicate, pale-faced girl and gently shook her hand. I wanted to hug her, but hoped the tenderness reflected in my eyes was enough to make her feel welcomed.

Ava smiled at me, the tears fresh on her cheeks. "I'll tell you what the fuck they were doing, feeding kids mind-control drugs. It's to sway them into doing bad things for bad guys…I think they're all in the CIA." Ava paused, eyes darting around, as if making sure no one was within earshot.

Anna piped in, "Come to think of it, I overheard my dad talking about this when I was just a young girl—during his Vietnam horror. He was programmed and exploited to kill."

"How…how do you know that the agency is doing this now, Ava?" I asked. I too, had heard snippets of accusations that the CIA still did these things, yet was appalled a nineteen-year-old has this family betrayal in her mind.

Ava hesitated, the haunted look of a broken spirit creeping out of beautiful, light brown eyes. She resembled Jennifer Lopez, I thought. "Half my childhood, I thought my dad was a used car salesman. That's what he told us. I never questioned it—he had a classic car collection of old Porsches and Mercedes, so it matched his personality. Then I overheard him talking when he thought I wasn't home—it was just before I turned sixteen. So, I became my own spy. I snooped and found his agency badge in his sock drawer."

We remained silent a moment. This had to be therapeutic for her, and I wondered if she'd ever told anyone this, even her best friend Paige. How long has she held this all in? "Have you ever told anyone what your dad does?" I asked her.

"Only my mom, who made the mistake of confronting him. That's when she disappeared. I haven't seen my mother since my sixteenth birthday." Fresh tears slid from the girl's eyes, and she quickly looked away.

Without looking at either of us, she sadly whispered, "I've never fully trusted my dad since then." She turned her eyes back towards Anna. "I heard him yell at my mother when she asked him why he never told her the truth about his job, he screamed "I'll have to kill you if you tell anyone. Her mysterious disappearance was never solved, but I think he killed her or had her murdered. There was a woman named Debra he was seen talking to at a bar in D.C. that mysteriously disappeared around the same time."

God almighty. Connecting the dots.... Connecting the dots...

I'd heard the heroin epidemic in America is directly linked to the CIA, among other monetary areas within our political system. A multibillion-dollar industry with 90% of the world's opium crop coming from Afghanistan. "Omigod, it's just like when the CIA was feeding kids in the Army LSD cocktails back in the 50's through the 70's."

It was Anna who spoke now, "Yup, to lure them into clandestine military missions, make them submissive to killing abroad. Same behavioral control, different drugs—"

Ava chimed in, "My dad was working at that creepy place in the city with a head of Homeland Security who tried to strap *me* to a table—but my dad told him no, not yet." Ava's hands shook as she lifted her cappuccino.

"You too? Why?" I asked, wishing for a glass of wine rather than latte. This secret shit going down can drive anyone to drink. Yet, how secret is it all really? Homeland Security operates in plain sight, with crimes against humanity detaining ten thousand innocent refugee children in detention prisons.

"He thinks I should join the military like he did, and not follow my dream to go to Stanford. We are a military family, starting with my ancestors stationed in bases on Angel Island in 1863. My great-grandfather was sent to the Pacific during WWII, and my dad insists I should be carrying on the family tradition."

Similar to Julie, I thought. Holding onto her dad's hawkish legacy, not able to let go. I asked Ava, "Why are they so adamant on not making this *your* choice rather than theirs?"

Ava swallowed a sip of her newly refreshed Cappuccino and seemed to ponder this for a moment. "I dunno, but the whole team of them seem to think I'm a danger to our country for being anti-war. My dad said he should have me killed to '*protect the American people.*'

I blurted out, "Just following orders. Nice *defense*! You're a danger only to dark money."

Soft relaxing music played in the background, with the sounds of waterfalls. A weird contrast to the conversation.

Anna asked, "So, are they using opioids now on their test subjects?" I kept an eye on the Barista, so he doesn't think we're conspiracy nuts.

Ava nodded her head, "Pretty sure, yeah. I heard the men say heroin makes people feel like Superman and they think they can conquer all those phantom enemies, leap over tall buildings. They mentioned increasing the dosage for one of the kids, a black boy around eighteen, as he screamed, "you're next Ava, you're next!"

"God almighty, what monsters." I had a sudden recollection of a story I heard while working in the computer internetworking world, of a Stanford student that took acid tests to a lab in San Francisco long ago for this same purpose. This is unbelievable, yet I knew truth lay in these stories. Quite a world that has been spawned from the federal government and moneyed power.

The words tumbled out of Anna's mouth, "Of course, the glorified war narrative is told over and over again, furthering the naïve recruits into clichés and ideologies peddled by film-makers and eloquent politicians."

As if defending her father, Ava said, "My dad is as encoded like a robot as they make their victims. He has never been the same since Afghanistan."

We nodded our assent to this. "The CIA isn't acting alone on this either." Anna seemingly directed the statement to nobody in particular.

"No," I answered. "I figure it's a team of people at the top of the big defense contractors—way up in the overlap between corporate America and the federal government. I certainly never swam in the center of those dark waters when I worked in Silicon Valley, yet I learned more about it than I'd care to admit."

"I can imagine, since the intelligence community, defense contractors and tech-industry are so linked." Anna took a bite of macron raspberry as she said this. "Are you hungry Ava? This is dessert for us, we just chowed down French food. We can order you—"

Ava jumped in, "No thanks, I haven't had much of an appetite lately—but wanted to say there's something else strange. There was nude artwork splashed all over the prison-like place, mostly by French artist Henri de Toulouse-Lautrec. I wonder if my dad had hoped to steal erotic artwork the night we robbed your art gallery."

The way Ava so casually mentioned her part in the art theft unnerved me. This girl is not all there, kind of a "*Gone Girl*." Not surprising with her screwed up childhood.

I glanced out a window and saw the surreal shoreline and the tall tip of the Golden Gate Bridge, noticing the flowers all along the rocks. So peaceful.

Anna's eyes narrowed, then moved from side to side as if calculating something. "But...I never carried erotic pieces," she said while putting her coffee cup down.

"No erotic art at *Exotic Exposure*—sorry Mr. CIA!" I laughed, to which Anna smirked. "Erotic art, huh? So, was there sex abuse involved also?"

"Yup," Ava was still visibly shaking. "The CIA produce super spies and program their subjects as 'robot agents' through use of drugs, hypnosis and shock treatments, brainwashing them to conduct acts of terror, assassinations, and sexual favors. I saw records on this during my personal spy efforts through my dad's stuff—it all looked covered up in the name of 'national security.' More horrific revelations leaped from her tongue.

I grasped the meaning then, like something sharp and jagged in my hands. Like a sculpture made of broken glass.

The words escaped my lips, "They're using people, *America's youth*, as political weapons, just like the art. Fucking with their heads."

CHAPTER ELEVEN

Julie

The doorbell rang as I lounged in front of the TV hooked on *Homeland*—getting brainwashed about spies and secrets according to Caryssa and Anna. They think it's a murky portrayal that helps justify the twisted "War on Terror." Regardless, I think it's an amazing show that raises some thought-provoking issues.

Who could be here at this hour of the night? Who *would* be here? A slight tingle made its way up the nape of my neck. Perhaps watching this program wasn't a great idea; my paranoia is in overdrive.

I considered pretending nobody was home. But my lights bathed the place in brightness, the TV blared until I reached for the remote and switched it off, and Feisty happily chirped his bedtime lullabies. That nighttime bird-song was somehow simultaneously relaxing and annoying.

What if it was that good-looking guy I kept bumping into at Trader Joe's? First, we nearly collided in the produce section, and he smiled and asked: "Do these peaches seem ripe to you?" *No, but you look ripe for the picking*, I wanted to say.

After the produce encounter, we would often meet at the coffee station. "We need to stop meeting like this," he joked, flashing that dazzling smile. The most adorable crinkles formed under his eyes when he smiled. From that, I knew he smiled often. That instantly attracted me to him. *Okay, let's meet at my place instead.* By now he knew my name and that I live in Sausalito. Who knows? Is coming to my house assertive or stalker-ish? Nope, pessimism can take a hike; this was charming. If it is him, that is.

I dashed to my bathroom, leaned into the mirror, and applied a few flicks of mascara. My eyes seemed to double in size with just a few strokes of my mascara brush. Noticing my unkempt curls, I sought to tame and tidy them with a comb. Finishing off, I slid a coat of copper-glazed lipstick over my lips. I returned my weapons of beauty and gave myself a once over before answering the door. A white silk blouse hung at my shoulders, covering my torso. A pair of fitted jeans contained my legs. That's the best I could do in just a few minutes. All in all, I didn't look half bad. Hope my dream boy is still there. That would mean he possessed patience, which would add to his already growing list of appeals.

I flew through my living room neatening my attire, bare feet slapping the wooden beams, and Feisty chirped, "Pretty woman!" Nothing like a feathery friend to give a girl a dose of confidence.

As my hand moved towards the doorknob, I hesitated. Be optimistic but smart. Realistically, this could be anyone. "Who is it?" I asked, my hand hovering above the knob.

The same heart that raced with anticipation of Mr. Right sank to my gut upon hearing, "This is FBI Special Agent Flock."

The gruff voice was clipped in a legalistic manner—and most definitely female. A frown tightened my forehead. I could feel a migraine coming on as my brain spun in confusion.

What the fuck! It was as if the TV channeled itself into my life, and here is an obsessive-compulsive terrorist hunter at my door. Isn't she supposed to have a warrant? But I have nothing to hide. What do I do? My stomach churned with anxiety. I straightened my shoulders, taking a moment to compose myself, and flung the door open trying to mask my panic.

Her slight frame appeared through the swirling, misty fog of the night as if appearing from a nightmare. She was five foot nothing and a half, a little round about the belly, with flat-ironed blonde hair pulled tight into a low pony-tail. She was stuffed into a slim-fitted sharp black suit that didn't compliment her figure in the slightest. From her belt protruded a standard issue Glock, and her badge glinted under the street light.

I had nothing to say to Special Agent Flock with the Glock. But she had something to say to me, something that warranted an abrupt, unexpected visit. Without so much as an apology for barging into my personal space, she announced, "We have informants that tell us a Mr. Jackson Taylor is staying here, ma'am." Her words carried authority and were delivered from an expressionless face. Though her movements were measured and considered, her eyes already got to work darting all over the place.

Ma'am. Guess I have no name in the eyes of a federal officer. "Uh…um… I am Julie Taylor, Jackson's sister. Mind telling me what this is all about?" But I knew. I was no fool. I feigned disinterest and listened as if I had the utmost respect.

When the FBI Agent turned a smidge, the words "FBI Terrorism Task Force" were clear as day in big white letters on her jacket. I braced myself. My stomach tensed. My throat dried.

Special Agent Flock squared her shoulders, trying to look intimidating. "Shortly after a terrorist attack in New York City, your brother was seen taking photos at the Times Square subway station. He was arrested for not cooperating with the police. I'm sure you must know this. What you may not know is he was ordered not to leave Manhattan while awaiting trial." Her words lacked empathy and were covered in firmness with just a hint of aggression. This attitude made my bowels squirm.

Holy shit Jackson, why didn't you tell me? I had half a mind to ring his neck the next time I saw him, which hopefully wouldn't be behind bars. For a brief second, I wondered if my brother had something to hide. But before that ridiculousness set in, I remembered him as the kid who cried seeing his buddies shoot squirrels with b-b guns. The truth was, my brother is a pacifist who couldn't hurt a fly.

The irony of it all.

I stared into dead eyes set within a hardened face, and replied defensively, "My brother heads up a major high-speed railroad project. His motive was to protect people from getting killed in train accidents with our crumbling infrastructure." My own words became keen-edged the more I spoke, feeling a need to defend my wrongly-accused sibling. While I wanted to let my words hit her in the face I had to remember her position and ranking. I couldn't help if I ended up in jail for verbally assaulting a federal agent. Weigh your words, Julie.

"And my motive is to protect the American people from getting killed by terrorists. Is your brother here or not?" the FBI agent spat with too much force for my liking. When her words came to a stop her jaw clenched, followed by a slight flare of her nostrils. Weren't agents trained in emotional control and such? She wasn't doing a great job of disguising her feelings. She behaved as though my brother were some murderous monster who she wanted to kill. She looked almost inhuman, like a robot. I half wondered if her hand would shoot out like it was remote-controlled. I no longer cared to be in the company of this angry lady. I had to put a nail in this conversation which echoed an interrogation.

My brother is a pacifist, but I'm not sure I am right now. I wanted to strangle the bitch for disturbing my inner peace. I had to get a handle on this rage; wrapping my fingers around her neck wouldn't help the situation for me or my brother.

I narrowed my eyes, soaking in the scene in front of me. Agent Flock stood stiffer than her uniform. When she spoke, I heard the army in her voice. I'd bet the farm she's ex-military as she holds herself like a mannequin wearing tactical-like cargo pants. I tried placating her militaristic side.

"You are implicating the son of a man renowned for building our nation's first Liberty Ship during WWII, and I work preserving its history!" I blurted out uncontrollably. The words spilled from my tongue before I had a chance to wrangle them.

Her nostrils flared once more. If looks could kill, I'd be sprawled on the floor in a bloody heap. The FBI agent was not impressed, as she demanded fiercely, "Just answer the question, ma'am. Where is Mr. Taylor?"

Life seemed to lack color for this woman; there were no shades of grey in her existence. It was all black/white, legal/illegal, right/wrong. She didn't do 'in-betweens', only this way or that. She stood unmoving, like a Knight of Self-Righteousness. Scars on her otherwise pretty face made me wonder if she fought in Iraq or some other land of needless war and is still chasing the shadows of terrorists. Experiencing such chaos would no doubt scramble a person's morals and rationality.

I answered, in as calm a voice as I could muster, "He left a few hours ago with his wife and young children, headed home after a much-deserved getaway."

At this, the agent strode forward invading more of my private turf, puffing her chest out. Her heels clacked on the floor. She whipped her head from side to side as if suspecting my brother was here and that I'd just spun a lie. At that moment, Feisty came alive in his cage. "FBI phony terror," *chirp*.

The FBI agent halted. Every muscle in my body tightened. Her eyes locked on the bird, suspicion drilled into them. "How'd that parrot learn to say that?" Her words were drenched in an accusatory tone.

"On his own, he can mimic what people say." I realized at once that I just revealed conversations that had taken place in my home. I would have face-palmed myself had my body not froze in anxiety. Just as I was about to defend myself, Feisty chirped again, "CIA evil."

Damn it Feisty, shut up. Beads of sweat traveled the slopes of my face. I was sure my perspiration added a glossy sheen to my features and would soon emit a stench. Agent Flock's jaw dropped, and just when it couldn't get any more intense, the bird added, "CIA FBI *chirp* partners in crime." This bird was digging me deeper and deeper as my heart raced faster and faster. Why'd I have to get a bird that can mimic conversations?

The agent's eyes hardened further, if that was possible, as she fixed me a glare that could murder. What was she going to do? Arrest me? Detain me? Shoot me? Does she think I am involved now? Does she consider the bird's words as my own and think I am disrespectful and a potential security threat to our nation?

However, to my shock, she turned to walk out the door. The grip of tension that had squeezed my chest loosened. Though she didn't leave without a few words. "You ought to discipline that bird, teach it some respect. His freedom here is thanks to Uncle Sam."

And with that, she was gone, into the fog that swamped her patriotic wake.

I glanced at the clock, one in the morning New York City time. Jackson was still airborne. I scrambled for my phone, reaching into my jeans. I texted him, my nervous fingers twitching over the keys.

Somethings up. FBI came looking 4 U. B careful Luv ya.

What a lame text. But what could I say? I didn't want to berate him for not telling me he was told not to leave the city. I don't blame him for taking his family and getting the heck out of an apocalyptic showdown. Can't they see he is innocent? Or have their minds been warped so badly with militaristic PTSD that they no longer see logic or have time for common sense?

I needed to vent. Anna and Caryssa were still on their ski trips to the French Alps and Utah respectively. This doesn't mean I can't text them, why not add some exciting tension to their adventure? Just as I started a new text message my cell phone pinged. Jackson. He obviously has a Wi-Fi enabled flight and is using WhatsApp or iMessage.

Jules don't talk to the FBI. They need a warrant to come to your place. They've become rogue and have no right.

Shit! Now I wish I hadn't texted him. My fingers roamed over the messaging icon again, pondering my response before I texted him back.

Don't worry. Barely said anything. Just letting u know they r looking 4u.

But did I barely say anything? Had this lady been a word wizard and pulled more information from me than I remembered? Feisty certainly said too much, that's for sure. I was frightened for the safety of my brother and his family. That fright sat in my throat and fizzed in my stomach.

Restless, knowing I'd get no sleep, I texted Anna. Shit, only seven in the morning there. Despite knowing there'd be no response until later, my thumbs flew over the keys:

Sorry to bother u in paradise. An FBI Agent popped by my place. Just an-other night in beautiful Sausalito!

I had turned the TV off before my unnerving visitor demanded my brother's whereabouts, and it was now eerily quiet. No white noise to fill the void of silence. The weather sang a quiet song outside, that's about it. Feisty was curled up in a corner of his cage, oblivious to the damage his words had potentially caused. Lucky bird, to be able to get all keyed up about misled law enforcement, and still fall back to sleep.

Minutes later, I changed into a satin nightgown, so I could look sexy for nobody but myself. After brushing my teeth and using a wipe to re-move my makeup, I lay on my bed, lit a candle and turned to my Google Home Mini. "OK Google play some relaxing music with waterfalls." I de-cided to leave the bird sounds out, had enough bird show for one night. Feisty just pissed off a crazed FBI Agent—couldn't be a good thing.

While listening to the sounds of rushing water among the chirps of crickets outside, it dawned on me that the FBI Agent is not the only one hovering over my home like a vulture. Who is the man I've seen watching from the street, in a long trench coat and roaring twenties-style gangster hat? He remained to be an unsettling mystery. Caryssa has joked a lot about the CIA being gangster warlords. Maybe Feisty is right about them being partners-in-crime. My mind wouldn't let me rest, continuing to conjure more unresolved revelations.

I was surprised when my cell phone rang, shaking my rushing thoughts free for the moment. It was Anna. "To what do I owe a call from the beau-tiful snowy Alps so early in the morning?" I asked.

Anna laughed. What sounded like hot tub bubbles popped in the background. "I'm so sore after an amazing powder ski day, I *need* some edgy action to get me pumped for skiing again today! Stay away from the FBI Jules, they're playing out the theatre act of 'terrorism'—an overused word used as a fear tactic in the drama of 'security.'"

"You're so lucky to be there where it's not the main acting show—"

"Well…not so sure. Here in the French ski resorts it's all about 'eco-terrorism.' Another sensationalized term to round up rebels—some innocent of nothing but being a moral environmental or peace activist."

"Well, there was that arson at Vail—"

"Which is sabotage against corporate expansion, not *terrorism*. Anyway, France is having its own amphitheater using dramatic terror plots to keep the outlandish global war on terror afloat, don't get me going! I heard a skier today say, 'If we want to defeat ISIS, let's defund the CIA and Pentagon.'"

"Wow, even in the beautiful French Alps this stuff is being discussed?" I was surprised. Even among vacationers, this pandemonium leeches into conversations. "Must have been an American that said this?"

Anna's laugh sounded more like a snort. "Jules, it's a global thing, the CIA is the head of seventy years of organized international crime, doing the dirty business of the rich and powerful warlords." She breathed heavily. "It was a foreigner that said it—but enough of this stuff, my hot tub experience is getting ruined!" I sensed a smirk.

"Well, enjoy the rest of your trip, and say hi to Pierre and Jared for me." I was somewhat jealous of Anna's French Alps experience but didn't let that affect my tone.

We hung up. She returned to her serenity while I sank back into panic and dread, the unknown fate of my brother and his family spinning in my mind. It took me a while to reach slumber. Once again, I dreamed of a man in a spy suit, watching from afar, this time with a pipe hanging from his mouth like some tacky Sherlock Holmes wannabe.

In the morning, with dazzling sunlight splashing from every window, and fresh, crisp air cooling my home, Feisty sang me awake. I was delighted to hear him. Man, I love my bird. What would I do without his unstoppable happy?

I fed him pellets and let him perch on my finger before brewing coffee and treating myself to a homemade blueberry scone. With the ambitious sun painting the horizon in yellow, I decided a walk sounded good. A walk would clear my mind and get some fresh air in my lungs. I slipped out of my nightgown and stepped into more casual attire appropriate for a morning stroll on a beautiful sunny day. My hair was kept in place by a woolen hat. My clothing on the other hand, consisted of a breezy jacket, yoga pants, and padded shoes.

The fresh, sea-salted Sausalito air relaxed me, as I walked briskly down Bridgeway, then up a steep hill off a side street. I turned, taking in the breathtaking scene below. My heartbeat accelerated with the exercise high, releasing a batch of endorphins. The Bay, sailboats, Golden Gate Bridge gleaming to the right and Angel Island all reminded me of why I chose to remain in my little Bohemian beauty of a hometown.

I had purposely traveled in the opposite direction of where the mystery man seemed to await in the shadows. I decided he was merely in my imagination, with all that has happened.

Half an hour after setting out for my walk, I returned to my studio apartment. The minute I entered I knew something wasn't right. At this time of day, anytime I walked into my apartment, Feisty would chirp up. He'd say one of his favorites "Bright day, I love you."

But there was no singing and no chirping. The place was strangely quiet. When I looked at his cage, no Feisty. His cage door was open. He was gone.

I scavenged my tiny apartment like a frantic crazy lady despite knowing there was no way he was here. How was my door still locked if someone took him? How could they have gotten in? Was it that FBI Agent? Am I missing something? It's just a bird—they can't see him as a threat, can they?

I wandered back outside. That's when I noticed what I had missed. One bright feather lay on the cobblestone by the rose bush—and two words were written next to it. "Respect Authority." If that wasn't terrifying enough, the words were written in a crimson fluid. Blood. Feisty's blood?

A dark, uneasy feeling grew in the pit of my stomach, a sound roaring through my head as my knees buckled. My scream was the last thing I remembered before I lost consciousness.

I didn't even feel my head smash into the rocky driveway.

CHAPTER TWELVE

Anna

What a planet we live on. Picturesque!

That's what struck me at the top of the challenging run I was about to tackle. I admired the view. Majestic snow-capped peaks dotted the horizon. I felt small in comparison. Below lay the distant valley, where our rented alpine apartment was located. From this distance, it resembled a Lego piece.

I soaked in nature's wonders—then pushed off. I hurtled down the snowy mountain. Cassidy's skis proved to be a good luck charm, rather than a bad omen. I floated, performing badass turns through the soft bumps.

Over a snowy crest, I spotted Pierre taking a rest while drinking in the surreal beauty. Coming to a quick stop beside him, I sent a heap of snow over his skis and sprayed his face. A smile became visible as he scraped the snow off. Skiing was the best medicine for both of us.

"Just like riding a bike, hey babe?" Pierre was at his best. The fresh air and exercise brought out his happy. The nervous energy of losing our girls seemed to fuel his rhythm on the slopes, as he bashed the bumps with no less agility than a teenager.

"I feel great, and look at you, showing off for your petit fils, hey?" I playfully punched him on the shoulder as he smiled into the sunshine.

Rays of sun washed his face. The wind picked up, offering gentle and swift snow twirls between the twin peaks.

"Our boy has no fear, gotta say. But he also has no form," Pierre laughed.

I followed Pierre's eyes, which were focused up the trail. Admiration lay in them. "Here he comes! We should ask if he wants us to take a video." Pierre suggested, pride softening his tone.

But Jared didn't stop. "Wow, you're both ripping it up!" the boy screamed as he blasted past us, his open jacket rippling in the wind.

The flow of my mountain mojo was tentative at first, rusty from neglect. But by day three in the French Alps, I was confident again. Jared flew down a steep 45-degree edge, jumped off a cornice and landed into a narrow gorge somewhere beyond our field of vision.

The wind strengthened. What started as gentle snow twirls turned into fierce snow drifts coming off the steepest ridge, then again, a minor snow slide. Intense, then subtle. Suddenly, the smaller slide appeared to trigger the entire slope.

"Merde sainte!" yelled Pierre. "Anna did…did you hear those explosives going off at dawn? Fuck! Is that where Jared went?"

"The dynamite blasts? Sure, even after stuffing earplugs deep into my ears to try to go back to sleep." I instantly remembered bits and pieces of last night's Les Arcs newsflash over the TV. Something about the avalanche control team working overnight to assure safety with the heavy snowfall, and instability expected for the Aiguille Rouges trails.

Aiguille Rouges. That's where we're skiing now. Jared turned down the steepest lip.

Pierre piped in, "I heard more than dynamite, there were choppers overhead bombing the mountain, working to redistribute heavy snowpack up there." He pointed to the highest elevation, to a huge mound of snow hovering precariously on the summit—just above where Jared went.

Why was I trying to be such the superwoman, strong and resilient as if Cassidy's skis sent off a survivor steak? Shouldn't I be at least as brave as my grandson?

A ski patrol came flying from nowhere, "people, listen—you're far off-piste here. We need you to move towards the ski-lifts. Please ski left toward the Combe des Lanchettes area." His gaze shifted upward, at the mass of snowpack Pierre mentioned. By now the wind was mighty, tossing ice pellets into our faces.

"But…but our thirteen-year-old grandson skied down that way!" I shouted, pointing at the steep bump run directly off the heavy snowpack hanging off the upper slope.

"That area's *fermé*—closed! Nobody should be skiing there!" The ski-patrol barked, bound in bubbly winter clothing with his eyes darting from slope to slope.

"It wasn't closed when *he* turned down that way!" Rage found my voice as fear festered in my gut.

One ski patrol started posting 'Closed Area' signs along the ridge of the steep narrow valley Jared had skied down.

"Oh, mon Dieu! why didn't you people close it sooner?" I screamed, my fists clenching and heart racing.

Other ski patrols gathered at the scene of the impending danger, and in unison backed up the lone guy getting cursed by two people frightened to lose their only grandchild. Their only offspring left…

Like a pack of wolves, they each roared at us, "you must move towards safety! Please, ski left towards the lifts—*à présent!*"

I watched in horror as a huge wall of snow broke loose from the top ridge. It crashed downward across the slope towards the ridgeline we stood on. My stomach sank. Before reaching us, it veered towards the steep slope Jared had skied down. It moved with haste and aggression, taking with it rocks, ice and heavy snow. Gasps and cries echoed in the air—from where was unclear.

It was as if a zipper was being ripped open. Then came a loud hissing sound, like air released from a bag mixed with the sound of a blanket dragged across sand.

Someone tugged at my jacket, "Anna, come on, we have to move fast!" Pierre was dragging me, yanking me, our skis crossing in a tangle of frantic madness. "Come on, Bebe! We need to go!" he panted.

I screamed with all I had in my lungs and as loud as my vocals would permit, cupping my hands to propel my words as far as possible, "Jared! Jared!" *What good will this do? Can he hear me?*

Now my survivor instinct kicked in and I skated with my skis, pushed off with my poles as hard and fast as I could. The avalanche rumbled in my ears, crashing down the steepest vertical terrain toward where our grandchild so bravely entered. I repeatedly turned around as if I'd see Jared fighting through the violent snow drift.

But there was no Jared. There was nothing but a total white-out of thundering, ruthless, never-ending rolls of heavy snow.

* * *

We sat in the ski lodge, our appetites stolen by stress. Time ticked slowly. Minutes were long and filled with anxiousness. An hour dripped by without any news of survivors—or fatalities for that matter. It was painful watching the three TV screens, with coverage alternating from national to *Les Arcs News*.

France 24 Live headline:

Aucune victime connue après une avalanche dans une station de ski française prisée.

No known fatalities after avalanche hits popular French ski resort

Les Arcs News headline:

Une avalanche spontanée frappe les Arcs. Les équipes de recherche et de sauvetage travaillent en masse, nettoyant la zone de debris

A spontaneous avalanche hit Les Arcs. Search and rescue teams have been working in droves, clearing the area of debris

One screen showed rescue dogs sniffing out the snow. *God almighty. Where's Jared?*

Pierre paced in front of the TV screens, attempting to walk off his worry. But there weren't enough miles in the world. His steps seized, and his head swiveled as someone said, "I heard the impact of the snow against the trees slowed the avalanche down a little at the entrance of the lower half of Aiguille Rouge…"

Someone else responded, "That's what I heard, the snowdrift slowed at the mouth of that steep trail used during the Albertville Olympics."

The trail Jared went down. I cast my gaze towards Pierre, who listened intently. There's hope!

Les Arcs News continued:

Une défaillance structurelle dans le manteau neigeux a provoqué une avalanche de dalle. Les hélicoptères de sauvetage n'ont pas pu s'approcher de la gorge la plus touchée. Ce que nous savons, c'est que l'avalanche a probablement englouti cinq skieurs. Ils peuvent être piégés.

A structural failure in the snowpack triggered a slab avalanche. It's been impossible for rescue helicopters to get close to the gorge most affected. What we do know, is that the avalanche had possibly engulfed five skiers. They may be trapped.

My heart sank; I gripped Pierre's hand. He remained wordless but squeezed so tight my hand numbed. *Dear God, you took my daughters, please don't take my grandson.*

We sat, silently. Two hours passed. Three hours. Nothing. Every new hour brought the possibility of information and restored my hope. But by the end of that hour, my hope fizzled away, hour by hour.

The voices from the TV screen seemed mechanical, a blur, the BBC reporter announcing, "According to regional emergency officials, several snowmobiles are running up and down the trail of the scene. No victims have been found…"

A voice shrieked beside me, "The warning level was raised to a five earlier this morning, and they had that entire area closed! Why the fuck did they reopen it?"

I shook off the negativity, realizing we cannot hold the ski resort liable. I just prayed. That's all anyone in these unfortunate situations can do.

My cell pinged earlier, and I ignored it thinking I had no wish to hear from friends right now. Something made me check messages. There was a text. From Jared!

Grand-mere! Grand-pere!

"Oh, mon Dieu, Pierre, look! With trembling hands, I flashed the cell phone in front of him.

"Well, answer, bon sang!" he ordered. All eyes in the ski lodge fell on us.

I texted Jared back:

Where RU? Are U ok?

The boy responded:

I'm the only one with cell reception, there's 5 of us

That's it? I frantically tried to call Jared's cell, and it went straight to voicemail. I texted:

Where R the 5 of U?

No response. I took deep breaths, hoping it would stay my patience. Now time moved even slower. I watched my cell obsessively. Every sound, no matter how loud or quiet, had me jumping, checking the phone. But nothing.

A young man attired in a starched blue shirt with a *Les Arcs Paradiski* label wandered by and I practically knocked him down with nerves. He spoke briefly with a guest before I could say my piece: "Excusez-moi, mon petit-fils de 13 ans a été pris dans l'avalanche, et m'a envoyé un texto! Il est avec 4 autres skieurs."

"Excuse me, my 13-year-old grandson got caught in the avalanche, and just texted me! He's with 4 other skiers."

His eyes widened. He burst out, "A-t-il dit où ils sont?"

"Did he say where they are?"

My desperate voice squeaked, "Non! J'attends une réponse!"

"No, I'm awaiting a response!"

He answered, eyebrows dancing wildly on his forehead. "Oh, mon Dieu, continue de vérifier ton téléphone et j'irai prévenir la patrouille de ski. Vous devez également informer le bureau principal." His index finger flew in all directions.

"Oh my God, keep checking your phone and I'll go notify ski patrol. You should also notify the main office."

I frantically raced to the office. I barged through the entrance, sending the doorbell into a frenzy. Cold air rushed in behind me. A young woman stood behind the counter, blonde and petite, wearing a smart and warm but colorful uniform. Her eyes instantly shot to me, followed by a frown that suggested an empathy to my concern. She spoke in English as if my years residing in the states had transformed me into a Native American. "Do you know someone that might be trapped in the avalanche?" She jumped straight to the point, aware of the current crisis.

"My 13-year-old grandson. Listen, he texted me ten-fifteen minutes ago, said there were five of them—."

The woman's entire body jerked upward to attention. Her mouth opened wide before words scrambled out. "Where? Where did he say they were?" A slight smile tilted her lips. Was she excited? Hopeful? Optimistic? I couldn't tell if it was due to some selfish desire to have her fifteen minutes of fame by being interviewed on the news, or from genuine concern.

"I don't know! He only said there were five of them." I watched as the woman played her keyboard, fingers whizzing and clicking as her eyes remained fixed on the screen, heavy on focus. Without prying her sight from the screen, she asked, "What is your grandson's name?"

"Jared. Jared Beauvais." I questioned how this information could help her—unless ski patrol could go out calling his name.

144 · T.L. MUMLEY

"What time was it when Jared texted you?"

Now, this made sense.

"Oh, I don't know" I pulled out my cell phone in search of a time-stamp. "At 1:45 PM he texted me." It was now 2:15 PM. Shit! Time was slipping through my fingers.

She hesitated, seemingly calculating a time in suspense, an unknown moment within an uncertain outcome. Her eyes widened as she nodded. "This sounds promising. It was three hours ago when a few witnesses, including our head ski patrol, counted five skiers turning down a backside route from Aiguille-Rouges—just before the avalanche hit."

"That's where Jared skied. So…so are the snowmobiles still running along the trail looking for stranded skiers?" My heart thumped like a sledgehammer. Pierre appeared from behind, wrapping his arms around my shoulders. I was momentarily lost in his embrace, feeding on a false sense of comfort and security. My eyes rolled around the rustic wooden counter and the window aside it, offering a picturesque view of the snowy mountains. Would I ever be able to ski again? Would I ever look at a powdery mountain the same again?

"There's…." She stopped talking, an unsettling frown forming.

"There's what?" Asked Pierre, his hold on my shoulders tightening.

"A…a blockage on the trail. The sliding snowpack got stuck at the narrowest part of a gorge, which is good for slowing the avalanche down—but the snowmobiles have been unable to move down further to search for survivors." Her eyes darted around as she ran fingers through her golden locks, brushing stray hairs from her face.

"But…but they must get down there somehow, did you hear my wife? Our grandson and four others are down there!" Pierre's hold tightened even further, as my stomach fizzled with worry. His chin sat on one of my shoulders. He trembled with fear, afflicted with the same great concern as me, that we may lose another family member.

I appreciated how her words were accented as only the French can do. It gave me a familiar, comforting feeling. "Sorry if we're pushy. We lost our daughters to tragedy and are frightened of losing our only grandchild." I explained, reigning back a full-on emotional breakdown. I fought off images of our grandchild's funeral, or yet more inner turmoil and crippling sorrow. We can't lose him too. We just can't.

Scary words heard throughout my life as a skier came to the surface of my mind: *After half an hour, the survival rate of avalanche victims drops to 50 percent. At 45-minutes, it's less than 30 percent.*

My intestines tangled with dread.

She locked into our eyes, nodding even more. "I assure you our emergency responders are doing everything possible. It's a delicate situation—the slightest disturbance can bring the snowpack crashing down further. Nothing upsets the balance of snowpack more than a snowmobile—well, that or a skier." She delicately explained, face softening and tone gentle and reassuring. But the words themselves and their meaning were anything but comforting.

I was relieved there were no TV screens in this office. The headlines were only stirring up more worry.

The brochures and magazines of happy skiers spread across the counter like Christmas decorations suddenly arose a rage within me. I irrationally wanted to launch them at the lady. I couldn't discern if this was from impatience of the crippling fear of losing yet another child. Either way, I suppressed my outburst. It wouldn't help. Instead, I continued breathing and tugged at the straws of hope.

"Is your grandson an experienced backcountry skier?" she inquired. It was then I noticed her nametag. *April.*

"No! He learned to ski on a tiny mountain in California—"

"Why was a minor who is a novice skier taken down dangerous terrain?"

So much for not sounding pushy. I was getting pissed, that outburst bubbling closer and closer to the surface. "Jared is a solid skier. And we weren't even skiing backcountry."

"Actually, the east face of Aiguille-Rouges is considered out-of-bounds. If your grandson was one of the five skiers seen turning down that steep, bumpy run, he indeed was skiing outside of avalanche control."

Pierre took my hand in his. I opened my mouth to speak but then shut it, worrisome that once the words flew, I wouldn't be able to control them if rage took hold. We hadn't skied for twelve years, we hadn't skied the French Alps for over twenty. And one big difference with the ski resorts in the USA compared to France—is that no trails are marked here.

An all too familiar emotion of guilt filled my heart, accompanied by flashbacks of that horrid day outside of court long ago:

Is it true the parents are at fault for letting their 12-year-old-daughter skateboard on a narrow street with no sidewalks in inclement weather?

No! No! No! I chased the thought away, and only said, "We do not need to validate letting our adventurous grandson lead the way to where *he* felt he could ski." My words were firm but controlled.

Now April couldn't speak, yet her eyes spoke volumes. "I…I'm so sorry, I didn't mean to sound insensitive." She toyed with the collar of her uniform, clearly uncomfortable.

We glared in silence. The woman was merely doing her job: protecting the Les Arcs image. Mother Nature hampered by Human Nature is no match for ski resorts, whether from lack of snow or too much snow mixed with rapid warming. It's too unpredictable.

I was ready to ask Pierre if he wanted to walk back to the main lodge with me. There could be an important news update that we were missing. When suddenly, derailing my thought, April's two-way radio squawked to life.

"Venez à la réception, vous y êtes? Plus de." The male voice spoke with unbridled urgency.

"Come in front desk, you there? Over."

April unclipped her walkie-talkie from her belt, "Bien reçu. Vous obtenez mon message sur le garçon adolescent? 10-12, les parents avec moi. Plus de."

"Roger that. You get my message about the teenaged boy? 10-12, the parents with me. Over."

The radio crackled with high winds, the ski patrol's voice coming through punctuated with static; "Bien reçu, *fizz, fizz, fzzzz…* Je ne peux pas dire si boy...*fizz, fizz, fizzzz*...lunettes et équipement...*fizz, fizz, fizzzz...*"

"*Copy that, fizz, fizz, fizzzz...can't tell if boy...fizz, fizz, fizzzz...goggles and gear...fizz, fizz, fizzz...*"

We froze in our spot. I felt nauseous. April's head turned our way. She pressed the talk button again, "10-1. Tue es en rupture. Sur."

"*10-1. You're breaking up. Over.*"

A few minutes passed, mimicking the feel of an eternity. Then April's radio squawked to life once more: "10-2. Deux mâles trouvés enterrés, les deux employés. Cinq survivants invités comprennent un enfant mâle, deux femmes adultes et deux adultes mâles. 10-38 Bas Aiguilles Rouges. Sur."

"*10-2. Two males found buried—both staff. Five guest survivors include one male child, two female adults and two male adults.10-38 lower Aiguilles Rouges. Over.*"

One male child. My eyes filled with tears. I clasped a hand over my mouth. Pierre squeezed his shut, while clutching my free hand, the one that wasn't curled over my mouth. He left, scurrying back towards the lodge as if he couldn't stand it anymore.

April stood motionless, unmoving until her radio came alive again: "Réception vous me recevez? Sur."

"*Front desk, do you copy? Over.*"

She snapped to attention, "10-4. S.A.M.U. déjà là. Besoin de mains supplémentaires? Sur."

"*10-4. S.A.M.U. already here. Need extra hands? Over.*"

As April awaited further response from the ski patrol, I slipped a note over the counter. I had nervously written: *Please ask if the kid is Jared. If so, tell him we love him.* My handwriting was squiggly with emotion, but I was confident it was readable.

I realized how hot I was in my snow clothing. I yearned to tear off every layer and dive into a cool shower. The adrenaline and terror had caused my temperature to skyrocket. But now I had greater things to worry about, such as the safety of my grandchild.

She didn't press the talk button to ask the question, yet I realized she was awaiting a response from the mountain crew. Her radio beeped into action again, "Négatif. 75 patrouilles s'étirent. Nous sommes couverts. Sur."

"Negatory, 75 patrols probing down the stretch. We are covered. Over."

That *was* reassuring. 75 patrols. That's plenty. Come on Jared. Make it back to us.

"10-4. Le garcon est avec toi? Sur."

"10-4. Is the boy with you? Over."

An immediate response, "Négatif. Un enfant mâle envoyé sur le tobog-gan. Fracture de la clavicule. Nous avons un héros. Sur."

"Negatory. One male child sent down on a toboggan. Broken collarbone. We have a hero. Over."

Both April and I opened our mouths yet couldn't speak. *A hero? Who? Jared?* Pride added to the already generous mixture of emotions coursing through me.

I said to nobody at the front desk, "Thank you for everything, I gotta run."

As I sped between buildings towards the main lodge, a strong gust of wind blew into my face. I stared at the parking lot mid-run and saw a scattering of ambulances, police vehicles, and fire engines. Chaos was in full swing. People buzzed around like crazed bees. Everyone rushed, weighed with the pressure and fatal consequences of one mistake. Sirens, engines, chatter, wind, and general discord filled the atmosphere. Ski patrols still roared up the mountain in snowmobiles, probing for any more buried skiers. A Helicopter hovered just above, chattering into the air, propellers a black blur above its metal body.

Pierre came from the lodge, running in my direction, "Bebe, Jared's on TV!"

My stomach dropped. "Oh my God!" I moved towards the lodge, but he stopped me.

"No, he's over there, let's go to him!" He pointed to the mountain base near a chairlift. A small crowd was gathered around a toboggan, including two reporters wielding tablets and a hunger for tragedy, decked out in sharp suits. As we approached, the reporters were leaving, presumably having been shewed away like annoying felines. We stared at Jared's bloody, cut-up face. His eyes were closed, with an expression of discomfort. He held onto his left shoulder. The male child with the broken collarbone?

I knelt beside him. "Jared, we're here. We love you." Those words almost came with a complimentary serving of tears, but I stayed that impulse.

The boy's eyes fluttered open as he attempted to lift his head. Wincing, he murmured, "I hurt. A lot. But see the totally rad sled I rode in?"

Boys will be boys, I couldn't help but think.

Pierre took Jared's hand, "Hey big guy, you hung in there!" he replied, likely to sound light-hearted.

Wind howled amongst our conversation, along with the hysteria unraveling behind us.

Jared smiled at his grandfather, mumbling, "Actually if it wasn't for Dusty, I'd be buried alive."

"Dusty? Who's that," I asked, cringing at the thought of Jared trapped in snow-like concrete. I shoved that thought aside and focused on the present. This cherished moment. *My grandchild is alive!*

"The avalanche trained rescue dog, she's a big German Shepherd." He explained, with magic in his eyes, as if he'd just met Lassie.

"The hero we heard about!" Oh, so it was the dog, not Jared. Either way, he was alive, that's all I wanted.

I turned to see Pierre exchanging health insurance information with other patrols, including the medical permission slip Josh had given us. *Josh!* I needed to contact the boy's father.

"Tell your grandparents, Jared. Go ahead, I permit you bragging rights." The voice came from behind. I turned to a man in a black ski jacket emblazoned with a big yellow cross. The ski patrol continued, "Turns out, our rescue dogs and ski patrols aren't the only good Samaritans of the snow," he smirked.

At this, Jared's red, puffy face lit up, "Dusty sniffed and found me, and she helped dig me out with the ski patrols. They carried me to the warming hut and told me not to leave. That's when I called you Grand-mere. But then…then I saw her."

"You saw…" I held out the word 'saw', waiting for Jared to finish the sentence.

"I looked out the hut door, and from afar saw a shadow cartwheeling down a snow-white sheet, tons more snow was crashing down—"

The ski patrol interrupted to explain, "The blockage at the gorge broke loose while the mountain crew probed for skiers—"

"Then I thought I could see a purple glove sticking out of the snow about fifty yards away." Jared jumped in again, the two cutting each other off with nervous energy. "I was dizzy and in pain but scared someone was buried. So, I stumbled through the snow, then touched the glove and could feel fingers! I hobbled back to the patrol hut, grabbed a cool plastic shovel and dug her out!—well, her head anyhow, so she could breathe."

"With a broken collarbone, mind you. This is one special young man here." The ski patrolman kneeled beside the sled and looked like he wanted a high-five, but Jared's face contorted in pain. "He saved the life of a 52-year-old woman. If her face was buried for even five minutes more, she would have died of asphyxiation."

So, he was a hero. Jared. My Jared. My incredible grandson. I planted a kiss on my grandson's forehead, "So we have two heroes today, you and Dusty. I'm so proud of you Jared, I love you." I looked up at the man and noticed the "National Ski Patrol" label over his front pocket. "I'm sorry, we have many heroes today, and thank you…what's your name?"

"Paul. They call me Paul the Patrol," he answered with an air of comedy.

Jared laughed through the pain, "They should name you Paul's Paw Patrol, since you said three of the rescue dogs are yours."

"Oh, so you're the one April was speaking to on the walkie-talkie?" I asked.

"Ahhh…not me. We have a few Pauls' on patrol."

Pierre returned to the sled saying, "We have all the medical insurance papers set. And Jared—something for you!"

Two ski patrols came to each side of the sled, one knelt down and presented Jared with an award medal. He gently placed the ribbon with a silver Les Arcs token around Jared's neck. "We hereby award you '*Outstanding Young Adult Skier*.' Thank you for your bravery."

Tears froze on my smiling face. I was far more concerned with the fact Jared was alive, than the hero stuff. But, triumphs are triumphs. "So…so the woman he dug out is okay?"

"She was unconscious when airlifted to Bourg St. Maurice Hospital, but is recovering well. Speaking of, we need to get you checked into the hospital young man. That clavicle fracture was not likely as bad until you shoveled snow as heavy as cement. We'll keep you strapped in that cozy sled and lift you into the ambulance."

Jared laughed about nothing, giddy and punch-drunk. It occurred to me he was drugged up with painkillers. "Can we ride with him?" I asked.

Pierre quickly added, "I pulled our rental up close to the medical services vans. We need our own wheels, Bebe."

We carried our ski equipment down to the car. While loading up I realized how famished I was, too nervous to eat for hours. My appetite came rushing back after being gifted with the knowledge that my grandson was safe. I pulled our uneaten lunch from the back, consisting of roasted chicken in a jus, couscous, a baguette and red wine. Comfort foods for the road.

Soon we were following our happy hero to the hospital, laughing from relief like two young lovers.

CHAPTER THIRTEEN

Caryssa

"You're the coolest ski mom," Tyler declared while adjusting the straps of his goggles, stretching them over his helmet.

"Oh boy, I'll sleep better knowing my teenager thinks his beyond-middle-aged mom is cool," I responded while buckling my ski boots, smirking to myself.

Tyler let out a goofy 14-year-old laugh, "I said you're a cool ski mom—but you still embarrass me all the time."

And there it was; he'd taken me off my parental pedestal. Ahh well, I'll take praise where I can get it. Teenagers aren't the easiest to impress.

I stood to grab my ski-jacket and gloves. "Ah-ha! So, I'm an embarrassing cool ski mom. Okay." I scrunched my lips, nodding.

"No, you're totally rad on the slopes. It's just everywhere else you embarrass me," Tyler insisted while zipping his jacket.

"Just so I know how to stop embarrassing you, give me some examples." I prodded. Perhaps if I figured out what I did that was so embarrassing, I could claim my 'cool mom' status with no exceptions.

"Let's just go out and meet Dad, forget it," He huffed with an air of laughter. I swear I saw an eye roll behind his goggles. Tyler snatched his ski pass, wedged it into his pocket and started for the door, ready to carve up snow and catch some air.

Following behind him, I raised my skis over my shoulder and begged, "Just one example." I stepped from wood and indoor heating that came courtesy of the condo, to white powdery snow crunching underfoot. Treading through deep powder in ski boots proved a workout before even hitting the slopes.

"Like, I don't know—like when you yelled my name across the high school gym in front of my friends. Really Mom, was that necessary?" Tyler shook his head, his words heavy with disappointment.

"Well, if you answered your texts and paid attention to the time, that wouldn't happen." I defended myself, feeling I hadn't done anything wrong. Okay, maybe I had embarrassed him, but justifiably so. "We were late for your orthodontist appointment." Maybe I needed a teen-manual. I wonder if you can find those at your local retailer. Parents would bash down the doors of bookstores to nab a copy.

"Sorry, I forgot." He mumbled.

"Just like you forgot to do your homework, forgot to show your teacher your binder—" I was loaded with examples, firing off a list before he cut in and shut me up.

"Aggghhh! This is when you're so uncool!" Tyler stomped briskly ahead, lugging his skis over his shoulder.

I admired the sunny plateau; the mountain peaks a stunning backdrop. They were huge and fluffy with heaps of snow. The wind knocked off sprinkles of white that misted the air. Lovely wooden chalets dotted the rising mountains.

It was crowded during the kid's spring break, full of laughter, conversation, and banter. Colorful ski suits whizzed along the abundance of white, catching big air as they leaped high, or bombing as they soared down the mountains, leaving snow sprinkles and chuckles behind. It was somewhat chaotic. But being such a beautiful day, I couldn't complain.

Really, who could complain after skiing five mountains within eight days? We just finished skiing at Snowbird and Alta in Utah, skied Alpine

Meadows this morning, and are now at Squaw Valley. We were connoisseurs of the slopes. Or as fellow skiers might say, carvaholics. Yesterday we met friends at Sugar Bowl. Life doesn't suck.

I caught up to Tyler, feeling the need to air my justifications, "Okay, first off, remember this: I'm your mom, not just a friend. If you think me being your parent is 'uncool' well tough brakes. And second, the gymnasium scene is not a good example, I need another." I explained over the ruckus of chortling school kids and the whoosh of snow being cut up by hungry skiers and snowboarders.

Tyler clicked into his ski bindings and stretched his legs, releasing a mighty sigh. "Since I know you'll ask for yet another example of how you embarrass me, I'll give two. During carpool when you drop us off, that music you play—"

I jumped in here. "What's wrong with classical?"

"Nothing, it's just a little boring to start school with Chopin ringing in my ears. You wonder why I zone out during first period?" With that, Tyler took off for the chair, and I skated with my skis up to him in line, carrying further questions with me.

"Okay, so do you feel that way when I play rock?" I asked, intrigued by the psyche of a teen and what classifies as good or bad tunes. Perhaps I'll crack the code and write the manual myself. I laughed off the image of hundreds of thousands of parents thanking me on a daily basis for writing an essential book in the raising of teenagers, talking on popular daytime chat shows, and becoming a deity for parents everywhere.

"No, but how' bout some Rap or Brazilian Jazz. Bossa Nova!" He suggested.

We laughed, razzing each other playfully. With this level of cooperation, he might co-write the book with me. "Wow, I'm impressed. I didn't even know you like music from the 50's and 60's—" I'd managed to raise a cultural person, not just obsessed with fads and junk food.

"It's a new wave now, Mom, get with it!" Tyler scooted over to let two other skiers around his age queue for the chairlift with us. "Did Dad say where to meet him?"

"Yup said he'd be at the top. So, what's the second way your old mom embarrasses you?" I couldn't let this go now. I was fascinated in a funny sort of way.

"I really love you Mother, but seriously—please don't hug me in front of my friends!" He said with rolling-eyes. Okay, hugs off limit in public, got it.

With that, the two other boys on the chairlift laughed, joining in. One said, "Oh man, my Mom does worse than that! She'll plant a big ole kiss on my cheek right in front of the school as I leave her car."

Shock. Horror. What a monster, showing a sign of affection. I shook my head.

I was outnumbered by three teenagers that no longer thought their moms were the center of their universe. I remember a time when Tyler was basically joined to my hip. Of course, back then, he only came up to my hip. Now my child stands in a 6'1" body. It's not a bad thing I guess, and I love who my kid is becoming—himself, as I slowly give him independence. And he takes it.

Looking behind us from the chair, the far-reaching view of impressive peaks stretched for miles. I saw the chocolate-box village with its fancy boutiques, cafes, and high-fashion skiwear.

My cell rang bringing me back to reality; I figured it was my hubby and retrieved it from my pocket. A glance at my screen proved me wrong.

I swiped-to-answer the call while watching skiers with an eye out for George in case he decided not to wait for us.

"Hello Anna, this couldn't be a chairlift chat, since it's ten at night your time…What? You're in California?…

I jolted up in the chair, alerting Tyler. In the reach of my periphery, Tyler's head shot my way.

"Why'd you cut your trip short?… An avalanche!?" The words spilled from my mouth louder than I'd intended.

"An avalanche!" Screamed the kid sitting hip-to-hip with Tyler. "Cool, where?" His eyes darted around.

I again spoke into the phone, almost in defense of the child's common sense in case she overheard:

"That's not Tyler talking. So, did they close the mountain...oh, my God, he got caught in the avalanche?!"

"Who got caught in the avalanche? Jared?" Tyler asked, leaning towards my side of the chairlift with concern in his voice.

The lift cranked to a stop, likely someone having trouble getting on or off. We sat, suspended in the air some 200-feet from the ground. Two of my biggest skiing concerns: avalanches and falling from lifts. My heart beat that much faster. Being held at this height didn't help any.

After hearing about Jared caught in the avalanche, I became wary and pulled Tyler close to me, a maternal urge taking hold. "Hey guys, I'm pulling the safety bar down now!" We had ridden halfway up the mountain with no bar, which typically doesn't bother me. I brought the bar down before the kids were ready, and the bar crashed into one of the boys' helmet. "Oops, sorry about that!"

The kid seemed undisturbed about the little head thump, merely looking the other way without a word to say, no 'ouch' or 'watch it' to suggest I'd affected him whatsoever.

"Oh Mom," his gloved finger pointed out, "that's another way to be so uncool, riding with the bar down." Tyler joked.

Anna had responded during the safety bar fuss. I moved my mouth toward my smartphone again:

"What was that? Oh my God, he's okay though? PTSD, poor kid! he saved the life...holy snowballs I gotta hear more about this!"

Tyler was chomping at the bit for details, "Jared has PTSD? He saved who?" He became a needy puppy at my side, begging to be petted or fed.

"Yes Tyler, Jared got caught in an avalanche. It's not all bad. He saved the life of another skier, a mother of two kids." I informed Tyler, causing his mouth to make an 'O'.

The chair cranked to life as my pulse found a gentler pace. *Finally!* Must have been stopped for five minutes. I said to Anna:

"We're going to be at the top of the mountain soon, sorry I need to go. I'll come to Sausalito when we get back. Give Jared a big hug."

Before we ended the call, Tyler piped in, "Wow, there's been lots of avalanches everywhere. There were two in California this week!"

The boy next to Tyler said, "There was one here—people got injured."

I answered, "Yup kiddos, avalanches are becoming more common thanks to accelerated climate change." *And no thanks to our policies putting profits before people and the planet.* I kept that thought to myself.

I gave my final goodbyes as we approached the top. George waved from the edge of the face run. My departing words to Anna before shoving my cell phone into my fanny pack and slipping off the chair were, "Even snow is political."

Infused with a sense of well-being, I carved turns leaving a dust of powder behind me. I tried not to piss off any skiers with a dose of snow-covered goggles. Skiing was effortless as I switched into autopilot. At that moment, I became weightless, free of worries and concerns, experiencing a fleeting bliss of escapism.

The sun casts a magical glow over the rolls of snow. People, in their colorful attire, swerved and turned and rode the fluffy slopes. Skiers maneuvered with control and grace, whereas snowboarders performed impressive feats of acrobatics, toying with gravity.

After several runs, George stayed off-piste in the trees while Tyler and I cruised groomers. We raced to catch the last run of the day, tucking it to the bottom for speed.

"Sorry folks, lift is closed for the day," the lift operator grumbled.

"No, no, please one more run!" begged Tyler.

The lift operator glanced at the last group that had settled onto a chair, then back at us, "Okay, go ahead."

"Yay, thank you!"

"The squeaky skier stays on the slopes!" I joked while scanning my pass on the newfangled electric chip gates.

"Well, make it a good one; it's the last of the day! The lift operator nodded. "And be sure not to venture off the backside as that chairs already closed, you'd get stranded."

And off we went.

The snow-blanketed mountains surrounded us on the chairlift. At the top, the shimmering turquoise and blue-hued water of Lake Tahoe made me stop and stare at its beauty.

I let Tyler take the lead. His choice was the terrain park, which elicited a silent groan from my arthritic right hip. I watched as he flew whooping over the jumps and through the halfpipe, completing tricks across the rails, taking an impressive crash at the base.

Laughing, he raised his arm, "I'm okay!"

When we finished for the day I asked, "Want to take a stroll through the village?"

"Ahhh…Nah…I want to go back to the condo and get out of my boots," he answered while flipping his goggles onto his helmet.

"Tyler, I'm going back to take off my boots also. I mean after that, see the sights and sounds."

He was shaking his head, "I'm kinda cold and tired, wanna veg out."

"And play video games?" I asked. "You can warm up by the fire-pit in the village—"

"No Mom, I just need to chill and take a hot shower."

"Suit yourself. I'm heading to the hot tub in about an hour. You and Dad can join me."

I lugged my equipment back to the condo with Tyler, locked it all up, switched into my après ski boots and headed back out solo.

The crisp mountain air intoxicated my senses while strolling to the village. Alpine forests with fir and pine trees, mixed in with other scents—newly baked cookies, fresh popcorn, the smoky, savory smell of fire-roasted pizza. And another distinctive scent wafted past my nose—marijuana. It ebbed from a twenty-something group standing around one of the fire-pits, giggling like hyenas.

The combination of earthy—almost fruity aroma of marijuana and laid-back ambiance radiating off the group somehow lured me in. I wandered to the opposite side of the fire-pit palms held out to catch the fire's warmth. Conversations traveled over the flames.

Words came from a barrel-chested man with a bushy beard and *Aspen Meadows Resort* bandana. He sported a flannel jacket and jeans, boots that came to his knees. "Dude, we thought you were lost, a goner, like that snowboarder found a few days ago."

"I was lost, gotta admit. I don't know this mountain like I do the ones at home." A small-framed guy answered as he passed a pen-like vaporizer to the woman standing aside him. She was a vision: a leggy blonde bombshell in a one-piece gold ski outfit that fit her like a glove.

"You need'ta shred faster on your board to keep up with us." Bearded-bandana man teased.

I was wondering how with the smaller guy's bright lime-green ski jacket that stuck out like a neon light his friend couldn't spot him. Maybe he was preoccupied chasing the ski-bunny.

"Dude! I shredded too fast, then landed head first in the pow! Took me half an hour to dig myself outta a ditch. That's some strange snow out there!" He replied defensively.

"No stranger than the snow we've had in Colorado this season," Big Guy laughed. "You're blaming your snowboarding mistakes on the snow cond—"

"Hello global warming," the blonde interjected. "The snow *has* become unreliable. She rolled her eyes. "Knock it off Steve. Billy could have been dead out there and you only mock his boarding skills."

A look across the hazy glaze of the fire into the owlish brown eyes of the girl gave me the impression that her mind and soul are expansive. The type of sexy woman who gets wrongly stereotyped as unintelligent or narrow-minded—like the only thing that matters is skin-deep.

Billy shook his head in the flickering light, "You really think global warming has anything to do with me getting lost in a snow pillow Steph? It's colder than a witches' tit in a brass bra out there."

"It's not simply local weather, it's changing temps across the globe. Remember how it was hotter than a June bride last week? There'll be no snow left for our kids!" Stephanie said while pulling on a stylish hat with the words *Aprés Ski* emblazoned in gold complimenting her body-fitting outfit.

Steve bypassed the topic, "Dude, you gotta learn to put pressure on your back leg, man. Be the boss a ya board. And I care more about buddy Billy than his bad boarding." He swung his arm around Billy's shoulders while handing Stephanie the vaporizer. "Just joking out of relief! Take another tokey-smokey and chill out girl."

She fanned her hands with a disapproving look, "No thanks, one hit off that thing was enough to make me feel like I'm floating off this rock." Stephanie had climbed on top of the rustic cropping near the fire-pit.

I no longer find it surprising fellow skiers and boarders talk climate change, despite being shiny happy people that tune out reality on the slopes. Words rolled around in my mouth, finally spilling onto my tongue, "I was just saying to a friend today that snow has become political."

They each shot me a surprised look, complete with raised eyebrows and taut eyes, with Billy responding first. "Ha, what's not political?" He took a hit...then raised the high-tech-looking vaporizer, "The herbs we vaporize...*politics*." His vocal chords sounded raspy.

Steve laughed, "The fact we hold medical marijuana cards making it legal to toke for pain management and breathing the air while skiing... *politics*."

Stephanie added from atop her little rock, "The gas we buy to get to the mountain and pulling out of the Paris Climate Accord fucking up future generations of skiing...*politics*."

Oh God; I've met my match in being the political satirist, I thought. A couple walking by overhearing our conversation joked, "The sky is falling Chicken Little!"

I smiled into the last moments of sunshine for the day and added, "Yup, we better get our powder turns in while we can!" As I glanced toward the mountain, the sun lowered like a glow-ball among the towering statues of snow-clad peaks. It resembled an oil-painting dusted with powdered sugar.

The big bearded guy, whose name was apparently Steve joined in, "Where I'm from—The Rocky Mountains—the opioid epidemic is about the worst in the nation. I think it's cuz so many skiers get hurt, and good ole doc doles out addictive pain meds. Happened to a good friend of mine. Now *that* makes it not just political but personal."

A moment of silence brought the conversation to an uncomfortable lull. *Beautiful Day* by U2 bounced off a pub speaker. It blended well with the atmosphere of laughter, skiers walking by and a couple dancing with their poles in their hands.

"What I don't get," added Billy, "If the ski resorts are hurting so bad with climate change, why some of them fund anti-climate action politicians."

"Ha, that's an easy one." Stephanie slid off her rock nearly stumbling into the fire-pit, stayed by quick footing. "See that! I was between a rock and a hard place," she laughed, pointing to the flames swaying in the wind, too close for comfort, "Just like the ski resorts. I have one answer, *water*. They need water not falling freely from the sky to make snow, and fear their water rights are infringed—"

"That," I added while holding up a pointer finger for emphasis, "and *oil*. Ski resorts use a lot of this black magic to run equipment…."

"And the biggest cause of global warming is burning fossil fuels," finished Stephanie.

"Argh man, all this talk' bout climate change makes me wanna change the topic. A great day skiing today, hey?" Steve looked high as a kite, eyes rimmed red and a slackness to his words.

"Seriously, we'll take our passion to the grave talking this shit—but to be a political denier is to float endlessly in a powder turn." Stephanie did a little nervous laugh.

I'd had enough powder politics with the stoners. "Well, I'm taking my passion to the hot tub, see you all on the mountain," I announced, offering a wave.

While sauntering away one of the guys, likely Steve, spoke up, "I'd love to take my passion to the hot tub with ya girl!"

Oh Lord, I don't have any response to that. Knowing I'd never see these people again, I sped back to the condo, where my husband and son were asleep on matching couches. The cozy fireplace flickered flames of yellow and tangerine while the TV blared. How can they sleep through that squawk box? Must be all the fresh air and exercise.

I freed myself from the ski clothes and slipped into a non-revealing tankini bathing suit and spa robe, slinging a towel across my shoulders. Fumbling in the kitchenette, I poured a little Chateau Laffite into a plastic cup. I learned the hard way that nice wine glasses and hot tubs don't mix.

By 6 p.m. I was simmering in a bubbly hot spa, gazing at the gathering dusk in the slopes. The quiet solitude of the night and jets hitting my tired ski muscles brought me to a place of serenity. The only sound breaking through the silence was a trickle of children's laughter from the clubhouse.

And then I heard the scream...

Alerted, I slipped out of the hot tub, grabbed my towel and spa robe and dashed into the clubhouse. There seemed to be nothing going on, just a few people laughing. "What was the scream all about?" I asked.

"Oh, everything's okay," was the only response I got. What could I do to help if there's no problem? Yet, the woman was still screaming, the sound coming from the bathroom. Should I check it out? A soft knock on the bathroom door issued a too-quick, "Just a minute!" So, I figured she'll survive. Maybe it's a girl that just got her period and she thinks she's dying.

Back out to the hot tub, I sank deeper into the water trying to get the jets to cover the screech of the woman's voice. Any deeper and I'd need a snorkel to breathe. I let myself drift in the current while my mind and body eased, but it was no use. I could not only hear her high-pitched scream, it sounded louder under water.

I propped myself up on the edge of the hot tub as two children came running out of the clubhouse. "We need to get Daddy and tell him Mommy's on fire!" A little boy yelled.

Fire? I looked through the glass doorway into the clubhouse and saw a guy emptying a fire extinguisher onto a blazing inferno. *God almighty, I was thinking a firepit by the hot tub would be nice—but this isn't what I had in mind!*

I grabbed my cell phone out of the pocket of the spa robe and dialed the front desk. "Hello? There's a fire at the clubhouse! I heard a woman screaming in the bathroom and was told she's okay. Yet she is still scream-ing—could someone check it out please?"

After the front desk assured me they'd send someone to check out the scene, I hung up.

A young man around thirty came out of the clubhouse calling after the children, "Boys? Don't go alarming your Dad. Your Mom's Okay," he an-nounced.

"What happened?" I asked.

"Oh, we're barbequing, and my sister is a novice at lighting the gas grill. The igniter button didn't work, and she tried a grill lighter. She waited too long. A cloud of gas built up and a fireball came at her face."

"Wow hope she didn't get burned?"

"No, but her hair, eyelashes, and brows got singed. She ran to the bath-room screaming, expecting her face to be disfigured. Sorry for ruining your hot tub experience," he laughed.

"No problem, I'm relieved your sister is Okay."

I got out of the water to press the hot tub jets, ran across the spa deck in the crisp night, *brrrr!* Then sank deep into the tranquil darkness. The stars shone as I stretched my legs, getting my muscles ready for the last day of skiing.

* * *

I dropped down Alexander Ave and stopped at Bridgeway Café for a latte on the way to Anna's place. The drive was beautiful through the sleepy Mediterranean seaside town of Sausalito.

When Anna greeted me at her door, she looked her radiant self. Flawless skin meets flawless heart. It seems her grandson shares her human compassion based on the rescue mission he performed while hurting with a broken bone.

"Hello snow sister can't wait to hear your ski stories," Anna expressed as she took the bowl of strawberries mixed with blueberries from my hands. "What's this, I told you to only bring your smiling-self."

"Fresh berries from my garden. And a wedge of cheese to go with it," I reached into my bag and presented the Camembert. "You are the one with a *scary* ski story. How's Jared?"

"He's fine, thank God! He's asleep in his room." Her eyes moved in the direction of *the ghost room*.

"*His*…room?" I noticed the subtle yet obvious switch from referring to it as the "girls' room."

Anna looked up while placing the bowl of berries on the table. "I worked with a contractor within days of leaving for the French Alps—and transformed the room into one that fits my grandson's personality."

She poured tea into the fine porcelain cups from her French collection —a white ground with blue and yellow modernist abstract pattern. The enticing aroma of tea helped me forget I left the latte in my car.

"Mmm…is this cinnamon black tea?" I questioned while raising the teacup to my lips.

"No, it's L'Artisan Tea for Two. I made it myself, with bergamot, cinnamon, ginger and a touch of vanilla extract."

"Wow!" I said. "You are amazing. Transforming the room into Jared's, almost losing your grandson in the French Alps, then coming back and making homemade tea…"

"Shhh!" Anna put her finger to her lips. "We'll wake him, he's been traumatized, and I want him to sleep—Doc says PTSD."

"I'm not asleep, Grand-Mére," Jared's voice echoed back.

I turned towards the hallway, my eyes landing on Anna's La Paloma *The Dove* leaning against a corner wall.

Before I could ask about her rendition of the Picasso painting, Jared appeared at the threshold. "Hi Caryssa!" The boy's enthusiastic tone belied the vision I saw before me. There were cuts and bruises on his face, neck, and hands. His left eye was puffy and bruised as if someone had punched him. *God almighty, the mountain beat this kid up.*

Jared seemed to sense my surprise, and he said "Don't worry, it's not as bad as it looks. I'm feeling good now."

I smiled at him, my heart melting. "You're amazing, saving a woman's life with a broken collarbone!"

"I didn't have pain when digging her out—only a grinding sensation in my shoulder. I was worried when I saw her rolling in the snow. I thought she was...she looked like..." He glanced at Anna. "She looked like you Grand-Mére."

Anna nodded her head, wordlessly acknowledging the stress the boy experienced. We remained silent for a moment while sipping tea.

Finally, I said, "that must have been a scary experience for you, Jared, getting caught in an avalanche."

He shook his head, "I had no time to be scared—It happened so fast. I only had time to survive. It's now I am freaking out."

It was then I noticed how exhausted the boy looked.

Jared continued, "When I was rolling down the mountain I only thought of what I learned in surfing lessons. To push up with my hands, swim to the surface. I thought, *stay on top, stay on top!*"

Anna wrapped her arms gently around her grandson, avoiding the arm in the sling. "Jared, why don't you go try to sleep some more?"

I noticed the swelling and bruising of the collarbone area and his wince at even the slightest touch.

"Yeah, I do need to sleep." He waved goodbye and walked back to his room.

After he shut his door, Anna said quietly "He's been having horrible nightmares, screaming out in the night. Like he said, it's now he's frightened. He was so brave during the experience."

We talked and sipped our tea for an hour more, and I realized Anna also needed to rest. Her big almond eyes were glazed over, and she seemed to struggle to keep them open.

I used the bathroom before leaving. As I walked past Anna's painting, I lifted it and looked at the back. And there is was, Ava's handwriting with the Picasso quote:

I stand for life against death. I stand for peace against war.

Since Anna had enough on her mind, I decided not to ask how and when she got her painting back from the police. As I was hugging her goodbye she asked, "Have you spoken to Julie lately?"

"Julie? No, I don't talk to her as much as you do. What's up?"

"Her pet parakeet was murdered by either FBI or the creepy CIA dude hanging around her street spying on her brother. They are on the Joint Terrorism Task Force."

"What the...? How do you know it was the feds that killed the bird?"

"It would be too much a coincidence not to have been—an FBI agent stopped by her apartment the night before the bird was found dead. Apparently, Feisty said a little too much."

"God almighty...it's like the doves Ava killed—with a symbolic message, '*if you kill the dove, you kill peace.*'" I insisted. *What's up with all the dead birds in this otherwise peaceful, open-minded, and caring community we live in? Strange.*

"Only the opposite. This was a federal agent, possibly two involved, that silenced her bird who was exposing the CIA and FBI for their roles in promoting war."

I looked directly into Anna's tired eyes. "Anna, you need to put this aside. You've been under enough stress with Jared's ordeal. Go get some rest."

"No, I won't rest. I'm going over to Julie's right now to comfort her. Come with me—you might want to hear what I have to say about how it's all connected to the murders at my art gallery and the prison."

I was jolted back to the reality I tried to escape. The reality that Diego Ramírez is my former bosses' brother. The former boss in Silicon Valley that once had me working undercover in competitive intelligence. It was a fabulous position. Respected. Highly paid. Yet, so intrinsically related to technology itself used as a sword.

I was hooked in now.

CHAPTER FOURTEEN
Julie

My head continued to throb a week after I fainted. A week after I'd smashed into my rocky driveway. A week after my beloved Feisty was murdered by a federal agent.

The local cops won't do anything. They'd sooner toss me into a looney bin for insisting the FBI or CIA silenced my bird permanently. Despite a DNA test confirming the words *Respect Authority* were written in Feisty's blood.

I decided a third call into the station wouldn't hurt. I grabbed my cell and dialed, hands trembling. The police answered on the first ring:

"Dispatch."

My vocal chords seemed to fold while holding my breath. I cleared my throat, consumed by the urge to ask for a specific officer, one whom I trusted. If Anna's prediction of his discharge was incorrect that is. It didn't hurt to ask.

"Hello, may I speak with Sergeant Coral please." *Am I really doing this?*

"Can I tell him who's calling?" The dispatch lady inquired with a clipped tone.

My heart raced; I wasn't about to give my name. What would I say? *Oh, it's the crazy lady that's been calling about the FBI murdering my bird.* I went on a whim:

"It's Anna Beauvais." I lied.

The woman spoke with clarity and a hint of monotony, no doubt from years of saying the following phrase, "Just a moment please."

He picked up promptly. "Sergeant Coral." His voice was a calming balm to my wracked nerves.

"Sergeant Coral!" I replied with an unexpected shrillness to my tone.

Silence filled the line until the realization struck. "Anna?"

"This is…I'm a good friend of Anna's."

He prodded. "Okay…and your name?"

"Julie Taylor."

"Oh, yes. The woman that claims the FBI killed her parakeet."

My breath was shaking as I took a heavy inhale before continuing. "Sergeant Coral, you of all people have seen we have a weird dead bird thing going on in Sausalito. Oddly, they seem connected—"

"I'm not on that case anymore, for the same reason I won't talk about this."

"Oh, so they did open a case?"

"No…no case. Not even a report was written. We don't have enough evidence to implicate a federal agent—"

"Please Sergeant Coral, my beloved Feisty mysteriously disappeared with the words *respect authority* written in his own blood. An Agent Flock with a Glock busted into my apartment threatening my brother, me, and my bird the night before that. And you think we don't have enough evidence?"

A brief lull stayed the conversation, until, "Your brother was a fugitive, on trial as a terror suspect."

I palmed my forehead. "Not you too! My brother is entirely innocent. He was taking pictures of the subway for his job!" The reality of how saturated our nation is in this bull-shit for billionaires was sinking in.

"I'm sorry Ms. Taylor, but I must go now." And with that, the dial tone hummed in my ear.

Something Anna had mentioned rumbled in the back of my mind: *I think Jason was fired or taken off the case because he said too much—about Ava's dad, the rogue CIA agent that murdered both Johnny and the prison guard.*

In my gut, I suspected that Sergeant Coral wasn't merely worried about losing his job, but also losing his life.

Later, while hunched down tracing a fingertip over the bloodstain on the cobblestones, a jasmine-colored car pulled into my driveway, the sun bouncing off its hood. Anna and Caryssa casually stepped out, a subtle breeze sweeping through their hair. They were both dressed in jeans and casual-chic tops.

I straightened, stretching lower back, relieving aches. Anna approached wielding a vase of colorful flowers. "For your rooftop garden," she explained. She threw her arms around me, "I'm so sorry about Feisty."

"Wow, these flowers will be beautiful up there, thanks! I feel better already." A tear slid down my cheek as I admired the mix of sunflowers, dahlias, scarlet penstemon and lush foliage plants.

Caryssa commented, "A Hummingbird paradise." Her eyes moved to the smudge of blood I had tapped with my finger as if willing my bird back to life. "Holy crap is that—"

"Feisty's blood? Indeed, proven with a DNA match." I didn't want to stand near the spot Feisty's blood was used to inscribe an authoritarian threat. "Let's go inside, Anna I want to hear how you think this relates to the doves."

Knowing how my friends adore their afternoon tea, I had a pot of water heated and an assortment of tea bags ready and waiting. But Anna insisted, "We've had enough tea at my place—how about some wine?" She asked with one eyebrow raised, reaching for her hairline, while the other stayed put.

"Sounds good to me, it's 6 pm on a Friday!" added Caryssa, justifying our transition from brewed tea to a sophisticated alcoholic beverage.

"Sure, I have a bottle of Merlot I can open. It will pair well with the beef stew I cooked." I dialed the crockpot to warm, watching the juices bubble ever so lightly.

"Mmmm…so that's what I smell cooking? Yummy!" exclaimed Anna, hunger in her eyes.

"It's been slow-cooking all day. Do you guys want to eat some now? Are you hungry?" I asked.

"Not yet thanks," answered Caryssa, presenting her palm. "We've been munching on Anna's scones, paired with her lovely homemade French-style Tea for Two. Maybe in half an hour?"

We wandered the three feet from Julie's tiny kitchenette to her living room, which was essentially in the same room, and rested our rumps on her couch.

"Okay Anna, spill your detective work." I insisted.

Anna sat straighter. "If it gets too intense, say so Jules. You just lost your soul mate—I know how much you loved that bird."

"You lost both your daughters, your security guard, your fine art was stolen and destroyed which caused you to close your business. Come on Anna, just talk to me!" Her skirting around the issue teased my frustration. Maybe it will be difficult to hear, but it could also help me find Feisty, dead or alive. I'd like to give him a decent burial.

"So," Anna started. "Ava Ramírez 'dad, Diego—the CIA dude who murdered both my security guard Johnny and the prison guard at the facility his daughter was locked up at, is tied into dark money from criminal elites. He's buddies with the Lock family, billionaires behind the rise of our radical political system."

"Isn't that a surprise—*not*!" laughed Caryssa.

"What's 'dark money,' I asked. "Although I can make a good guess."

"It's big money in politics with the financial source unknown," Anna responded. "The Lock family and others hide behind masks of philanthropy—but they're shady nonprofit fronts faking support for the social good."

"Bloodthirsty swamp monsters." Piped in Caryssa. "Pimps and whores for wars."

"I heard one of the Locks' defective oil pipelines exploded, killing two teenagers," I mentioned.

They nodded, with a look of human kindness twinkling in their eyes.

Anna continued, "There's a secret network conducting surveillance in 'competitive intelligence.' They gather information on community citizens working towards peace, renewed infrastructure, healthcare for all, clean air and water, LGBT rights and other truly positive areas of human rights."

"So...so...my brother was seeking funds to update the scruffy subway system of New York City to protect citizens from train crashes and was mysteriously pulled aside as a terrorist suspect." My nerves had been stirred up. "Do you think the incentive came from someone high up on the chain—"

"Yes, if not directly then indirectly from the likes of this bloated apparatus: A strangling network disguised as a social activist for the security of America." Anna took a sip of wine. "Your brother is a key executive for transit projects and wanted at least $30 billion for New York City. The Lock family is hostile to anyone that reduces our dependency on oil."

"Oh my God...my sweet brother was a direct threat to dark money." My stomach rumbled while bile crept into my throat.

I shook my head as Caryssa inquired, "Are you still floating on a fantasy freedom cloud, Jules? You must see by now there's a dark force driving our nation to oblivion."

"I've hopped off the freedom cloud, Caryss. Or I was pushed off when my innocent brother was brought in as a terrorist. Then the freedom facade was squashed for good after my bird was killed for speaking the truth." I gave Caryssa a stare that could kill. "But Anna, how do you know all this?"

"I've researched this stuff since seeing what my father went through." Anna hesitated, then added, "You know what's the most powerful weapon in the world?"

I debated the answer as Caryssa chimed in, "The truth."

"Yup," answered Anna. "And the moment anyone tries to expose the truth, the shady elite fan the flames with their fat checkbooks. Jules, I know all this from experience. My dad was used as a pawn when I was a kid, I connected the dots. And so are you now. I can see it in your eyes."

"Either with their fat checkbooks or their greasy Glocks to silence any person or creature attempting to unmask our homegrown oligarchs," Caryssa uttered as she glanced out the window at the calming palm trees swaying lightly and picturesque bay.

My eyes followed hers; I was reminded of what inspired me to rent this tiny, expensive studio apartment. The amazing views of Sausalito Bay, Marinship Park, and the Bay Model Visitor Center. Anchored ships, part of Angel Island and other beautiful sights were all within reach of our glances.

Anna remarked, "the oligarchs of our nation do nothing but operate a bunch of controls behind a curtain."

I took a deep breath in and out, then sipped my wine. "Well, my beloved Feisty was a creature that repeated what people say. And he ripped open the curtain to reveal the sham of intelligence 'wizards'."

"Oh, yes!" exclaimed Caryssa. "And you be like 'Toto come back!' when you told Feisty to not say another word."

"Ha-ha, my Feisty was the loyal watchdog like Toto…"

Caryssa didn't seem to sense my increasing anxiety and continued to let the words roll from her wagging tongue, "Then the wicked witch of the west came to your apartment and killed Feisty to symbolize going against the 'wizards' of the world."

Anna stood, scooped up the wine bottle and replenished each of our glasses. Glug-glug-glugs brought a temporary lull to our conversation as the wine filled our glasses. "The political fringe ideology of 'keeping America safe from threats' is a fear tactic. It's only about a 'threat' to the keepers of global power. A push back on anything that threatens this dark money."

"A threat to big oil, big war, big money in politics." Caryssa declared, with a look of purpose tightening her face. "All in the name of stopping sensationalized and even fabricated atrocities abroad."

Okay, I get it. I wanted to tell the girls I understand the metaphors to the political governing so-called elite and Feisty. But I was still not clear on the connection to the doves and felt like we were squashing my father's heritage of building Liberty ships. I asked, "So what does all this analogy have to do with the doves?"

Anna came to the rescue, "Ava Ramírez's dad is high up in the CIA, and he's a Lock family puppet."

"Just like the current pick for Director of that rat nest agency," Caryssa replied. "Nothing surprises me anymore since the CIA blew JFK's brains out."

"Let Anna finish please," I advised, with an outheld hand and gentle tone.

Anna's eyes fell from me to Caryssa. "Yes, the CIA is backed by oil and gas billionaires—a dark force driving our nation to its forever wars. Ava suffered a lifetime of abuse from her dad, both physically and emotionally. She loved her pet doves, loved what they stood for: *peace and love.*"

"I think I know where this is going," I blurted out.

"Let Anna finish please," Caryssa retorted, words razor sharp.

What the fuck is up with Caryssa? Okay, she's been trying to change the world since her kid was born. I remember her saying she is frightened America has been at war since before her child was in her womb. I splayed my hands, palms up towards Anna. "Go ahead."

Anna nodded, smiling at both of us as if to soothe the unsettled waters. "So, Ava killed her doves as an act of rebellion against her dad. She explained to me that her father killed her inner peace, killed her family love —*her mom.* The symbolic message with bloody tears below the dove's eyes and on its breast were meant to resemble her dad's hawkish ways."

Caryssa placed a hand on my shoulder, "So sorry Jules, this must be hard for you."

I considered Caryssa eyes and a deep compassion flickered within them. I saw Love. An emotionally charged love—a *'what-the-hell-is-this-nations-elites-doing-to-my-kid'* love. But it was there. It made me glad I never had kids.

"I get it…Ava killed her doves to symbolize killing peace—an anti-war message. I remember you saying Anna, *'If you kill the dove, you kill peace.'*

But the FBI or CIA, maybe together, killing my parakeet certainly was not as a message for peace."

"No," Anna responded, heavy on her word. "Just the opposite. It was a message of pro-violence for profit. To silence those revealing the shadowy spies controlling the world from behind the curtain."

"God almighty," sighed Caryssa. "I try not to think about my former boss as Diego's Ramírez's brother. He was the best boss I ever had!"

I relaxed into the moment. The bitter irony of letting go of my dad's Liberty Ship Legacy for fear of betrayal was at odds with my spirit wasting away with holding on too tightly to the conspiracy theory that it was ever about freedom.

"If you kill the dove you kill love," I added to the mysterious equation. So, if you kill a political-talking parakeet, you kill—"

"World peace," Anna replied. "Remember, peace isn't profitable and threatens dark money."

I had an aha moment, and blurted out, "It's a way for the war wizards to say, *'Pay no attention to the man behind the curtain'*"

Chapter Fifteen

Anna

My doorbell chimed as I whizzed around my art studio, organizing for the next class. I figured it was the delivery of a new easel I ordered. Little Billy was disrupting the class again, this time breaking his station's easel. I considered sending the bill to his parents, who believe their mini Van Gogh is without flaw.

The children's next class was to be focused on cubism, collage, symbolism, and surrealism, with an option to choose their project from one of these themes. Given that I like to display my own work, the rendition of Picasso's *La Paloma* will be set on an easel in front of the room.

The painting's striking white dove contrasting against a black background fuses my emotions—what emotions I'm not sure. Perhaps America's white supremacy against black suppression. Or something more abstract: like our political system on the dark side, hidden behind a symbol of peace.

All I know is that my emotions are stirred like a witch's brew bubbling within a cauldron.

I was in no rush to answer the door. Typically, the guy rings to alert me to the package's arrival, followed by a bang of the box being set on the step. But what came next was not the usual clunk of a delivery box.

Thump, thump.

Knuckles pounded the wooden door of my loft, disrupting my thoughts. I tried to fake oblivious, returning to the task. I needed my young students focused on their projects rather than this mess—so the *Space to Create* décor on the wall doesn't give way toward little Billy making space to destruct.

And there's no reason this guy needs my signature for art studio furniture—be gone!

It came again. Thump, thump. My pulse quickened.

I sat the polish on a nearby table, breaking from my shine and shimmer mission. I wasn't imagining the sound. It was there.

The unmistakable presence of someone lingering at the front door barreled me back to the moment. Given recent revelations, my imagination was running wild and uninhibited. Another fed agent? My chest tightened.

The knocks came faster and louder now, drilling a sense of urgency into me. *Bang-Bang-Bang*! My throat got dry.

A soft voice cried out, "Anna, are you home?"

You've got to be kidding me. Now I regretted each minute I waited. I dropped everything and dashed to the front door, flinging it open.

There, at my threshold, stood Ava Ramírez: the girl who helped rob my art gallery. The girl whose father killed my security guard. I had recognized her voice behind the door. I wouldn't have recognized her otherwise.

The sheer image of her blew my mind. Tears ravaged her blouse. Trails of crimson spilled from each nostril. Her right eye was swollen shut. Blood dribbled from her lower lip, and the side of her face was shadowy in a blackish purple. She wore one sandal, the other going without, her feet blistered.

What the fuck is she doing here? Then again, I've invited her to my home and a coffee shop to talk openly about her part in the art theft and lifelong family hardships inflicted by her dad. And the recognition her dad became mentally unstable due to being suppressed into the army. Why wouldn't she trust me?

"They're after me," was all she spilled out in a shrill, panicked tone. She collapsed at my feet. I reached to help her, and a ticket fell from her pocket. *Golden Gate Transit. Good, she took a bus and didn't run the whole way.*

Carrying her into Jared's room, I realized she weighed no more than 90 pounds soaking wet. I fanned dark strands of hair away from her bloodied face. She whispered, "Please don't call 9-1-1. Nobody would understand."

I stared into Ava's brown eyes; the amber hue of a fine cognac. Then a flashback—only the eyes staring back at me were no longer hers. They were eyes as blue as the sea—sparkling and thrashing and churning. A purity of soul reflecting from an anguished young man that tragically, accidentally struck my twelve-year-old daughter thirteen years ago.

I elevated her head with pillows. "No…no Ava I won't call anyone. Hold on, I'm going to take care of you."

My hands were a tree in a violent storm. I rummaged through the medicine cabinets, snatching sterile bandages, instant cold packs, ibuprofen, a wet face cloth, and water.

Back at the girl's side, I squeezed the cold packs then gently wiped her face. "Let me know if I hurt you and take these." I handed her two ibuprofen and a glass of water, which she chugged down.

Looking around my girls' former room, a calm washed over me. I seemed to hear my daughters' voices. "You're doing the right thing, Mom. Take care of her."

The branches of a camellia tree scraped against the window, like bony outstretched arms. The wind picked up and whined a mournful note—emotional and desolate.

Odd…here's a girl lying in my deceased daughter Bianca's bed. A girl who helped steal then destroy my art—*my livelihood*—what I was so absorbed in at the precise moment Bianca was killed riding her skateboard.

Yet…I knew that just as condemning Brandon Garth would never have brought my daughters back, treating her with anything but tenderness would not restore those art pieces.

Forgiveness. Compassion. Acceptance. Concepts often lost in a world of strife with twists and turns—where reality and fantasy are dangerously blurred. I wanted her to rest, but asked softly, "Who is after you, Ava?" But I knew…. My *gut* knew.

Her one good eye found me, staring through me. "My dad. He wants to kill me."

Even though she's twenty, she appeared—and sounded—so small. Fragile. Broken. Like an unnurtured child.

I asked, "Why?" But I also knew why. I just didn't want to believe it.

"I told my dad I was planning on letting the cops know they're bad guys." Ava's voice cracked, and her bloody lips trembled. "They advertise that mind control lab in the city to help kids to be their best and prepare for a career. They call it *America for Success.*"

"That's...are you talking about the place where the kids were strapped to tables?"

"Yes! The kids enter thinking they'll get more career options than at their high schools. It starts out with paperwork and seems legit. Until they're told they'll be given a drug that helps relax them for admissions tests for college."

They're building their sales pipeline of prospects for future profitable war games. I kept the thought to myself.

Ava looked better already. I was happy she wasn't as physically hurt as I had first thought. I directed the cold pack over her wounded eye. "Keep this on to help the swelling go down," I advised. I stroked Ava's hair, moving a few more strands off her face.

She nodded, like a sad puppy. Helpless, I knew I couldn't call anyone. Any law enforcement would think I sounded as nuts as Julie. What would I say? *I have a girl from Tiburon that helped rob my art gallery to pay for college. Her dad is a rogue CIA agent trying to kill her.*

Which reminded me of her father's partners in crime. "Ava, who did this to you? Who is working with your dad?"

Her fists clenched. She turned away and chomped her lower lip, causing it to unleash fresh blood. High-pitched laughter escaped before she spoke.

"My darling father beat me up, but that's nothing new. I'm used to it." She hiccupped and started to cry. Gaining a little composure, she said, "His long-time army buddy who is a big-wig at a huge private security company is one of the guys—he goes by the name *Vanquisher.*"

Ava wiped her eyes with her sleeve, trailing a line of black mascara over her torn white blouse. Her hands were shaking violently. "His real name is Victor Prince. He's forever bragging to the others about the weapons he makes.'"

Ava continued, as I handed her a tissue to blow her nose. Blood soaked the tissue and she looked down at it with another nervous laugh. "The other guy is a top defense dog. He's brutal, the one that shoots the kids up with opioids or whatever the fuck is in those IV drips. Even that's kept secret." She sobbed into the fresh tissue I handed her.

Furrowing my brow, I leaned toward her and gawked into her unhurt eye, I could feel her emotional pain, just as I'd felt Brandon's.

"Ava, you don't need to talk about it now if you don't want—"

"I need to talk about it, it's killing me keeping it all inside! The drug… the drug they inject into our veins makes us feel euphoric while they have us watch violent videos of military ops. It's like they try to get us addicted to heroin or something…and digital warriors."

The power of the poppy, I thought, *has conquered contemporary America. That, and the power of the digital revolution and violence. Follow the money.*

Glancing out the bedroom window, lay a gorgeous field of little orange California poppies. I thanked God these were not the opium brand.

Ava coughed, then added, "There's another guy too, but he isn't directly involved in drugging us or the violent videos. He's some top dude at Homeland Security. They call him 'Watchdog.' He's always walking around the outside of the building, like the immoral Ironman made out to be keeping us all 'free and safe.'"

I tapped a button on the top of Jared's Apple HomePod, turning up the relaxing music. Violins, flutes, and pianos flowed along with the ethereal vocals, neatly and artistically tying the words together.

Ava's facial expressions relaxed, until her eyes found something outside the bedroom door. I tracked her gaze, to my *La Paloma* painting leaning across the hallway.

"I'm sorry." Her eyes begged for forgiveness, brimming with remorse. "I didn't mean to do it. My dad…he—"

"Masterminded the entire thing," I answered for her with an under-standing smile. How I knew this came from intuition more than evidence.

Ava nodded, an empty, haunting expression on her face. She tore a hole into the tissue in her hands, then ripped it to pieces with twitching fingers. In a tentative voice she asked, "Did you ever clean off my writing on the back?"

I grabbed the painting and swiveled it around. "I kind of like it and will show it to the children in my art class tomorrow as a lesson in symbol-ism in art. After all, it's Picasso's quote."

The girl grinned; the first time she'd shown a smile. I handed her a fresh tissue, which she used to wipe the blood dribbling from her lip. Picasso's quote, written in black against a light beige canvas, shouted its message:

I stand for life against death. I stand for peace against war.

Ava seemed somehow transformed. As if the internal black hole of yearning was starting to get filled with an ounce of love and acceptance.

More confidently now, she asked, "What about the other art pieces, the statue of the nude woman and the battle painting. I really did a number on those. God, I am so sorry." She grimaced and twisted her lips into what looked like a forced smile.

My mind was telling me I should be angry at Ava for the destruction of a few of my prized art possessions. My heart was seeking hope and under-standing, not hate. I couldn't think how to answer, so I gave a weak, "It didn't end all bad."

Ava's hands started doing another tremor as she looked down at the floor. She stuttered, I…I guess I wanted to play my dad's game and use art as a political weapon—but against violence rather than for violence like him."

This yanked my attention. "Hold on, I want to show you something." I scrammed to my art studio and grabbed my rendition of the Delacroix, *Liberty Leading the People*.

The minute I carried it in, Ava exclaimed, "Wow, it's as good as new!"

"It's amazing what a good art restorer can do," I remarked. I decided not to mention my artistic eye can see where the torn parts were, or that my bronze Pradier statue will never be restored.

We stared at the painting of the bare-breasted flag-waving woman wielding a gun and leading a charge through battle depicting the French Revolution. Ava piped in, "Kind of reminds me of the Statue of Liberty."

"Yes, that association is often mentioned in the art world. Of course, 'Liberty' is not an actual woman. It's an abstract force." It dawned on me the connection of these 18th and 19th-century art pieces to modern global warfare.

My personal motivation to paint versions of Picasso and Delacroix was driven from the same passion for peace that inspired Picasso to paint his works —using depictions of the brutality of battle then contrasting the dove of peace.

Both artist's works are about deceptions of war and social change. I had also attempted the brushstrokes of Picasso's Guernica, which reflects the horrors of battle. But after the girls' deaths I needed something uplifting, which birthed my art gallery.

Almost thinking out loud now, I asked Ava, "Do you think it was a coincidence your dad grabbed these specific pieces to use as political weapons?"

The girl looked straight at me and said without emotion, "It's no coincidence. I've seen the artwork the CIA has at Langley. Including Kryptos. There was a "bring your daughter to work" week, and I flew to D.C. with my dad, caught a glimpse of the sculpture. It's kept hidden from the public. It's a work of secrecy and elusiveness of truth…"

Kryptos. I've researched Sanborn's works of encrypted sculpture, trying to figure out this secret code. The artist is as mysterious as the Kryptos itself. I left this alone for now. Too complicated to get into with the clock ticking…

Looking at Ava, I could see that talking this through was helping, not hindering her progress. She had trailed off, so I asked, "Did you know the original Delacroix painting was defaced in Northern France in 2013? At the Louvre Lens, a woman scribbled a cryptic code with a black marker, 'AE911."

At this, Ava jerked straight up, the good eye almost popping from its socket. "Yes, I read about it, it's a message how 2200 architects and engineers insist 9/11 was self-inflicted by America's historic war machine. I think the woman writing that message was sickened by paintings glorifying wars that cause such consequences."

"Did that woman's actions give you the idea to write on my painting?"

Ava shook her head. "I...I don't' know. But I overheard my dad saying the CIA withheld information that may have stopped the 9/11 attack. I was only three when it happened, but I remember. He thought I was asleep."

"Your dad worked for the CIA back then?"

Ava grabbed a wet wipe from the nightstand and slowly rolled her head while cleansing her face and hands. She answered, "No, he was fresh out of the army and offered a position with the huge search engine company, DataRodent."

Which got funding from the CIA. Ava's expressions softened then hardened as she responded to my inquiries. "So, resentment towards your dad motivated you to mark up my Picasso dove painting and cut apart my Delacroix with scissors?"

Ava hesitated, twisting a ring on her finger. "Maybe, I don't know. I went on a rampage with your art because of my anger with my dad dragging me and Paige into this mess—for his part in stifling my attempt at revealing the secret underbelly of the CIA's illusions onto the people."

She looked less nervous now, maybe even relieved. She continued, "I think the fourth message; K4 of Kryptos even has a subtle hint of how the passages and timeline of our violent history is untrue. I took my anger out on your art and I was wrong."

I believed she was onto something with the dark code of the Kryptos art sculpture, but I needed to focus on prepping for the kid's art class and getting her to rest before Pierre takes her away. This was getting too deep for me—so I simply asked, "Is Paige still in prison?"

"No, she's out and doing community service." Ava concealed her face behind a trembling hand, eyes zipping away from me. I waited.

After a moment, she broke the silence, "Paige's only guilt was being with me. She never even touched the art. It's me that should be punished. I'm the one that grabbed the art with my dad...I'm the one that vandalized your business."

Ava's hands shook with fiercer intent. I reached out and closed them in mine, whispering, "shhh,…it's okay, Ava—"

"No! It's not okay! My powerful dad bails me out of jail to control me, gets immunity from murder as a top CIA guy and Paige gets the watchful eye."

A vicious rage boiled inside me; *He gets impunity from murdering Johnny.* "Your dad should be in prison." I spat out, rather tactlessly.

Ava pondered this, twisting the ring on her finger even more, until it came off. I motioned for her to continue, and she did:

"No, he'd be a danger to other prisoners. He belongs in a mental institution with the rest of the crazed military torchbearers. He was once a gentle, kind soul—now drugging me to make me forget about how I can reveal the atrocities the CIA has carried out in the name of '*intelligence gathering*,'—trying to kill me to silence me. I'm smart enough to crack the final code in Kryptos as well."

Kryptos. There it is again. A sudden thought occurred, *somebody killed Julie's bird to silence it.* "Ava, nobody has been able to crack the final code—"

"I can."

"You think you can?"

"Yes, I'm a wizard at math and have overheard too much. His team is socially engineering me to silence me."

I realized she was even more emotionally damaged than I first considered. Remembering she said her dad would never pay for her college education and that she believed he killed her mom, I mentioned," It came to my attention your dad's choice to bludgeon Johnny to death—the Pradier bronze statue of a naked woman as a heroine—may be symbolic of his misogynist ways."

At this Ava squeezed her eyes shut and said nothing.

I realized I may have pushed her a bit far. "Ava?" Her eyes were closed. "Ava look at me."

She inched open her eyes. I locked my own on hers before giving her what she so desperately needed: "I forgive you."

It was Brandon Garth all over again.

* * *

"She's been asleep in Jared's room for three hours."

Nervous energy turned me into an Olympic house cleaner. I emptied the dishwasher, mopped the kitchen floor, and wiped down the counter-tops within ten minutes.

Pierre paced back and forth, a glass of bourbon in his hand. He ran fingers through his silver-streaked hair. "We can't let her stay, ma chérie, they might follow her here. Think of Jared's safety!"

"She has nowhere to go—"

"Come on! She must have friends!" Pierre smacked the glass down so hard, amber liquid sloshed from it and spilled onto the table. We stared at the puddle, a splash of tawny shimmer, trying to find humor in it.

"Pierre, her friend's homes would be the first place they'd look for her. Her best friend has already been to prison and back due to this guy's actions. This is her own father we're talking about."

My husband's mouth opened, his eyebrows reached for his hairline. "The log cabin!"

"I thought of that, even though we've yet to use the cabin ourselves."

We'd acquired a small log cabin in South Lake Tahoe at a bargain price, figuring it would cost us less to ski more. Renting condos didn't come cheap.

But we assumed we'd have time to christen the cabin before providing a retreat for a girl we hardly know—before giving her a safe-haven from dark and hidden American power.

I glanced toward the hallway leading to Jared's room, and added, "Why must I always feel other people's emotions as if they're my own?"

"That's what I love most about you, ma chère. If I possessed this level of empathy, we would never have been apart for six years."

What could I say to that? My heart buckled and split as I chased away the pain of losing precious years of our marriage.

"I'll take her to our cabin and will have my new teacher's assistant Paula stay there with her," Pierre suggested. "Paula's single and loves Tahoe. She'd be happy to work from the log cabin for a while. It would give Ava a chance to sort out her rather toxic life—and get her away from our home."

I sensed Pierre's internal hesitancy to have anything to do with Ava. "How can your TA work from Tahoe, she helps with your students—"

"There's plenty for her to do with paperwork, and I thought of something else! You said Ava is interested in sculpture. I'll have Paula take materials up to the cabin with her. Let's see, I've extra supplies of chalk, brass, copper, pewter, clay—"

"Just clay to start, she's a beginner—don't go overboard with this." It struck me we are discussing the possibility of teaching art to Ava. The emotionally distressed girl that shattered my art business and killed her own pet doves. But I realized why I'm trying to save her; I couldn't save my own girls.

Besides, providing her with a creative outlet, art therapy, might be the best thing for her. She's damaged goods—the product of an evil father. Soul searching would do her good.

I added, "Too bad you don't teach encrypted sculpture. She's taken an interest in the corporate art at Langley—the sculpture. Says she can crack the code."

Killing her doves, Ava had explained to me, was a symbolic mockery of our violent militaristic culture right down to the sacrificial lamb mentality. The second dove resembled the U.S. Seal, with the serene dove replacing the Bald Eagle—a bird of bad moral character. It carried the message that war could never bring peace, even hinting at how the symbols on the U.S. Seal are blatantly masonic & occult despite what some hawkish historians claim.

Brilliant symbolism.

"Kryptos? The sculpture outside of CIA headquarters? You've got to be kidding me, nobody's been able to crack the last code," Pierre muttered. "Shhh…I hear her moving around in the room. We don't want her hearing us talk about her."

I whispered, "We need to be sure she's not here tomorrow when the children come to art class. I don't want to endanger them."

The bedroom door squeaked open, then the bathroom door shut. A moment later, water sprinkled from the showerhead echoing all the way to us.

"Great!" I exclaimed. "She'll feel better after a hot shower."

"Yes, but then we need to talk to her about the cabin. How long has she been here?"

My eyes found the kitchen clock. "Three and a half hours, maybe four."

"Shit. Do you think Diego Ramírez could track her to our house?"

I didn't want to say I'd been fretting about this. After all, she robbed my art gallery, inscribed a pro-peace quote onto the back of my painting and I've reached out to her. "No, unless she mentioned to her dad that I've spoken to her. I have the impression she's too smart for that."

Pierre mumbled under his breath, a faint whisper barely audible. "Maybe she's smart but something is odd. Why did she use your art gallery as the subject of violence, theft, and destruction?"

I nodded my agreement while whispering back, "She was manipulated by her renegade CIA dad looking to use my art for political gain."

"No matter, I am not happy with getting involved with this—"

I raised my hand…" Shhh, she's coming."

Ava teetered into the kitchen, her head cocooned in a fresh white towel. What a difference a nap and shower made. The bruises hadn't changed a great deal, but her eye was no longer swollen shut, and her skin glowed pinkish rather than the pale-like death she wore upon arrival.

"Did you have a nice nap?" I asked.

She smiled her appreciation, then said in a scratchy voice, "I feel much better. Thank you. May I have a glass of water please?"

Pierre grabbed a glass and moved toward the refrigerator dispenser. "Ice?"

The girl nodded while flashing perfectly straight white teeth against olive skin. She brought the glass of water to her lips and took a sip. She swished the liquid in her mouth before spitting it into the sink.

She grimaced. "Sorry about that," she began, "but my mouth is dry as dust."

I grinned. "No worries." Taking in her clothing, my eyes rested on her torn blouse and blistered bare feet. "I have fresh clothes, shoes and an unused toothbrush. We seem to be close in size."

"You are so kind. Especially after I was…anything but kind to you."

A gentle breeze shook the deck windchimes, bringing soothing melodic tones to my senses. I smiled at Ava. "I believe in the power of kindness. If you hurt me, it's because you were hurting yourself."

Ava drank small sips of the water, closing her eyes while seeming to savor the blissful moisture in her mouth. She eventually looked up at us. "Thanks."

"You must be hungry." Pierre nudged a bowl of fruit in front of her. "Eat."

Ava's face crinkled as she announced her lack of an appetite over the last few days.

"You must eat, Ava. You need nourishment." I saw a tormented soul in her that hadn't been fueled by any love for too long. Her body needed to compensate.

She picked at the fruit, slowly at first then grabbing by the handful. "Wow guess I did need to eat. These are the freshest berries, even better than the organic fruit at the store I work at."

"They're from our garden," I answered. As Ava enjoyed the blend of raspberries, blueberries, and strawberries my nerves tightened. I glanced at the clock. 5 pm. Time was ticking by, as was our likelihood of remaining hidden from a barrage of awful men.

Pierre sensed my urgency, directing a question at Ava, "Is there any way your dad could track you here?"

Ava forced a mouthful of food down and shook her head firmly. "I never told him I talked to you, Anna, so at least I don't think so."

Pierre glanced at the girl's cell phone shoved into her back pocket, shaking his head. "Anyone can track people's mobile phones these days… your dad's a spy, Ava."

I shuffled forward, grasped both of Ava's hands, and gently pulled her toward me. "Ava, we need to get you to safety. For your sake, for our grandson's sake. For all of us. Pierre will take you to our lovely new little log cabin in Tahoe—"

"No! I have a job. I wasn't there today and don't want to be fired. I'm finally getting my shit together!"

"You've got to be kidding, right? You should be more concerned with your life than getting back to work—"

"I'm broke! I live paycheck to paycheck and have to survive!"

"You need to survive by not getting killed first! We can lend you money." Pierre's sternness pulled his face taut, likely at me for getting so involved.

"Where do you work?" I asked. No doubt, the girl seemed a bit naïve to be more concerned with keeping her job over staying alive.

"Nugget Market in Tiburon. I like it, they like me and even might make me Assistant Manager! I can't fuck this up—"

Pierre piped up, "Ava, we will go there personally ourselves if we need to, and explain you are in danger—"

"I can't tell them I'm from a family of spies."

"We won't mention details, just that you are being chased by people who want to hurt you. Look, Ava, we need to leave soon." Pierre was adamant, his voice unbending to any other choice.

Fear sparked in Ava's eyes, like tiny streaks of lightning flashing in her pupils.

As Pierre was readying further encouragement to ignite rationality and motivation into Ava, a loud pounding came from the door, stopping us all cold.

They've found us.

CHAPTER SIXTEEN

Caryssa

Carpool duty time!

As the kids piled out of my SUV, I tuned into KPFA radio and was hit with the news of another school shooting in America, an all too common occurrence brought on by an economy of violence that sustains the violence.

With a sick pang in the pit of my stomach, I watched as the giggling happy-go-lucky boys scrambled into the high-school building, disappearing behind the heavy industrialized doors. They were slap-happy during the last week of school, ready for fun in the summer sun.

I sat there for at least ten minutes, immobilized with a sense of sensitivity.

On auto-pilot, I decided to try out the new "Get It Now" App I had downloaded. Nothing like hiring someone to run my errands. I tapped in my wish list: Notebooks, *check*. Grocery items, *check*. A bottle of Montoya Cabernet, *check*.

How we've yet to stop squeezing out Earths vast oil supplies to fuel all the gadgets we are convinced we need to make life easier, remained unchecked—lingering on an unfinished "to-do" list of humanity.

I drove home and awaited the courier to come while trying to get some work done in my home office. I couldn't concentrate, looking every half hour for an update on the heart-wrenching shooting thousands of miles away. I prayed my own kid stays safe even in this peaceful community—and that irresponsible politicians and business leaders will finally make the policy changes necessary to stop the insanity.

A voice in my mind repeated something I overheard at a recent party in Discovery Bay. I remembered the comment stuck out in the sunny attitude of the moment. We were on boats—water-skiing, tubing and floating on California's beautiful stretch of Delta. Music was playing, palm trees waving, boat grills were fired up with sizzling steaks and chicken mingling in the air with the scent of Coppertone.

The topic seemed to exist within every conversation, glance, plan, and gathering. *School shootings*. The words as common as the air, blending in with the beauty around us, like water. During the laughter, sunshine, floaties, and fun, a parent had said, *"It won't stop until guns and war are no longer in a central position of our government and political economy."*

It was no use—work was not going to get done. I grabbed a water bottle and strapped on my running shoes, then headed out to hit the trails of the East San Francisco Bay Hills. My gorgeous neighborhood—lucky me. At a good pace, I ran in nature past the views of the Golden Gate Bridge, Bay Bridge, Alcatraz and Angel Island. The fresh cool breeze slapped my face, the wind blowing through my hair.

Later, too wired to sleep, I read while burning spiced incense. The meditative fragrance of sandalwood brought an inner calm. The sound of the rain merged with winds and wind chimes. A cat meowed in the distance. My eyes struggled to stay open as I nestled into a lavender scented pillow, pulling the soft throw over my shoulders.

Sleep finally came and with it a reoccurring dream:

The chair moved back and forth as I held my tiny infant close to my heart, rocking him to sleep. The soothing lyrics of Rock-a-Bye-Baby engulfed me. Through the open window, peaceful sounds of birds were followed by booming fireworks. A group of children whistled and clapped. And then my baby was running with the laughing children. How did he grow so fast? The booming increased. The traumatized birds disappeared, and my cat freaked out scratch-

ing my leg until a vein burst into streams of blood. The exploding fireworks turned to bombs and the world went dark.

"Mom! Mom! Are you okay?"

I awoke drowsily. Fragmented images floated through my head. Is my baby okay?

"Mom?"

I turned and saw my baby. Wow, from short-legged toddler to fix-feet tall overnight. *And our nation is still raging and dropping bombs.*

Tyler's goofy teenaged energy propelled him to bounce on the back-end of my bed.

"What are you doing up so late?" I asked.

"You're screaming woke me." Tyler was frowning.

"Screams?"

"You musta had a bad dream."

Shaking my head, I pondered my dream. Nothing made sense. Scattered pictures. Yet, somehow everything did make sense. Subtle hues of our nation's built-in culture of violence haunted me in my dreams.

I looked at the clock—midnight. "Tyler, you need to go back to sleep, it's a school night. Come here and give me a hug. Thank you for checking in on me, sweetie."

Tyler hugged me a bit tight, my ribs feeling like they'd snap. "Just wanted to see if you're okay," he said, stifling a yawn. "Goodnight."

"Actually, good morning almost. See you in six hours." I watched Tyler move toward his room and blew a kiss. "Love you!"

"Love you as well." My boy's voice was that of a young man, and my heart felt like it was following him out the room. The vulnerability I've felt since he was born snuck out of my eyes and rolled down my cheeks.

I snuggled into my pillow. Falling back to sleep, I trained my thoughts on our recent family camping trip at Lake Tahoe. I wanted my dreams to be images of the wildflowers, lakes, the greenery along the hiking trails, the quietude of kayaking and other beautiful things we encountered.

* * *

The minute I turned my cell phone on in the morning, it pinged. A message from Anna appeared. *"I'm doing it again! Taking in distraught people."*

Oh no, what's she up to now? My dear sophisticated, multicultural friend Anna from Paris, always thinking of others before herself.

I speed-dialed Anna. She picked up on the first ring:

"So, you're taking in more stray cats, hey?…where did Ava go, seems no place safe…wow! how nice, you two haven't even used the cabin yet… Is Jules there? Sure, come over we'll talk in person…. Okay, bye"

I sipped more coffee, then took a hot shower, letting the heat run over my neck and shoulders. While rolling my head for added stretch, I realized both Ava and Julie, or maybe I should say Julie's brother—are running from rogue CIA or FBI agents, fearing for their lives.

With a towel wrapped around my head, I vacuumed and polished, nearly knocking over my Google Home Mini. *"OK Google play Nora Jones."*

The relaxing beats and sultry smooth voice flowed through my house as I dressed in jeans and an oversized blouse, did a two-minute application of makeup and dried my hair.

I sat at my laptop trying to work, focused on the community improvement grant proposal for the "Sustainable World" contract gig I took on.

The doorbell broke my concentration. Certain it was Anna, I was all too happy to take a break. "Come in, girlfriend!"

Anna stepped into my living room dressed casual-chic in a white sundress, straw boater hat, and flat strappy sandals. As always, she complimented her style with a classic beautiful smile.

"Well, I'd never know you've been through such stress. How's the home-shelter going? Those women couldn't get a lovelier loft in the Sausalito Hills." I pulled my blender off the counter, filled with the thick, cold pureed raw fruit I prepared before she arrived. "Want a smoothie?"

Anna lifted the glass as if she was inspecting the color of the drink. "Looks like plain orange juice." Then she took a healthy sip.

"It's an orange-ginger smoothie," I answered. "Infused with immune strengthening secrets."

"Mmm…taste great, thanks! The home-shelter will need to go out of business soon, or else I'll go mad." Anna's delayed response was announced while still smiling. "At least Ava had left before the children came for their art class."

"Where's Julie? You said she was at your house now. I figured she'd be with you—"

"No, no, no. I'm overwhelmed and need some personal space. She was asleep when I left—hasn't slept for days in her apartment. She's too spooked about her bird being murdered and brother threatened by the feds. She babbled on about a rumored sting op across America."

"Accusing innocents of terror plots," I added. "We both know it's no babble, Anna." I thought of the innocent eighteen-year-old boy in a small town outside of Boston arrested on "terrorism charges" for merely posting a self-created rap song on Facebook. So much for freedom of speech. And then there's Julie's brother.

We moved into my living room taking our smoothies and the bagels I had toasted. I placed a small plate of brined salmon, cream cheese and capers on the table. "I have more fresh coffee if you'd prefer caffeine, I've had enough already."

"No thanks, I've had two cups this morning and it made me jittery." Anna's eyes seemed to be admiring the view from my house.

We sat quietly for a moment, appreciating the clear sky highlighting the fiery-orange of the Golden Gate Bridge and the huge expanse of murky-green San Francisco Bay.

I turned to Anna and said, "It's so kind of you to help both Ava and Julie. I've got the impression you reach out to Ava because you lost…" I stopped, wondering if I'd be pouring salt in her wounds.

"My own daughters. Yes, that's the biggest reason I can feel her hurt even though she helped sabotage my art business. She's trying to survive child abuse. She's running, frightened and has been all her life—running from the evil driven into her own once-loving father."

"And Julie too—"

"No, Julie never hurt me. Oh, but…sorry to have cut you off. Yes, I feel Julie's pain. She too is running from hidden political malice that threatened the lives of her beloved pet and innocent brother. Her world has been crushed, ironically by the same war economy her dad's livelihood came from."

A song popped into my head and escaped my lips. "Imagine all the people living life in peace…"

"World peace will only be attained without the global money in politics," Anna declared.

We sipped our fresh-fruit smoothies, enjoyed bites of lox while looking out at the white sailboats that seemed to magically appear out of the light fog rolling over the windblown water.

I continued with Anna's mutual compassion: "And Brandon Garth. That's when I first connected to you—I saw you could see through the media circus to the innocence of that boy."

At this Anna sat straight up. For a second, I thought I'd said something wrong.

"Yes! The unjust justice system wanted me to toss the precious kid into prison, take the millions and run all rich and happy. But I felt *his pain* even though his car tragically struck my daughter. My husband thought I was nuts, blamed me for both daughters' deaths and left me."

I nodded, both our eyes gleamed with tears. Slowly—a bit hesitantly, I added, "I think I understand. The pain for your girls was transferred to Brandon. I feel a love for my child so deeply it hurts. I sense any pain, any hurt, he experiences."

Anna simply nodded, turning her eyes toward a framed photo of Tyler and me when he was three-months-old. A turquoise border emphasized his blue-green eyes. The word "SON" emblazoned the label on the top. My heart skipped a beat.

I dropped a few capers onto Anna's plate to compliment the salmon. "You know, when I hear of school shootings, I feel as much for the alleged child-perpetrators as I do the kids shot. I think, *what dark cultural forces are causing these once innocent children to shoot children?*"

Anna shook her head with a look of disgust, "Well I wouldn't go that far. If it was your kid shot at school, you wouldn't feel that way—"

"Come on Anna, yes I would! The same deplorable forces chasing Ava and Julie's brother are linked to the negative influence causing those kids to lose it! For Christ's sake, the CIA and other 'intelligence' agencies are sponsoring terrorism and we go on as a society—"

"You don't need to explain…I realize they use violent and illegal means to achieve political aims. I lost my own father to this! Yet I don't think you'd pardon any kid for shooting up your own child's school."

Anna walked over to my living room window, glancing out at the captivating view. Her eyes scanned the vast open space as if to search for unanswerable questions—like, why are humans so fallible?

I love how open and kindhearted she is but a bit annoyed with her now. Then it hit me…*She lost her own children. Does she feel a déjà vu with forgiving the boy whose car fatally struck her daughter? Is she feeling guilty for what is her moral virtue?*

Recalling my scattered dream last night, I saw the connection to what I was trying in vain to say to Anna—my kid and others inundated all their lives with nonstop unwarranted wars and deceptive obsession with '*going after bad guys*' since before they were born. A huge imposition to their social-emotional well-being.

But Anna's children never had the chance to find their life position while wading through such political impositions. Anna doesn't have the chance to worry about her girls getting exploited by military powers, like what's happening to Ava. Or simply the chance to be concerned with the lack of nuance of "superhero" movies portraying violence as a virtue.

But she has Jared…*Sweet, beautiful Jared*. I inquired, "How's Jared doing? Is he healing well from his scary ski trauma?"

"Yes! Thanks for asking. Kids heal so quickly physically and emotionally! Jared is doing so well, he's bragging to his friends about surviving an avalanche and saving a lady's life. We are all counting our blessings!" Anna's skin seemed to glow with happiness and relief.

"Fabulous to hear! So...you mentioned Ava is staying at your unused new ski cabin in Tahoe..."

"Oh...yeah, Pierre drove her up this morning. His teaching assistant Paula followed behind to stay there with her for comfort and support. I don't know how long we'll let her stay, but we needed everyone safe—especially our loving Jared."

That we were trying to keep her 'free and safe' from our own military might lingered in the corner of my mind. "Why do you think she showed up at your doorstep rather than at a close friend's place?"

"She arrived beaten up by the bastard that calls himself her father. She thinks he wants her dead to silence her."

"To silence her for speaking up about the secret power at the root of our nation's violence we are talking about now," I blurted out.

Anna at once seemed shocked and recharged. She said, "You know, that's what drew me to build our friendship, to begin with, Caryssa. I could see the almost clairvoyant connection you have with your boy and how you'd help me see through legal bias to Brandon's humanity. And something else—"

"And our shared ability to see through the lies within global power." I finished. "We are not mushrooming in the dark enabling those powers to feed us bullshit."

Anna chuckled, placing her smoothie on the coffee table. "We strive for truths."

"Anna, I love you for your honesty and the human compassion you show the world. But be careful. You can't let yourself be bled dry."

"I was bled dry as a young girl during the Vietnam War, Caryssa. At age eleven, I heard my uncle say my dad was killed due to CIA covert ops. I ran through the streets of Paris crying, seeking a purpose to keep living..."

At that moment Anna's cell phone rang. Her face turned white when she answered it. "Oh my God, Jules, don't do anything rash. Sorry I left. I'll be right there!"

Anna turned with tears rolling down her cheeks. "I have to go, Julie said she's having suicidal thoughts."

* * *

The happy hour parties on Friday night for years at our home had been stalled with life's crazy busy. My little family has been having its private happy daily, but we needed to have a summer gathering tonight.

I decided to connect with a circle of friends we haven't seen in a while —the old playdate group.

"Do they know Tyler is away camping?" George called from the backyard. He lifted a spade and stopped digging in the soil while harvesting potatoes.

I glanced out the open bedroom window. The sunset cast a mystic, rather strange light and shadow over the San Francisco Bay. A light fog rolled over the Golden Gate Bridge. The surreal beauty from my backyard reminds me to live in the moment.

"Yes, we even joked about our teenagers having no desire to hang out with a bunch of beyond middle-aged parents fussing over their grades and futures."

My hinged window caught the wind like a sail, blowing it shut in my face. *Arrrggg!* I opened it back up, announcing to George, "Forget about setting up the fire pit, too windy—we'll burn the house down."

He looked up from getting his hands dirty in the garden, something we both love to do, and asked, "So who's coming?" I wondered if it was dread I saw in his eyes. Although he's a social animal, George would rather hang with his old Cal pot-smoking crowd than be pulled into chatty Mom's trying to change the world for our kid's sake.

"The only ones able to come are Bryan and Charlotte Garrity. The rest are either on summer vacation or have other commitments."

This seemed to get George's attention, "Oh…that sounds fun. I figured Bryan and his family would have whisked off to Copenhagen or some expensive city in Switzerland by now with the multi-millions they inherited."

"Nope, they still live in their modest small home near Eucalyptus Park, where we went after our boys played ball together." It struck me Tyler was only five then, maybe eight by the end of little-league baseball. An entire decade has slipped by and our kids are young adults now. I love who my kid is becoming, such a purpose behind all the pain. At the same time, I'm frightened he's growing faster than our bank account.

Still talking through the bedroom window, George asked, "So what did they do with the twenty-five million Bryan inherited from his dad?" He was referring to the trust fund Clarence Garrity, a former U.S. Senator, finally handed to Bryan after twenty years, long after disowning his only son at age eighteen for not following in his shady political footsteps.

"I told you, they invested a huge portion to charities with a positive impact on our own nation like *Americans Helping Americans* since half our populace is in poverty. They didn't want to live like Bryan's parents: egotistical rich asses that never gave back to society." I said this while realizing the window was shaking on its rusted hinge, so I pulled it shut.

That rusted hinge was a subtle reminder of other home improvement projects needing attention, including the peeling paint around our house exterior that confronted me lately.

The scents of sage, citrus blossoms, and pink jasmine wafted into my room with the gush of wind, lingering in the air as I tidied up for our guests. I lit scented candles, put decorative towels in the bathrooms, vacuumed and polished.

In the kitchen, I pulled the goat cheese and rosemary pita bread out of the oven, then stuck toothpicks into the smoked salmon bites. George came in with baskets full of green beans, potatoes, and lettuce from the garden. "Don't go overboard with hors-d'oeuvres. I'm cooking chicken on the barbeque."

I was grateful it's not windy in the front yard where our grill is. "Don't lecture me! Of course, I'll have a few appetizers for our guest—"

"They won't be hungry enough to eat my entrée. Don't insult the chef!" George, forever the culinary control freak.

"It's not like we'll eat the minute they get here, chill out! I have two light hors-d'oeuvres I'm proud of making myself, don't insult the assistant cook!" Eighteen years of marriage is a beautiful thing until we bicker over nothing.

"Only two people are coming, not twenty like we used to have for happy hours. We'll have enough food to feed the world—"

"*Blah, blah, blah!* Two simple appetizers to go with the wine—don't worry, your yummy meal won't go to waste." I kissed George on the check, and he turned a loving gaze my way.

"Nice outfit by the way," he complimented.

I had on a blue and white striped one-piece shorts ensemble with cut-out shoulders. My blonde hair was piled on top of my head, a few strands spilling out around my face. "Thank you, I feel like the late fifty-something trying to look twenty."

George's smile was more of a smirk, "Works for me."

* * *

A decade didn't seem to age Bryan or Charlotte—if anything they both looked younger. "Wow, like a rich and famous Hollywood couple that never ages!" I laughed.

Charlotte's eyebrows raised, her mouth forming a frown, "Neither of us have resorted to Botox or plastic surgery after Bryan got his family windfall of money if that's what you mean. Just good healthy living!"

"Oh, believe me, I'm all into daily exercise, fresh air, sleep and natural beauty to stay young!" I responded. From previous conversations with Charlotte, I knew that talking money was never taboo with them. If anything, they loved joking about Bryan's rich little poor boy days.

We sat in my living room, enjoying the ambiance of candles, music, and wine. The usual panoramic view was encased in heavy fog, yet still looked magical in that quintessential San Francisco way. An otherworldly low fog with burning clouds above it—casting off a bright yellow mellowness blended with the sinister gray blanket.

The two men were deep into a conversation in the kitchen, standing by the food and booze like moths to a flame. I often wonder why people hang in my messiest, least favorite room after I work like a crazy lady making my house so cozy for guests.

"It's much warmer out than you'd think with the fog and wind," Charlotte announced, "Looks like we dressed alike for the occasion."

She had on a colorful skirt and matching bohemian-chic style blouse with ruffled edging, the gypsy Berkeley look. Her hair clip had worked itself loose and dark hair fell in waves around her forehead. Hair that once matched the color of Bryan's, his now salt and pepper.

"I had a grand plan to have us sitting out in my backyard among the flowers, fire pit, view and fresh breeze but that didn't work out. So nice for us to get together after bumping into each other so much around town over the years. You look fab, Charlotte."

"Thanks, I lost fifteen pounds since our baseball in the park days with our boys, without even trying. I think I put less stress on myself." Charlotte's skin seemed to glow with contentment.

"So, the old saying 'money can't buy you happiness' is a lie?" I joked.

Charlotte looked surprised for a second, then smiled and said, "I'd like to say the money we got from Bryans family trust has nothing to do with it, but gotta admit it helps ease the worry of paying for the kid's college tuition."

I nodded, all too familiar with the concern. "I'm impressed with you, still living in your modest home, giving to charities and living a simple life of beauty—"

"Oh, we are living well enough, mostly in travels and learning multiple languages. So far, we've traveled to seven countries and the twins are learning a fourth language. We just got back from Costa Rica and didn't want to leave!" Charlotte exclaimed.

George walked in carrying the tray of hors-d'oeuvres, Bryan following behind. Bryan chimed in, "The boys loved the troops of monkeys swinging from the trees, the sloths and snakes, zip-lining through the rainforest and surfing—"

"Costa Rica is so lucky the monkeys are their *only* troops!' I exclaimed.

Charlotte seemed energized, jumping in, "So peaceful. We surfed and snorkeled every day! The biodiversity, sunny beaches, warm climate. We'd move there in a flash."

"You wanna move to Costa Rica, hon? It can be arranged." Bryan scrunched his face up, his dimples digging deeply into his cheeks, giving him that charming indulgence when he laughed. The dimples humbled him, made him human. "But what about our jobs?"

"Oh, come on Bry! We can both do our work in Costa Rica. In fact, my profession of Ecology is the biggest there. Costa Rica is the most protected natural environment there is—no mutilated frogs like here!"

I studied Bryan's face. Still that tall handsome man I met ten years ago at a ballpark while watching our boys play. Same sparkling blue eyes and crooked Irish grin. Only his hair seemed to change with the silvery locks adding to his distinction. He remained reserved. Quiet. Seemingly waiting for his wife to continue. Which she did:

"Costa Rica is so politically stable and prosperous within its education, healthcare and safety net. It abolished its army seventy years ago and has enjoyed peace ever since!"

"We could learn from that example; regardless how much bigger we are. They saved from spending on 'defense' and instead invested in education, healthcare and this beautiful thing called life and happiness." I uttered.

George piped in, "Bryan doesn't have to worry about our nations fucked-up financial priorities. This here Harvard drop out is doing quite well since his sugar daddy stepped in…"

The rest of the sentence evaporated in a slow recognition of surprise, as George good-heartedly pushed on Bryan's arm. The wide-eyed raised eyebrows of our guests sent an uncomfortable silence through the room.

I attempted to smooth over my husband's rough-edged comment, "Um…George, I think Bryan is proud of his Cal Poly education and career and—"

"It's not that." Bryan held up his arms as if in surrender. "I'm okay with the Harvard thing and sugar daddy comment. It's just that…well, my dad died of Parkinson's last month. He held on and we tried to mend our ways but…"

My hand went to my mouth, "Oh my God we are so sorry Bryan."

He nodded, and we remained quiet for a moment. I sensed Bryan didn't want to talk about it now.

Charlotte quickly wrapped an arm around each of us and said calmly," No harm in the comment George, I mean, the sugar daddy thing is true, and we even joke about it! We may not need to worry about our boys' financial futures. Yet it's the cultural hegemony we concern ourselves with for our kids. The ruling class manipulating our culture, imposing their worldview on our children. That's what makes me think about moving out of the country."

We all nodded, taking sips of our drinks and pondering this.

As if to change the topic yet not, Charlotte asked, "So how was your recent family trip to D.C.?"

"It was wonderful thanks. Lots of fabulous food and wine, seeing the sights and sounds, kayaking the Potomac. It's nice to be able to bring Tyler with our own agenda, rather than the hawkish politicalized version the schools seem to send the kids on."

"Oh, I hear you—with the deceiving glorification of our history of violence. That's what I mean by cultural hegemony."

"Seriously, what is politics anyhow, but a manipulation of symbols? An adoration of globalism and nationalism? Rather than take photos of flags, war monuments and oppressive graves, we focused on the wonderful art museums, multi-cultural exhibits, gardens, architecture, good food and the positive innovations our nation *has* achieved."

"So, you didn't see the history and space museums?"

"Oh, we saw all the museums, The Holocaust Museum, Smithsonian American History, Air and Space—all the main attractions. I meant we didn't highlight or waste photos on the scheming political fluff such as engraved clichés like "freedom is not free." Although of course, you can't miss this type of preachy marketing slogan while there."

Charlotte nodded rather than spoke. "What was Tyler's favorite?" she simply asked.

"The Natural History Museum—the huge bear and other wild animals. I personally loved the Butterfly Exhibit. I found the American History Museum a rather amusing twist of good and bad and couldn't help see a pattern etched directly into our growing war economy." I mused.

"It's been a while since I've been there, explain your thoughts." Charlotte seemed a little wary. Yet, from our previous conversations I know she shared my vision.

"An unhealthy cultural mold of superhero hoopla, onto Hollywood glitz and war worship. We start out innocent enough with childhood toys and TV series: the Batmobile, Romper Room, Mickey Mouse, Sesame Street and the infamous Barbie Doll darling of our childhood." I started to say....

"Heck yeah! I remember Barbie really gets around the museum. She's rather popular," laughed Charlotte.

"I think she may even have been on display working the factory making plastics or something," I added.

"Or she's sprinkled among the exhibits making metals and burning fats for the 'war effort,' joked Charlotte. "Can't people connect the dots to money—merely getting us out of an economic depression?"

"But the almighty dollar is critical!" I laughed. "We move onto the Wright Brothers and their incredible invention of the airplane. All good until they make an unethical business decision with the war department to make a buck and then the exhibit goes from virtuous design to "*The airplane goes to war!*" *Weeeee!*""

We could hear George and Bryan laughing outside at the barbeque, and George called to us, "Dinner is ready!"

"Smells great, we're coming!" responded Charlotte.

As we moved towards the bistro area for dinner, I mentioned, "Oh, and the last night in D.C. we stayed at a ritzy hotel near Reagan National airport and were sleeping with the enemy!"

"Sleeping with the enemy?" Charlotte gave me a quizzical look.

"There was a picture of the Pentagon on the wall of our hotel room, creepy!" I laughed. "Nothing like shoving a not-so-subtle reminder of our nation's unhealthy obsession with nuclear weapons and war in our faces the last night of our trip! The freaking Death Star itself on the wall, I was half expecting Darth Vader to knock on our door."

"All in the name of '*national security*,' George mocked in the background. We all laughed at the political absurdness, what else could we do? "Scary knowing that evil empire in Star Wars is so metaphorically America."

"Yikes, I wouldn't have slept all night with a picture of what amounts to a potential Illuminati headquarters staring back at me!" Charlotte commented. "As an Ecology expert I can tell you the Pentagon's actions are directly linked to Earth being destroyed, increased fires, and our air and water getting polluted."

"I didn't let it ruin my last night of such a fabulous trip. I only laughed about it, the stark reminder of how my cherished Silicon Valley is too married to the Pentagon, putting dangerous weapons into minds and hands as bad as the NRA." All guilty of putting toxic profit before the people.

The evening was full of laughter and good cheer. No more talk about world politics or the federal government's incompetence. After dinner Bryan got us dancing for hours in my living room, with the city lights and bay sparkling outside the big windows. George worked the music with an eclectic mix of rock, jazz and traditional ballads from all over the globe.

As Charlotte and Bryan were leaving my cell phone pinged and I received a text from Anna, who was in Hawaii with her husband and grandson. I read the text:

Just letting u know, Jules is OK. She's not suicidal, just stressed. More good news-her brother is off the hook!

A sense of relief floated with me as I got ready for bed. Julie's red-hot temper matched her red-hot lips and hair. Her stress got away from her, but she'll survive.

Julie, a never married, childless woman holding on tightly to her dad's legacy of building warships for all that '*liberty and freedom*,'—now caught in the web of a culture of politics, technology and the corrupt legal system. I wondered if through her brother's ordeal she is appreciating a different perspective of life: Parenthood.

I wondered also how her brother's case got dropped and what it took to get off the hook.

I had my suspicion.

CHAPTER SEVENTEEN

Julie

"Jules, Jules, you're crushing my ribs, girl!"

I couldn't let go of my brother, afraid I'd lose him forever—this sweet man who went from trying to save the raccoons as a young boy to saving humanity from more train crashes, only to be accused of being a terrorist.

"Well look at you! There's nothing left of you. It wouldn't take much to break your bones!"

Making light of Jackson's stressful ordeal seemed to be working, as his laugh lines were put to the test—a wonderful sight I had no plan to smooth away.

We stood at the edge of my garden rooftop, with a clear view of Angel Island. Jackson became silent. The only thing escaping his lips were nervous laughs full of obvious relief. But something else hovered.

"So, I told you your buddy Steve stopped by here months ago, pissed at the injustice—said he'd get a team together to fight for you. Looks like it worked! I signed the petition, by the way. Is that what got you off the hook? I read that over one-hundred thousand people signed it."

Jackson pulled two wine glasses from my new cabinet. Ignoring my statement about the petition, he remarked, "Nice wine rack, looks like solid cherry wood!" As his fingers grazed the natural finish I noticed his hands shaking. He then stood rigidly and jiggled the contents of his pants pockets.

As much as I loved my new wine rack, it wasn't important. My baby brother was free yet fidgety. "Jackson?"

He looked into my eyes, and I saw emotions I've never seen in him. Anger. Fear. Doubt.

"Jack…you're free, you're okay. What's up? You didn't answer my question. Did the petition get you off?" I wanted to hug him again but had already nearly crushed his fragile spirit.

"The petition helped. If anything, it made a statement." He sat down on my patio recliner chair, squirming to get comfortable. He adjusted and readjusted the cushion under his butt. His eyes closed, and he rubbed his temples.

"But it's not what set you free?" I had a sick feeling in the pit of my stomach thinking of the million-dollar bail statement Steve had mentioned. "What *did* it take?"

Another nervous laugh escaped Jack's throat. He tensed and threw a searching glance into the mist of the evening darkness. What was he looking for? His dignity? *Those fucking bastards look what they've done to my baby brother.*

"Oh, the same thing that makes the world go around—or is the root of all evil depending on one's perspective." Jackson took a sip of wine and smiled. Only, it was a forced, unhappy smile. His lips pressed together with squinted eyes.

I thought about college tuition for his kids and tried to push my own resentment aside to offer support. He needed my love, not bitterness. Then I remembered the Change.org petition Steve started as a fundraiser. "Jackson…how much came out of your own pocket?" I braced for the answer.

Jackson held the wine glass to the soft beam of light radiating from my apartment and pushed the recliner back further. His silhouette was suspended in darkness and I could not make out the expression on his face as he looked across the bay.

I could feel him trying to reestablish the simple childhood love and joy that connected us. As if to buy a moment, he took another sip of wine. We sipped together in a silence broken only by the sound of crickets. I waited.

Finally, Jackson answered. "Just 100K."

"*Just?* That's a tenth of a million dollars!" I felt my hackles rise and for a split-second almost smashed my wine glass against the brick wall.

"Jules, it is what it is. Would you rather me rot in a cell for no reason? My friends raised a lot of cash to get me out. It's water under the bridge—I really don't want to talk about it." He got up, grabbed the bottle of wine and with trembling hands poured himself another glass. I wondered about Jackson's drinking—but now was hardly the time to broach the topic.

"Now I feel guilty for my small contribution." I sulked.

Jackson looked at me with a fierce tenderness. "You give the best support anyone can, Jules—sisterly love."

I liked this answer. It gave me a warm and fuzzy feeling. My brother is the deepest soul mate I've ever had, other than Feisty.

Feisty. My parakeet was not only able to mimic what humans said, he could decipher what was said and decode meaning. My beloved social animal got himself killed for saying too much.

A sudden flashback to the words of Agent Flock with the Glock as she stood exactly where we stood now, "*Shortly after a suspected terrorist attack in New York City, your brother was seen taking photos at the Times Square subway station. He was arrested for not cooperating with the police.*"

The warm and fuzzy feeling disappeared. "Is your job still secure? I asked, feeling disconcerted.

"Yes, but not the five billion budgeted for the first phase of the high-speed-rail project I spearheaded. It got dropped. There are some powerful people killing public transit projects—"

"Caryssa claims the Lock Family has people canvassing neighborhoods," I interrupted. "Political activists for those oil tycoons trying to stop high-speed-rail progress."

Jackson leaned toward me with a furrowed brow. "Actually, we've discussed this in meetings. It's happening. People *are* going door-to-door saying to voters, '*do you want to stop higher sales taxes?*' Then saying, '*can we count on you to vote no on public transit plans?*'

"But…*really?* I had wondered if it's another of Caryssa's conspiracy theories—she even thinks big dark money came after you in the subway." A creepy sensation ran down my spine.

The creepy sensation only intensified after Jackson said, "I actually *believe* the Lock family is behind this, as my proposed project ran counter to their promotion of pipelines."

Trying to act brave, I insisted, "If anyone came to my place saying this shit, I'd slam the door!" I was defending my brother's livelihood more than the ideology.

Jackson sucked down the last drop of his wine, throwing his head back. "Let's go inside, I'm cold, it feels chilly."

I followed him back down the loft ladder into my studio apartment, shutting the latch behind me. The fog was rolling in, but not enough to make me feel cold. I worried about his strange symptoms.

Jackson was staring at me, or past me. I followed his absent-minded gaze to my corner desk where a twelve-inch Liberty ship model was proudly displayed. He slowly proclaimed, in a near whisper, "Dad hand-built that model. He was likely as excited about making this tiny replica as the real cargo ship."

"I remember watching him create it, with his dental technician friend that helped him. It wasn't all that long ago in the scheme of things…what, the late 90's? He sculpted in from wax and cast it in metal." My mind floated back to my father scratch-building the model with no use of any kit. He was not only a skilled ship-builder but a master modeler.

Jackson stepped closer to the casting and peered in. There, with a light rust appearance for realism, stood a small model of the SS William A. Richardson, the first Liberty ship our dad helped build. It sat on an authentic mahogany wooden base, an accurate replica of the original ship.

"Dad had quite the sense of humor," I mentioned. Rather than label his model with the ships actual name, he had tagged his little toy, '*Ugly Duckling One, Marinship.*'

"He always made us laugh." Jackson opened the latch to the display case box, and a newspaper clipping fell to the floor. I looked down at the yellowed paper dated October 16, 1942. An edge tear on the front page made it difficult to read: '*Twenty-thousand people flock to Sausalito to witness the first Liberty ship launched at Marinship.*'

Stooping to pick up the paper, Jackson said, "So interesting seeing all this unravel in the news long before either of us were born." He turned the sticky yellowed front page and pointed to a photo. "Good looking dude!"

A photo of our handsome father stared back at us, with a headline: "Thomas Taylor—engineer, built ships for the War Effort."

"You look just like him." I gently kissed Jackson on the cheek.

Jackson shoved the paper back into the case, almost forcefully. "He must be rolling around in his grave," he declared in a snappy tone of voice. "I remember overhearing him tell mom his only regret was how he made money, especially going into the '*defense*' industry after the war."

I was taken aback and couldn't respond. Jackson seemed to recognize my shock, and he added, "I mean…really? We need to invest in infrastructure, not our war economy! My means of supporting my family is being squashed due to this—this negative historic buildup."

"Well don't take it out on dad's livelihood!" I didn't want to argue with him, he'd been through enough. But I'd heard enough. "If it weren't for his high salary, we never would have enjoyed our childhood living in the Sausalito Hills, vacations in Carmel and Shell Beach—"

"It's not dad I'm mad at. It's…it's…all connected, Jules!"

"What's connected?"

Jackson ran a hand through his hair, then raised both arms and shrugged, "I don't know. Everything, I guess. Me being accused of being a terrorist, your bird being murdered, even Anna's art gallery robbery and murder scene. And those freaking stinking bloody doves!" He spun in a circle as if to take in my apartment.

Then he stared at me. "Don't you get it? Can't you see this? Jules...they came looking for me *here*."

Shaking my head in denial, I headed to the kitchenette to open a second bottle of wine. He spread out both hands against me as if to stop me. "Jules...Jules, somebody killed Feisty—angry after not finding me here. It's my fault—"

"It's *not* your fault, nothing's your fault! Don't even say that!" Bewildered with this mysterious outside force tainting my loving family bonds, I hurled the corkscrew into the sink hard, causing a loud crashing sound. Jackson jumped, overly startled.

A string of mental images flashed before me: The FBI terrorist task force appearing at my place, Fiesty's blood on the cobblestones, Anna's description of the symbolic messages left behind with the doves. My eyes darted from my dad's model Liberty ship back to Jackson. I caught a reflection of my bright red hair in the mirror and made a mental note to get to the hairdresser to tone it down a bit.

Jackson continued, '*Liberty.*' The word is the first victim of war fought in its name! Now Washington continues to claim the need to export all that liberty."

Then the words written on Anna's Picasso painting, by the daughter of a rogue CIA Agent slapped me in the face. "*I stand for life against death. I stand for peace against war.*"

As if reading my mind, Jackson said, "Think, Jules! What was the message that girl who killed her doves tried to convey? Seriously, what is terrorism? War is terrorism on a bigger budget!"

Now my hands trembled as much as Jackson's as I frantically twisted the corkscrew. I turned to him and repeated; "*bloody teardrops left under the dove's eyes symbolize being blinded by an elusive enemy. Three blood drops left on the breasts symbolize a removal of our society's heart.*"

It was like a light bulb turned on. I frowned when recognition dawned. Jackson is right. It's all interconnected—to billionaire industrialist.

For money.

Chapter Eighteen

Anna

"She's not here, ma chérie. Nobody's here!" A calm but alarming intensity in Pierre's voice over the phone made me sit up straight and pay attention.

My chest tightened, and a vague sense of unease seeped through me, winding its way into the thick rivers of emotions that clogged my senses. "But what about Paula?"

"I told her to go home, Anna. She can't stay in Tahoe forever—the girl has to work. She has her own life—"

"I'm not suggesting she had to stay at our cabin, just...just wonder if she's okay."

"If who's okay, Ava or Paula?"

"Both of them!"

"Paula is more than fine, she's at my classroom now. She said she and Ava had a nice time, and I see the clay sculptures they created together drying. Ava seemed to like horse sculptures. I'll bring them back to my class for bisque firing."

I smiled. How nice to have brought normalcy through art to Ava's crazy world. The happy thought vanished as soon as it came. "Pierre, what if they tracked her to our cabin through her cell phone? We could jeopardize ourselves—and Jared."

"There's no sign of any struggle. The place is cleaner than we left it. Looks like she simply decided to pack up and leave. The only thing remaining of her presence is a lingering scent of perfume—smells like Caron's *Poirre*. Don't worry about her, ma chérie."

The mention of the perfume reminded me of the night my art gallery was robbed, and my security guard murdered, since that perfume lingered in the air afterward. "She could be dead somewhere. What if they dragged her back to that mind control lab?"

"Anna, it's not our job to look after this troubled girl—"

"But you think I failed at looking after our own girls!" I chocked down the words.

"Please don't start. Our girls were not troubled and have nothing to do with Ava. You need to let go. Don't let her crazy world ruin ours."

Were our girls not troubled? One stormed angrily out of our loft, took her skateboard on a winding street in the pouring rain and got killed; the other committed suicide. I took a deep breath and changed the topic. "I miss you, when are you coming back?"

"I'm heading home now but will hit traffic. Anna, there's something else here."

"Oh no, not another dead dove?"

"No, a painting."

"I know my replica of Picasso's *Guernica* is there. I packed it during our last trip to Tahoe, remember? How could we miss it, it's huge and you complained about it fitting in our car, so I had to roll it up. I was concerned it would damage the painting, especially since it's only half done."

"But it's been removed from the cabin basement, mounted onto a stretcher and placed leaning against the desk where the sculptures are as if Ava created a mini-art gallery." Pierre hesitated, and I could tell there was more to it.

A mini-art gallery. Now the fateful night at my art gallery was coming even more alive in my mind. I cringed at her mounting my painting, did she ruin another of my art pieces? "Please don't tell me she attacked it with scissors or something."

"No, but there's writing on the back—lots of writing."

I braced for the message the girl wrote this time. "Let me guess, another anti-war message that matches Picasso's original intent of the painting?"

"Hmmm…looks like the decrypted text of Kryptos, with a clue for the fourth yet unsolved message."

Kryptos. There it is again. An art sculpture located at CIA headquarters at Langley, Virginia. Installed in 1990 by artist James Sanborn with four encrypted messages, of which three have been solved. The fourth is said to be impossible to decipher.

"Holy Christ, she said she was going to solve it. Imagine if she's ballsy enough to be on her way to Langley?"

"The least unsafe place for her to be—"

"I'm not serious, that's not where she'd go. Read the first message please."

"Over the phone? You don't want to come and see for yourself? A couple of them are somewhat long.…" Pierre's voice trailed off as if he was moving away from his cell phone, turning the painting over. "And it's all mumbo jumbo.…"

"At least read the first deciphered code."

"Okay, here goes—they are all marked with 'K's'. I think it stands for key:

K1: Between subtle shading and the absence of light lies the nuance of iqlusion.

"Iqlusion. It's not a word—"

"I know…it's all coming back now. I studied this sculpture in an art class. The artist, Jim Sanborn, purposefully misspells words and if I remember correctly, some words are backward."

"We can easily say the word is 'illusion,'" I insisted.

"Oh, it is. It's known worldwide that's what he meant. Anna, don't worry, your painting is fine, although it's totally covered with writing on the back."

"*Totally?* My painting is the same size as Picasso's original! It's eleven-feet-tall and twenty-five-feet wide!" I bellowed.

"And as I mentioned the Kryptos four encrypted messages get a bit long, plus she wrote the messages kind of big."

"Oh no, in a black marker like before?"

"No, she compromised this time and used one of my charcoal art pencils I had supplied for their session. Look hon, I want to take off and head home. I'm tired."

"Read the second Krypto message before leaving please!"

"Come on, Je t'aime, ma chérie *Just google it*! Ava wrote the same words the artist did. "

"Okay, but…but at least tell me the clue she left about the fourth message."

"Oh, you're a beautiful pain in the ass. You have no patience. It's complicated. She wrote *K4: Only words known are 'Berlin Clock.'* Then below that clue, she wrote *"Time itself is circular, not linear. So, all the world keeps repeating misdeeds."* Then her third line is, *"By 1987, 6 million people died because of CIA covert ops. Dark and light; Shadows and secrets.* The last line of her personal clue simply reads, *"American Holocaust."*

"Wow…deep and creepy! Ava told me she thinks Kryptos resembles the CIA's grand illusion to the people about America's true history or timeline. Well—drive safe and see you in a few hours."

After hanging up, I sat immobilized thinking about Picasso's *Guernica* painting. Its been over a decade since I attempted replicating the original with oil on canvas. I simply could not paint death and destruction after losing my daughters. The details of the painting were now as fuzzy as the obscured painting itself.

The first thing I keyed into the search engine was *Guernica*. There, staring back at me, was the mural-sized masterpièce Picasso had painted in 1937, displayed at the Paris World Fair.

It struck me as admirable Picasso was brave enough to display this piece—*this antiwar icon*—at an art fair with a theme of modern technology. It stood alone, challenging the notion of war as "heroic." The painting was deemed too risky to use as a backdrop for President Bush as he raged against Iraq.... Or perhaps too moral.

Why did Ava choose this painting to display the Kryptos messages ?

The overtly political painting, as confusing and dark as the Kryptos sculpture and encrypted messages itself, speaks volumes of the inhumane brutality of war. Was she trying to show a potential fascism in America ?

Chills ran down my spine as I looked at the painting. It was hard to distinguish the scattered figures but I recognized the ones I had already painted myself: A woman, head back and screaming in anguish while holding her lifeless child. Death and dying in chaotic images throughout. In the center, a dying horse with a sword sticking through his mouth. Perhaps most telling is the soldier, looking frightened rather than the brave facade put on by too many art pieces.

I googled Kryptos sculpture solutions, and read the second encrypted message :

K2: It was totally invisible Hows that possible? They used the Earths magnetic field X

The information was gathered and transmitted undergruund to an unknown location X

Does Langley know about this? They should Its buried out there somewhere X

Who knows the exact location? Only WW This was his last message X

Thirty eight degrees fifty seven minutes six point five seconds north

Seventy seven degrees eight minutes forty four seconds west ID by rows

Wow, Pierre wasn't kidding about the spelling and punctuation mistakes intended to add mystery or ambiguity. 'WW " must mean William Webster, an active member of America's shadow government. I scrolled to the third message :

K3: Slowly, desperately slowly, the remains of passage debris that encumbered the lower part of the doorway was removed. With trembling hands I made a tiny breach in the upper left hand corner and then widening the hole a little I inserted the candle and peered in. The hot air escaping from the chamber caused the flame to flicker but presently details of the room within emerged from the mist x can you see anything q?

This one refers to the opening of King Tut's Tomb. But the theory of secret chambers within its walls has been scientifically debunked. My next thought is a metaphorical reference to the elusive Vatican secret archives, of which scientist are now trying to decipher through artificial intelligence.

And then maybe...*just maybe*...it's allegorical to the secret post-apocalyptic bunkers built throughout our nation laying await as a hideaway in the event of a nuclear armageddon those fleeing to them would have caused.

Ava claims she can solve section four of the mysterious art sculpture on the grounds of her father's work headquarters. I wonder if her deeper desire is to get away.

I know that Sanborn designed Kryptos in 1989; the year the Berlin Wall began to come down. But what does this have to do with the Berlin Clock? It's all as secret as the agency itself. The Berlin clock tells time through a complex scheme—Illuminated light. I also recall an art professor mentioning another agency involved in solving the first three messages: The NSA. *As if they can be trusted?* Now, we have certain American leaders that want to build our own suppressive wall...

Where's Ava? I wondered if she was dead or alive.

CHAPTER NINETEEN

Ava

I learned from my father. CIA spies are famous for moving freely throughout Europe on fake passports. But I'm not going to Europe. There's too many of my dad's pack of wolves to pick up my scent there.

I found it ironic while shuffling through SFO that I was as nervous about my Hispanic looks being questioned by immigration officials as the counterfeit document I clutched in my hand.

We stepped up to the security checkpoint podium. *Maybe I'll need to do something else to throw them off—fake a suicide or accident, or—?*

"Ticket and I.D. please." The burly uniformed guy glared at me over his eyeglasses. He wore the typical bright blue latex gloves ready for over-eager pat-downs. My real ID's were stuffed into my socks. I handed him my phony passport and airline ticket.

Shit!

I rallied a smile to distract him from any hint I wasn't who the documentation claimed. Out of nerves, I rambled, "I'm a U.S. citizen." *Why am I saying this as if I'm an illegal alien fleeing my own country?*

My words were met with silence—too much silence as he repetitively stared at my passport, then back at me. Finally, he asked, "Any relation to

Jerry García? I like the Grateful Dead," without much personality or human touch.

Act normal. Look normal. Radiate confidence and wit. "No, but I was thinking of taking up the guitar and bringing him back from the dead," I said, an attempt to humor him.

Instead, it made him seem colder. "Wait here, your microchip isn't passing the scan."

Double shit!

My boyfriend Chris, whom I both love and loath for his calm demeanor that could sleep through a bomb, wrapped his arms around me. "Don't worry girl, everything will work out."

"Easy for *you* to say, you have a legit passport," I whispered back.

The security dude returned, "excuse me Ms. García, has your passport gotten wet, been left out in the rain or anything?"

Lucky me! I sweetened my smile. "Oh, yes," I lied, the rainstorm yesterday came unannounced and I had left it outside in my open jacket pocket."

The security man nodded, studied my credentials again, then to my relief said, "Go ahead Ms. García—but be sure to get your RFID chip reactivated before your next trip outside our borders."

I raised my chin, almost skipping like a happy child while pushing my bags through the x-ray machine. Luckily, with so many people passing through the airport, no one seemed to be paying attention.

I turned just on time to see Chris being subjected to what looked like a karate chop to his crotch, and I cringed. *What the fuck?*

After we gathered our belongings I asked, "what was *that* all about?"

"Oh, they found a Chapstick in my pocket during the full-body scan."

"Chapstick. Of course, always worth a ball-busting pat down—never know what one can do with lip shit."

A chuckle escaped his lips, "Well babe, let's get to our gate. Look, they didn't even stamp my passport." Chris pondered.

I rolled my eyes at his naïve remark. "They don't stamp it until we enter Costa Rica. Mine's not stamped either."

I looked at the passport I held in my trembling hands and for the first time realized that running scared with a false document can be more daunting than staying still. The name glared back at me as if to say, 'this is who you are now, don't fuck up.' *Jamie García.*

I like it, especially after the reference to the singer-songwriter with the free spirit. I imagined turning my new identity into a conversation piece with all the new Costa Ricans I'll meet.

As we moved toward the jet bridge to board the airplane, an increasing excitement and sense of relief began to overshadow my fear. *I made it through security*!

Just before the airplane entrance, there was a split second of trepidation upon seeing two Latino millennials arriving at SFO being questioned and asked for IDs. The men interrogating them had three letters emblazoned on their dark jackets; ICE.

I nearly laughed hoping they would question me. I'd say, "*I'm fleeing North America for a better life, Goodbye, Good riddance!*"

Our seats were in the last row in the back of the plane, where the engine makes the most noise. Even while boarding, the auxiliary power unit hummed so loudly my own ears vibrated with it. Perfect. Nobody will hear us talking.

"How'd you get the fake passport?" Chris asked. "Online?"

"Heck no, I wouldn't trust anything on the Internet. I have connections."

"Connections?"

Shaking my head while tossing an incredulous look his way, I said, "*Come on*, Chris! I'm the daughter of a CIA agent." The plane was not yet full, with nobody anywhere close enough to overhear. This didn't stop us from whispering the entire conversation that ensued.

"Your dad…A CIA dude who tried to kill you for knowing too much —who killed two men then blamed and framed you and your friend Paige. You are running from him, he certainly didn't help you—"

"No, but his brother has always cared about me—"

"*Of course!* Your Uncle Rob. I should have known since he helped us break free from those scary dudes to begin with," Chris recognized, eyes wide while pressing his hands against my shoulders.

"Who else but my Uncle Rob working corporate espionage would know how to create an identity through thin air?" I laughed, realizing this just might work to keep me alive.

"Shhh…" Chris raised an index finger over his mouth while pointing to people putting bags into the overhead bins.

I heard each engine starting and the ignition fire up to a roar, so I was not concerned. I said, quietly, "Scary thinking what they'd do my Uncle if they found out he helped me get away."

"Especially the tough guy with the weird tattoo looking like an all-seeing eye, the one drugging us trying to get us to join their underground operations…whatjamacallhim, Bob, Bret or whatever his name is."

"That's Bret Solomon. He's known my dad for years, a former army buddy who now works for a trans-national defense contractor. And his partner-in-crime, he's Bob something, big last name but acts like he has no balls."

"Seems to have enough balls to me, he nearly crushed me trying to get me strapped to that table—"

"His freaking badge is bigger than his balls! The guy's an idiot works for Homeland Security recruiting his army of brainwashed youth."

"*Homeland Security?* But they protect our nation from—"

"Illusionary enemies made up by the CIA. Why do you think they're after me? I've overheard too much through the years from my dad, who was typically few on words but would get so drunk he let secrets slip out."

"But lots of people expose their secrets, conspiracy theories on the Internet—"

"'*Conspiracy theories?*'. That term itself was invented by the CIA to cover up their atrocities, to discredit reality. Homeland Security has good, bad and ugly, and this dude is ugly."

"Well, let' forget all this, we are going to Costa Rica, a pristine land lucky enough to have abolished its army sixty-five years ago. No military predators will chase us there."

"They've had a President wise enough to break down their own wall with a mallet, symbolizing an end to their military spirit. Too bad U.S. is going in the opposite direction—"

Chris tapped my arm and pointed to the aisle. A flight attendant was walking toward us, looking me straight in the eye. "Excuse me, are you Jamie García?"

I tried for a resting calm face, "Yes."

"There's a gentleman on board to see you, says it's urgent. Please follow me toward the cockpit."

My hand went automatically to the fatty tissue between my shoulder and elbow, covering the bandage. Chris whispered, "you had it removed, didn't you?"

"Yes," I whispered while the flight attendant made her way toward the front of the plane. "My doctor cut it out from my arm." We were referring to a tracking device involuntarily implanted just under-the-skin while we were guinea pigs for drug experiments conducted by my dad and his cronies to lure us into military madness.

"I have to go," I announced as I stood and headed down the aisle.

"I'm coming with you," Chris insisted. I was about to advise him to stay but he was hot on my heels, so close I felt his body heat against my back. My palms sweated and my heart beat faster as I made my way towards the front of the airplane, only grateful all the passengers were now seated so I wasn't also fighting against a flow of people.

One man stepped outside of his seat to put something into the overhead bin, then apologized to let me through. "Oh, no problem finish what you are doing," I said, only happy to delay any confrontation. Chris pressed against me, laying his hands on my shoulders. My sense of dread deepened as I anticipated being dragged off the plane.

The airline hostess greeted me as I came just shy of the cockpit, wondering who I'd find. "Just outside the passenger boarding bridge, Ms. Garcia. Please be quick, we are about to taxi to the runway."

Before I even turned toward the airplane entrance, I heard Chris say, "Hello Mr. Ramírez."

Bracing myself, I took a deep breath and turned, expecting to see my father. It would not surprise me if he had a gun pointed to my heart.

The eyes I met were indeed my father's. But the smile and look of kindness were not. I let out a sigh of contentment as I ran into his arms, hugging him. "Uncle Rob!"

"Goodness gracious niece are you crying?" My uncle placed a hand under my chin, softly lifting my face to his. A single tear squeezed out of my wild eyes, as I explained, "I thought you'd be—"

"Shhh…I know, and I'm not. I wanted to see you off safely, my beautiful niece. And Ava, I warn you, don't come back."

* * *

It won't be difficult to never return even though I love beautiful California. I hadn't been able to relax for years—since my father was sucked into the violent stream of the intelligence system.

The magical rainforest of Costa Rica changed that. I no longer have the constant ticker tape of thoughts charging through my head. I live and breathe by the wind, the waves and the wild things.

The wild things. I look around our tiny treehouse, a jungle haven set deep outside the small town of Cahuita on the Caribbean side. It's constructed around a massive tree within a thick tropical forest, suspended in nylon straps tied around the branches. A mosquito net is the only thing separating our bed from the tree itself.

The sounds of birds, frogs, monkeys, sloths, and other creature's burst in the misty darkness, drowning out the sounds of our lovemaking. *Our very drunk lovemaking.*

Something is missing within me making me sad. Chris said he desired me for many months, from the moment he laid eyes on me when I played a role in our escape from madness. I never gave myself to him—I could never let go.

The first time I make love to the man I'm falling in love with, I'm so smashed there are only hazy flashbacks of the intimacy we shared. We had stumbled back from the reggae bar last night, nearly falling off the rickety wooden ladder as we climbed up to our hideout—our exotic escape from the world and fell into bed in a mass of limbs and loud noises. Were the noises I remember ours? Or the critters in the tree?

This place is spicy. Sexy. The people we met at the bar so present, living in the moment. All night the words, *"pura vida,"* for pure life or *"con mucho gusto,"* which means with pleasure, infused the atmosphere. I was at ease. For the first time in my life, I felt something I never had. *Gratitude.*

Nobody is in a rush here—except me. Today I am in a rush to get out into the lush forest with my boyfriend and to get my hands on him again —with a clearheaded intention this time. I've been emotionally and physically numbed too long.

I look out the window and see Chris walking around the base of our treehouse. White, sandy beaches stretch ahead, the surrounding scenery— beautiful. It's sheer bliss. I feel alive, awake and want adventure. I want to climb those mountains, feel the rainforest against my skin, do crazy stuff like have sex in the great outdoors. I slip my panties off for good measure, figuring my sundress is enough for what I have planned.

After grabbing my cell phone and a light jacket, I float down the ladder and call out to Chris, "Let's go take a walk through the forest!"

"I thought we'd planned a beach day? Or zip-lining?" Chris is swiping his finger across his phone viewing photos. "Check these out!"

He has captured a sanctuary of waterfalls, flowers, amazing creatures, views and even what looked like a vulture. "Wow, that frog, it's bright red and blue!" I squealed.

"There's lots of interesting animals out there."

"Let's go find more!" I urged, racing into the thicket, mysteriously thrilling and alluring. The wilderness called, unraveling the passion within me. I was the queen of the wild things, beneath my sundress I was becoming as moist as the rainforest surrounding me.

I sense Chris behind me on the forest path, a mammal after his prey—a welcome thought to my repressed sexual desires. Deeper and deeper into the lush tropical tangle of green upon greens we move, trying to run as we trip over tree trunks. Gigantic ferns and mist-filled mountains swallow us into the jungle.

We stop, my eyes on Chris's as he gently presses me against a huge tree, the bark spongy from the rains. He removes his hat, and I untie the jacket from around my waist, sweat pouring off my brow from our jaunt through the steamy forest. Chris drops both garments carelessly to the ground.

He kisses my eyelids, then my lips. The kiss continues onto my neck, my breast, down, down—desperate, achingly hungry. As his hands find their way under my dress, a loud groan escapes his lips, "Mmmm…I hope the lack of underwear is for my benefit, and not our furry friends." Chris points behind me.

I turn and see dozens of white-faced monkeys peering at us, mocking us from their perch in the trees while rubbing plants all over themselves. A river rages just beyond, adding to the primal energy—drowning me in ecstasy.

Then another pair of eyes are watching, big, black and haunting. A large Margay cat lounges in a tree so nonchalantly it appears to have melted down a branch. The mix of danger and eroticism increases my arousal.

Not another human soul was within sight, but all around us, sounds of the wild blended with our moans, groans, and panting—echoing through the badlands. It was as if the animals were saying, "*We're here, welcome to our jungle and thanks for the show.*"

Rather than the wild animals intimidating me, they become a turn-on. My screams are as loud as the howler monkeys and toucans. There was a rustling of leaves and little critters scattering in every direction. Eerie insect sounds added to the overwhelming magnetism—my carnal senses height-

ened to each one, *A cricket? A moth? A grasshopper and Cicada?* The forest
and its inhabitants joins our rhythm.

Chris whips his t-shirt off and I admired his tall, wiry physique. No
bulging biceps or popping pectorals. "You're beautiful," I whispered breath-
lessly into his ear.

"That's my line!"

While back in the states, I'd been more concerned with survival than
accepting his compliments of my "curvaceous Latina body."

A strange confidence suffuses me, running through my veins, pulsing
my groin. I was a jungle beast, hungry for flesh. I felt empowered—domi-
nate and desirable. There was a small clearing on the ground and I kick
my soft jacket there to cushion Chris's back.

After removing Chris's boxers in one quick pull, I grab his manhood
and pump it a few times before pushing him to the ground. We roll
around panting, and he kisses me in places I've never been kissed, a praying mantis munching on its prey. Our tongues and groins become linked
until I can't take it anymore.

Mounting him, I slide his penis inside me and take control. "What if a
poisonous snake joins us?" he gasps while groaning with pleasure.

"Be a brave boy! We are doing it with the bugs and beasts." I ride him
like a horse starting off slow, then alternating between a sultry grind and
high-speed bounce. My braless breasts escape from my dress, flapping in
the breeze with each rise and fall. He calls my name over and over, and I
call his.

"You're the best, Ava!"

"Jamie! Remember, I'm Jamie!"

"Fuck! Who will hear us, the animal kingdom?"

"Oh…Chris, *you're* my animal!"

In my ecstasy, I hadn't even noticed when he lifted me, with surprising
gentleness shifting my weight back against the tree. I again become a tree
nymph animating nature. Swatting a swarm of mosquitos away, I was relieved we both applied repellant.

My legs wrap around Chris's waist, and I loop my arms around his shoulders as he thrust into me again, powerful and forceful, pushing me into the tree. My body writhes and meets his with thrusts of my own. I didn't want him to stop, and I didn't care anymore about anything I left behind, the power over me released.

My fingers claw at him, pulling him deeper into me. Small growls escape between my gasps and our orgasms rocket through us—escalating through the jungle. Shudders wrack my body as I'm liberated—from oppression, from near death, from a life of capture by a beast more dangerous than any in this forest.

A contented sigh escapes my lungs. I give his neck a lick and a kiss, "Damn, I can't get enough of you."

Guttural laughter vibrates through him, "Yes and I can't get enough of you either," he admits before thrusting his still erect penis inside me again.

We take our time now, kissing and stroking each other. I run my hands through his hair giving it a gentle tug before slanting my mouth over his. Our lips and tongues prod and plunge, mimicking the languid movement of our bodies.

Finally, I unwrap my legs and unsteadily stand up, the tree behind me supporting my shaky limbs. And that's when I hear it, the sound at once soothing and familiar—like someone blows across the mouth of an empty bottle. A low cooing.

My eyes follow the sound, and I see the noticeable white flash of the tail along the edge of the trail. And there, perched on a low branch is a white-tipped dove.

And I know I am home.

CHAPTER TWENTY

Caryssa

The angel that tapped my head when Tyler was a small child stopped appearing. Was it because he thought I no longer needed him? Perhaps my imaginary friend was my child's Guardian Angel—and he's flown off to watch over the next little kid?

While sitting in bed sipping coffee, I pondered my spirituality. A glance above my headboard brought my eyes to the small wooden crucifix I bought in the cathedral gift shop fifteen years ago when George and I attended mass at Notre Dame in Paris.

Paris, where we conceived our only child. After praying three years for a miracle, I had come back from Europe pregnant and passionate about world peace—which led to questioning the church and bowing to Buddha in a meditative Yoga pose.

A simple set of wooden rosary beads adorned the crucifix, making a decorative wall hanging. The rosary beads came from the Catholic church where Tyler made his First Holy Communion eight years ago. It dawned on me that was the time when I envisioned an angel tapping me and thought it may have been to guide my only child into becoming a good little Christian.

Climbing out of bed, I stretched and got dressed into dark gray comfy pants paired with an oversized sweatshirt and scarf. I intermittently glanced at my wall cross while applying makeup.

Tears welled as I gently touched the beads that once served as my meditation and prayer, whispering, "Dear Lord, I've not lost faith in you. I've lost faith in religion, in the Roman Catholic Church—the sinful secrets of Vatican City. It's become like God's bankers, an international business; sins for money."

The tears fell. I couldn't figure out if I was crying for my reverence or the nostalgic remembrance of Tyler attending religious education which got us to church every Sunday as I did throughout my childhood. Maybe all the above or none of it.

Opening my bedside drawer, I grabbed the Bible I used for the Bible study I did before we went to Paris. I hadn't touched it since recognizing the violent passages in Tyler's "Brick Testament" Lego's book he had picked out himself at age eight, which repulsed me—*how could they put such violent text in a children's book?*

I opened my Bible now. What I saw made me smile. It was one of the "Weekending" passages added between scripture:

REFLECT

The hard thing to understand is that faith is the one area in our lives where growing up means we must grow to be more like a child, trusting simply in goodness and complete knowledge of a higher power who has our best interests at heart

-Colleen Townsend Evans

I realized it wasn't my spirituality I questioned, but... *Christianity?* Does that higher power have to be the God any man-made religion *claims* he is—or the God in our own hearts?

Still focused on my crucifix I continued, "I don't go to church every Sunday because I believe you are within every being. You are everywhere, in a blooming flower, the sound of my son's laughter, at the peak of a mountaintop. Tell me, Lord, is not the antagonistic 'us vs them' thing a sin itself: creator vs creature, Catholicism vs Yoga, nation vs nation, even man vs woman?"

"*Who* are you talking to, mom?"

The sound of Tyler's voice broke my gabbing to God as I turned in embarrassment to my son. "I'm talking to my cross." I suddenly felt silly and uncomfortable talking to Jesus in front of my child.

"*O-kay*...well, have fun talking to the wall. I'm off to see friends."

With that, his mocking words left with him. I had a flashback of Tyler at age six, telling me about the difference between an angel and a person, and for a second, my heart tugged at whether this crazy world already squashed *his* awe for goodness. No doubt, he and his friends will be glued to their laptops over the next few hours—headphones on, immersed in a violent virtual reality.

Which brought me to the next thing I felt compelled to talk to the wall about, "I fear, Lord, that technology has grown faster than spirituality—especially destructive technology claimed to "save the world." The God in my heart is not a vengeful God. So, when the Vatican or church claims things like, '*souls are being saved while millions die for God or the church,*' it turns me away from such violent faith toward one of collective consciousness."

My phone pinged, and I realized Anna was waiting for me down the hill at the Golden Gate Grind. She and Julie were meeting me for coffee.

Dashing out the door, I said one last thing to the air, the wall, to God or whoever was listening, "Forgive me, Lord if it seems I've turned away from you. It is world violence I have forsaken, not you."

* * *

Anna was sitting on a tall bistro chair outside of the café, under a bright orange umbrella. The moon was behind the Golden Gate Bridge

230 · T.L. MUMLEY

this morning, with calm, clear skies. It was one of those early afternoons we could see Alcatraz, the entire city, and the Farallon Islands.

Anna looked the same as she did a decade ago when we first met—a tall willowy figure, light chestnut hair with blond highlights, and big almond eyes set within flawless skin. The only thing showing her age was a couple wispy gray strands of hair at her temples.

She had ordered us each a cortado with decadent dark chocolate truffles. I could hear caffeinated chattering, spoons tapping and the whoosh of espresso machines as I glanced into the cozy, contemporary coffee shop.

She broke into a gushing explanation of a message she received as I approached the bistro, "I got another text from Ava!"

"What's with the excitement? Isn't she at your ski cabin—?"

"No! Wow, we haven't spoken in a while, let me fill you in. She disappeared from our cabin and we didn't know if she was dead or alive with her father and his war-business cronies after her. Her text simply says, 'I'm safe.'"

"Well, that's good to hear, where is she?"

Anna was looking at the screen, "She didn't say. I don't recognize the cell number and think she was likely supplied with a burner phone."

"A burner phone?"

Anna tucked her freshly applied lip-gloss into her purse, "A disposable kind nobody can trace. My guess is her uncle Rob helped her escape. I remember her telling me he's good to her."

"Wow, I hope that's true, I can rest peacefully knowing my amazingly supportive former boss is not as shady a character as I thought!"

Julie's voice was a distant murmur overlaid by the ambient hum of the coffee shop. As she neared, the high-pitch of her voice whistled like the wind. "Hello ladies, good day to be by the Bay!"

And there she was, with blood-red lips that spoke volumes for her high-energy and rebellious flaming red-hair flowing out from beneath the big sunbonnet that adorned her head.

It will be an interesting girl-time coffee date, I thought.

After she settled in and sipped her latte, Julie announced, "Good news! My brother Jackson is doing well. The FBI even gave an excuse—their version of an apology I guess, for the harrowing ordeal they put him though."

"The nightmare they put your *entire* family through," I added.

Julie nodded her head, "I'd say, and Agent Flock hasn't apologized to *me* about silencing my bird with a bullet. The bureau's fear and suspicion are cancerous! I'm just happy for my brother."

"How did they apologize?" asked Anna. "Over the phone?"

"No, they went to his house and said, 'We ask you to accept our deepest apologies on behalf of the FBI.' The kids heard it as well which gives them hope in the system."

A woman with a yappy white poodle, its fur pulled back into a hot-pink ponytail, came out of the coffee shop. Her face was adorned by three piercings and her hair shaved into a purple Mohawk. She stopped at our table and said, "Excuse me, I don't mean to sound like I'm eavesdropping, but did you say the FBI *apologized* for something?"

"Yes, for accusing my brother of being a terrorist," Julie answered without any hesitation.

The woman clicked her tongue and shook her head, walking away mumbling, "Well I'd never!"

"What the heck was that all about?" pondered Julie.

"Beats me…maybe we should tell her it's not the FBI we blame so much as dark money in politics." I responded.

"Yeah…the same dark money making the FBI go after my innocent baby brother and kill my beloved bird." Julie slumped deeper into the bistro chair, then covered her face with her hands.

Anna raised her eyebrows, continuing what we thought was a private conversation in the corner of a public café. "So… Agent Flock showed no remorse?"

Julie's mouth fell open, "Are you kidding me? That woman seems locked into her army days. She shoots to kill anything that moves or goes against her orders. It was two guys that had the human decency to say sorry, two 'gentle giants' as Amy called them."

A glance around The Golden Gate Grind reminded me why I've always loved this coffee shop, apart from the unbeatable view. The outdoor seating is on a spacious patio surrounded by lush gardens and a fire-pit. I could see into the shop through a glass window to the stone walls covered with work from local artists, the quirky furniture and charming burlap ceiling.

Realizing I had tuned out of the conversation, I focused back on what Julie was saying...

"...they admitted to mistakenly linking his fingerprint to one found near the scene of an actual supposed terrorist attack on the subway."

Anna held both Julie's hands in hers, "And their blunder led to your sweet brother being tossed into prison. I'm so sorry they put you through this. But it's—"

"All over," Julie finished. She glanced my way and smiled. "Caryssa, I'm sorry for being so defensive when you mentioned it's connected to our growing surveillance state war economy. I think you're right. I just...didn't want to believe my father's beloved career...I refused to see the connection to the weaponized plague killing our population today..."

She trailed off. "Shh," I whispered. Now it was me unlacing Julie's fingers and taking them into my hands. Squeezing them a bit too tightly, her knuckles went white. "You need not apologize about anything, and I'm so happy your family has this whole senseless drama behind them."

Anna had pulled her chestnut hair back into a messy bun, with wispy strands escaping. She brushed a tendril of hair away from her face. "I wonder...how did they screw up on a fingerprint when everything's so computerized and accurate?" she pondered.

Julie shrugged her shoulders, "Hell if I know, the digital fingerprint looked like some bad guy's, I guess."

A misty breeze came off the Bay, bringing with it the fragrance of coastal sage. It mixed well with our lattes and chocolate. The modish stereo setup cast jazz and classical through speakers hanging from awnings.

I appreciated the sky, one of those moments that take your breath away —brilliant red strands shooting out in a fan from one spot, and then orange comes up and the hills turn to dark cut-outs against it. The air smelled like a campfire, and I was reminded the smoke was not coming from the nearby fire-pit.

The digital revolution always roused my interest. "We've come to over-rely on big data with everything in life—none of it precise. My kid has been rendered to a data point with 'PowerSchool,' an online app with daily 'upgrades' to their grades. Half the time it's bogus information be-cause the teacher forgot to do data entry."

"That's frustrating," said Anna. "Although, maybe teachers don't have time to keep up with such crowded classrooms?"

"Either way, it's not all good for students or teachers. The human touch is disappearing, buried by technology," I declared. A young man maybe mid-twenties with a serious buzz-cut looked at me through weird eyes as if accusing me of suffering from technophobia.

I don't know how he heard me surrounded with so many electronics. He toggled between tapping onto his laptop and staring at his smart-phone. A Google Glass hung from the side of his head. I noticed him ad-justing the volume on his stylish gold-accented earbuds.

But there was something else in his strange eyes. Something I couldn't place. Pain? Depression? He somehow looked so alone surrounded by all his toys—an empty, haunting expression on his face.

We locked eyes for a moment and I saw into his heart or mind. A past joy or love of life lingered beneath the pain. I was about to turn away when he spoke.

"Hi," he simply said, his lips trembling.

My heart raced for this youth I've never met, his eyes seemingly plead-ing to me for acceptance. For whatever reason, there was a split second I wanted to hug him. *This is someone's son*, I thought. Instead, I responded in as emotionally detached a tone as he had initiated.

"Hello, there." I hoped I didn't sound cold or condescending. Should I say more?

Julie repeatedly looked from me to gadget guy. As if to come to my de-fense or switch the focus back to our girl-time coffee, she said loud enough for him to hear, "*Too much technology?*—you're a former Silicon Valley techy! Are you getting all Stone Age on us, Caryss?"

"Oh, *come on* Jules, I've seen your love of the proverbial paper calendar and yellow sticky. You're like Wilma Flintstone. You even have her red hair," I joked.

"And you're Betty Rubble!"

"I see," I said—not seeing at all. "No, she was a quiet brunette that followed others like a puppy. I'm nothing like her." I liked today's feistiness in Julie, a fun version of it I'd never seen.

Anna laughed and said, "Caryssa has a good point when she talks about the technologies of a Sci-Fi reality. I'm half expecting to see a robot barista come by to see if we'd like to refresh our lattes."

We glanced around as if R2-D2 or C3P0 would make an appearance. Julie piped in, "Well, robotic arms are moving cups around inside the coffee shop, lifting levers and brewing the perfect cup of java for people—"

"*Shit*—I hope my kid gets a chance to have this thing called a job to make some cash for college. The robots are taking over," I uttered with an uneasy feeling creeping over me. I noticed a cop standing off to the side with his arms crossed in front of him. His kind eyes defied his closed stance—eyes that seemed to watch for something to happen.

"Have you become anti-technology, Carys? Don't forget the industry enabled you to buy that house of yours in the hills—".

"*Anti-technology?* Jules, you make it sound like I think technology is an enemy. It's just the..." I had a brain freeze realizing I sound like I'm demonizing my beloved high-tech career. I helped make this a better world—connecting hospitals, people, hearts, *didn't I?* "It's technology as a weapon that concerns me." *Or how it isolates people*, I thought sneaking another glance at the guy lost in a virtual world.

My mind floated back to the soul-crushing reminder of how that innovative land of technology and toys—that beloved tech-island where the *best* days of my career were spent—*Silicon Valley*, is so connected to the production of military technologies. How "defense spending" was integral to its development.

We remained silent a moment until I reiterated, "I love technology when it's used in a constructive way. Our nation being the biggest arms exporter in the world is *not a* good use of technology, and it's coming back to haunt us."

"We'll all be uploading our brains to computers to survive," Anna said, breaking the intensity. Ironically, she picked her cell phone up while saying, "speaking of, I want to read to you an email I got from Ava."

Julie's eyes went wide. "Wait! Let me get us fresh drinks and a snack first, want the same?"

"I'd prefer a mint iced tea," I replied while handing Julie money she refused to take.

"I've got this round. That drink sounds refreshing, three mint iced teas?" Julie asked. We nodded and continued discussing our techno-crazed humanity.

"I hear you about dehumanizing the world with manipulation of data, but I sure would love a robot to clean my loft," Anna suggested.

"Oh sure, Rosie the Robot would be nice, but she's putting the house-cleaning business to shame! Heck, there's lots of good use of Science out there—such as in medicine, environmental engineering, even self-driving cars. It's the bad use of Science I speak of—"

"Like 'smart' bombs and guns?" Anna questioned.

Nodding, I added, "The modern Mad Scientist isn't Frankenstein creating some monster-human. He's creating weapons of mass destruction and believing he's saving the world."

"Are we saving the world again, Caryssa?" Julie came back with a tray carrying mint iced teas and a bowl of popcorn.

"*Mmm...*this is *fantastic!*" I exclaimed while chomping a handful of the buttery, crunchy popcorn.

"Now let's hear that email, this will be like listening to an excerpt from a novel!" Julie commented. "With a bizarre twist coming from this girl—and why is she contacting you all the time?"

"I think she's leaning on me as a window to the world left behind her." Anna swiped her phone, then said, "listen to this:

TO: Anna Beauvais
From: Jamie Garcia
Date: October 20, 2018 2:14:33 CST
Subject: Kryptos and Shit

So…I'm done trying to solve Kryptos but I can tell you it's all about the il-lusion the CIA has cast over the world. The agency arms, trains and funds ter-rorism. It's an allegory to the darkness of history connected to shadow money today.

The third encrypted message of Kryptos is about Tut, the boy-king. He was a teenaged warrior, only nineteen! He tried to escape being controlled by power just like us!

It's a subliminal message connecting what happened then and now—right down to the Pharaoh's gilded funeral mask on display as a world-renowned piece of art. Like all soldiers, they turned this child into entertainment for the masses—like oppressive wreaths decorating graves.

All the gold, jewels, and shiny objects excavated from his tomb were han-dled with more tender care than the soldiers during the "Great War." Then the tragic death and discovery of this boy-king made a good story for a publicity show.

Same shit, a different era. The riches in King Tut's tomb resemble today's two top problems: Ignorance and greed.

PS: Remember my message on your Picasso painting: "I stand for life against death. I stand for peace against war."
Jamie Garcia

"Wow, Ava is one pessimistic girl," insisted Julie.

"Mmm…I'm not sure about that, I see her as one smart girl who can think for herself," I countered.

"Well, what's with her identity crisis?" Julie edged us on.

"*Identity crisis*? She's incognito Jules, using a fake identity and untrace-able device to survive." I blurted. "We live in a world where history, myth, and politics collide. And you know, she just might be onto something. I read that the fourth yet unsolved message of Kryptos reads 'Out of darkness a gold King Tut."

"I've heard that too," Anna piped in. "But like all the other encrypted messages, there's a misspelling. Darkness is spelled 'darknss.'"

"I thought it read 'Berlin Clock.'" Julie pondered.

"Maybe both are part of the fourth hidden message at CIA headquarters. After all, it's known that a sculpture of King Tut's stepmother, Queen Nefertiti—the *Nefertiti Bust*, is displayed in Berlin," Anna informed.

"Oh! And King Tut's tomb was rumored to have secret rooms with a hidden chamber where the queen's body was thought to be buried. It's all still a mystery although some claim she's been found." I added.

"Whatever...I don't know about you guys, but it seems the relaxing scene around this swanky café is starting to look a bit apocalyptic," Julie declared as she glanced out at the San Francisco Bay, now casting gray shadows.

We turned and watched a ferry boat make its way through the smoky haze toward Alcatraz Island. The sun was a bright burnt orange, casting an ominous glow over the water. "I pray for all the people losing their houses and loved ones in these fires across our state," I whispered. *Our nation.*

All the wise words in the world about climate change accelerated by human action and causing many fires entered my mind—whether through old policy, plastics, burning fossil fuels or cigarettes.

The girls nodded, no words leaving their lips. We decided it was time to head home.

I drove around town doing errands for a few hours, including grabbing groceries from Trader Joe's. The sun was a glowing red orb in the smoky sky. Later I was lounging on my couch, reading a Steinbeck novel while half listening to the news and sipping Chai Tea. The view from my living room was spectacular as ever, streaks of orange lighting up the sky across the Bay with the city and bridge lights twinkling.

The only thing I heard from the mainstream reality TV show our news has become were snippets of another mass shooting that I couldn't tolerate hearing. I picked up the remote to switch it off, and I froze. *This couldn't be real.* I covered my ears to block off the words, but it was no use. Fragmented pieces of the story hit me with a wave of nausea:

'*...mass shooting at the Golden Gate Grind...four people killed...heroic local police officer able to quell further damage...the lone gunman is an ex-Marine combat veteran...his motive unclear...*'

The remote dropped from my hand, making a loud crash as it hit the floor. *His motive unclear? —how about a built-in motive?* I thought. An Orwellian dystopia, our global arms race to nowhere. The money in politics placing swords over the heads of humanity. *How odd, we were just talking about this, at that café!*

Then, in typical media fashion, the image of the suspect flashed before me, giving him fame while the victims fade away. Victims that could have been my friends. *Myself.*

There, pictured on my TV screen, was the guy that had sat at the table next to us at the café, with the same haunted look on his face. That 'somebody's son' who had tried to reach out to me.

I heard screaming, then recognized it came from me, as my eyes landed on an inspirational plaque on my wall that reads, "Live in the Moment." At that moment, I wanted to throw my cup at it.

* * *

"Do you want me to videotape this, Ava?"

"Sure, Chris, just let me feed pellets to Harmony." I curved my fingers in another attempt to scratch the wild dove's neck, but his stiff posture told me he still saw petting as a threat.

Harmony is the name we gave our new forest friend. The low, continuous humming of insects and birds surrounded us. I felt better rested and happier than ever.

"It's amazing how you could train this wild dove, Ava," Chris commented.

"This gentle peacemaker will only feed on my hands though, can't pet him yet." Chris sent me one of those looks he gave before asking how a dove lover could have done what she did to her own. *I killed my own pets!* Oddly, to show how war hawks kill peace.

I silenced him with a stare, "Are you ready yet?"

Chris switched my burner phone into video mode, and stopped to ask, "Just tell me again, what was the symbolic message you tried to convey?"

"This is the last time I'll repeat it. I'm trying to forget! *The three bloody teardrops under my pet dove's eyes resemble being blinded by elusive, forever enemies. Three blood drops on the breasts symbolize removal of a society's heart.*"

Chris pressed the record button and said, "Here's our release hoping to send off love, peace, and compassion to heal the world."

I uplifted my eyes toward the sky. Raising both hands, I released Harmony, his majestic wings flapping—lifting him toward the lush forest canopy.

The End
Thank you for reading.
T.L. Mumley

Have you read my debut novel, **MASKS OF MORALITY**? Find out how it all started for Caryssa Flynn and friends! Available at Amazon and select bookstore shelves.

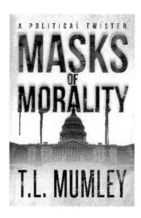

About the Author

T.L. Mumley is a former high-tech marketing executive, a writing coach for high school students and author of debut *Masks of Morality*. She lives with her husband and son in Northern California.

Visit her website at:
http://tlmumleybooks.com/

Connect with T.L. Mumley:
Facebook: https://www.facebook.com/TLMumleyAuthor
Twitter: https://twitter.com/tlmumley
Blog: http://tlmumleybooks.com/blog/